Business Ethics

Sunday Ethic – Monday World

Business Ethics

Sunday Ethic – Monday World

Ted Batson and Blake J. Neff

TRIANGLE PUBLISHING

Business Ethics: Sunday Ethic — Monday World
by Ted Batson and Blake J. Neff

Direct correspondence and permission requests to one of the following:

Triangle Publishing
Indiana Wesleyan University
1900 West 50th Street
Marion, Indiana 46953

Web site: www.trianglepublishing.com
E-mail: info@trianglepublishing.com

Batson, Ted and Neff, Blake J.

ISBN: 978-1-931283-14-4

Cover and Graphic design: Lyn Rayn

Printed in the United States of America

Table of Contents

Preface

One of the by-products of the industrial revolution is the compartmentalization of knowledge. Compartmentalization—separating ideas or processes into isolated categories[1]—has proven efficient in the manufacturing world, but it often leads to the acceptance of false ideas in the academic world. For example, universities have long attempted to train students to be ethical decision makers. Under a compartmentalization mindset, students are taught ethical philosophies and theories, management strategies, accountability procedures, etc., as if they were independent and somewhat unrelated elements in the business process. However, anyone working in the "real world" knows that these elements of decision making are inseparable. A decision in one area will affect all the other areas in some way.

In an effort to overcome the artificial barriers of compartmentalization this book teachs ethical principles intertwined with the five managerial functions. It uses a case study approach to stimulate students' analytical thinking skills, based on integrated instruction in basic ethics and managerial knowledge. Most of the case examples are drawn from real-life experiences, and all interviews are with owners and/or managers who have demonstrated managerial success and ethical decision making in the small business world. Names and selected occupations have been changed to protect the participant's privacy.

Students are invited to examine their own belief systems, challenged to investigate the strengths and weaknesses of secular ethical philosophies and theories, encouraged to explore biblical principles and teachings in the context of their personal lives and the business setting, and assisted in the development of a personal framework for guiding their ethical decision making.

To keep up with current events in the business world, it is recommended that the students apply their ethical growth to ethical dilemmas found in recent business journals, newspapers, and media sources. This publication includes list of ethics websites and their addresses for students' and professors' convenience.

It is the authors' goal and prayer that this book has helped the reader think through the sticky issues that are part of the journey for maturing managers who seek to glorify our God through interactions with the business world and its challenges and responsibilities.

Blake J. Neff and Ted Batson

Endnotes

1. Merriam-Webster Online Dictionary, "Compartmentalization," http://www.m-w.com/dictionary/compartmentalization (accessed August 20, 2007).

Introduction

"Unless the Lord builds the house, its builders labor in vain."

(Psalm 127:1a)

A father wanted to teach his adolescent son a lesson on managing the family business. The father sought to test the son's understanding of how to conduct business. The following exchange between father and son provides a glimpse at one-dimensional business thinking.

"Suppose a customer is shortchanged by $10 in a particular transaction. You know the customer has been slighted, but no one else is aware of the problem. What do you do?" the father asked.

Seeking clarification, the younger manager responded, "You mean, do we tell the customer or not?"

"Well, maybe," his father said somewhat tentatively. "What I am really asking is do we tell our partner?"

Such thinking reflects the norm in today's American business climate. The need for sound teaching in ethical management sparks little debate in the current business climate of fraud, deception, and "cooking the books." In Washington, D.C., the debate focuses on how to legislate morality. Should there be tougher penalties for white-collar crime? Would additional administrative regulations help? How about requiring the CEOs of major corporations to sign their company's financial statements, thus personally vouching for their accuracy?

Teaching Business Ethics: Contemporary Absences

In *Business Ethics*, we address what we see as basic omissions in modern approaches to the study of business ethics. We offer new approaches to the age-old problem of guiding a business and even one's personal life through the process of ethical decision making. In our view at least six major elements are absent from much ethical teaching. These absences lead to ineffectiveness in teaching ethical decision making and, hence, ineffectiveness in the practice of ethical decision making in American business today.

Absence #1: A Rationale

Throughout the twentieth century, national and state legislatures attempted to impose morality and ethical behavior on the business community. Prohibition, fair labor laws, equal opportunity, workplace safety laws, and the Family and Medical Leave Act (FMLA) are a few examples of these legislative efforts. This altruistic view of the law's impact has led to a belief that if it is legal, then it is ethical. In response, business schools have designed courses in business ethics that amount to little more than a rehash of current legal guidelines already imposed on the business community. Hence, many managers develop a one-dimensional ethical system that might be summarized in this statement: "As long as I obey the letter of the law, I behave ethically." While the vast majority of managers exercise their citizenship responsibility to obey the law in their business dealings, obedience to the law is not an end in itself, but it is a solid foundation for building a higher level of ethical management.

Absence #2: An Integration

The application of an industrial model with its compulsion to subdivide each entity into individual parts has led to greater efficiency in the assembly of automobiles. However, the compartmentalization of ideas, knowledge, and skills in the educational world—facilitated by separating disciplines, courses, and topics—has not been tremendously successful in training managers to behave ethically.

In an attempt to rectify this shortcoming, a major university recently declared that every course offered in its college of business was to include an ethics component. While this attempt to integrate ethics into every aspect of the curriculum is admirable, what this really means for most courses is a finer degree of compartmentalization. One chapter or a lecture or two fulfills the department's ethics requirement for the course. A more real-world approach to impacting managerial behavior would be to integrate ethical concepts and their applications with accounting, management, human resources, marketing, etc. principles.

Absence #3: Entry and Mid-Level Examples

A review of textbooks for undergraduate and graduate ethics courses reveals that the majority of business-world examples studied involve the headline makers and top management officials in well-known mega-corporations. The implication is that if students examine the sensational ethics cases involving top management in the Fortune 500, they automatically will see comparable applications to entry and mid-level management decision making situations.

We believe this top-management approach to the study of ethics creates a false and unethical illusion that all business graduates will become CEOs of major corporations. Further, such an approach creates "disconnect" between what the undergraduate business student studies, and where his or her business career will begin. Logically, those few who eventually become headliners will have developed lifetime habits of ethical decision making at the lower and middle management levels. Utilizing case studies and other applications depicting small businesses and entry and mid-level management dilemmas will provide the novice manager with more useful preparation for successful ethical behavior in one's budding career.

Absence #4: The Application Step in the Learning Process

A review of most ethics textbooks in schools of business reveals an almost exclusive teaching of secular ethical systems. The reader is encouraged to analyze the various philosophies and theories, and then formulate a systematic approach to decision making. The assumption is that a thorough study will help offset the weaknesses in various philosophies and contradictions in various theories. Contingent on this assumption is the belief that a student who learns about ethical philosophies and theories automatically will become an ethical business manager.

David Palmer writes in the *Columbus Dispatch*, "It seems as though every time public employees are caught in the act of unethically or illegally porking out at the public trough, some anointed apologist claims additional ethics classes are required." Palmer concludes, "Remedial ethics classes for adults are akin to requiring public employees to undergo potty-training courses prior to being employed."[1]

We believe that a more effective approach lies in reexamining the very premise that the mastery of ethics theory creates ethical managers. Too often students fail to master the most important step in the educational process, which is application. *Business Ethics: Sunday Ethic/Monday World* provides practice cases designed to emulate the real-life dilemma of entry and mid-level managers and small business owners. Our prayer is that through the use of this text, students not only will gain the mastery of theory, but also will learn to apply ethical principles in their own real-life dilemmas.

Absence #5: The Power of Scriptural Truth

Years of teaching undergraduate and graduate business classes have led us to an alarming observation. A large number of current and future managers believe that a successful business cannot be managed utilizing God's Word as a guide in decision making. A greater faith exists in economic theory than in biblical truth to guide ethical decision making. Sadly, such an attitude prevails even on evangelical Christian university campuses. Many students are oblivious to the Judaeo-Christian roots of moral values. Others simply reject solid biblical teaching as impractical.

Several successful entrepreneurs challenge that conventional wisdom. S. Truett Cathy, founder of Chick-fil-A restaurants, recently told a House of Representatives Subcommittee on Commerce, Trade, and Consumer Protection that he "balances the drive for profits with personal responsibility by using *biblical principles*" (emphasis added).[2]

Similarly, Dallen Peterson, founder of Merry Maids, says that Christian principles have led to his tremendous business success. Merry Maids, which was acquired by Service Master in 1988, is the nation's largest housecleaning service. After selling that business for a reported $25 million, Peterson wrote *Rags, Riches, and Real Success*, wherein he outlines his seven principles of real success.[3] Much of the wisdom in these seven principles comes directly from the pages of Scripture.

Each of the interviews in the "Ask the Pro" section of chapters 5 through 20 of *Business Ethics: Sunday Ethic/Monday World* has been conducted with a businessperson who attempts to integrate Christian faith with business practice. These managers offer valuable solutions to the case studies outlined in each chapter.

Even more important, by their example they prove that successful businesspeople often do live out their faith in the everyday world of management and work.

Absence #6: Identification and Analysis of Personal Motivation

The modern approach to education also has failed to address the personal goals, needs, and drives that compel individuals to act as they do. Such an approach denies the human element in the transference of ethical philosophies and theories, as well as biblical principles, into everyday decisions in the real-life business world. By contrast, *Business Ethics: Sunday Ethic/Monday World* seeks to aid students in identifying and applying their personal ethical systems; careful interaction with the text should give the student or manager a well-refined statement of ethical guidelines for future use.

Ethical Decision Making: A Cord with Four Threads

Business Ethics: Sunday Ethic—Monday World is based upon the belief that these absences in the teaching of ethics are best addressed by viewing the study of ethics as a cord with four threads. Like a cord with four threads, four major continuums influence ethical decisions. The stronger the component threads, the stronger the cord. Conversely, weaker component threads produce a weaker cord. A weak or missing thread creates an increased likelihood that poor and unethical decisions will occur.

Thread #1: Managerial Knowledge

Figure 1. The Knowledge Continuum

Knowledge Continuum

Lack of Knowledge				Much Knowledge
-10	-5	0	5	10

Knowledge of managerial functions is a very important thread in the ethical decision making cord. Of course, a high level of managerial knowledge will not ensure a high level of personal or business ethics. Not knowing managerial function, however, provides fertile ground for the germination of unethical practices and unethical decisions.

For example, in chapter 6, the failure of management to develop a long-term business plan at "Hur Ministries" leads to an ethical dilemma. Similarly, at "White's Garage" in chapter 9, management clearly does not understand the staffing function, which also produces an ethical dilemma.

Good managerial skills not only can downgrade circumstances that contribute to unethical decisions, but they also can defeat a manager's sense of inadequacy. Helping the student understand the interconnectedness between managerial knowledge and the other three threads is an important component of every chapter in *Business Ethics*.

Thread #2: Managerial Skill

Figure 2, The Skill Continuum

	The Skill Continuum			
Low Skill				**High Skill**
-10	-5	0	5	10

How well a manager can implement managerial functions reveals his or her true managerial skill level. It is easy to see that the potential for higher skill development is directly proportional to the manager's knowledge. For example, one cannot become a skilled planner with only limited knowledge of the planning process. The same holds true for the other four managerial functions. Like lack of knowledge, lack of skill in any management function opens the door to situations that contribute to unethical decisions or unethical actions. Conversely, the higher the skill level, the lower the probability of inadvertently making unethical decisions or acting unethically.

In the "West Park Apartment" scenario of chapter 11, a manager understands the importance of providing quality leadership. However, she lacks an adequate skill level with regard to implementing authority as a leader. This managerial deficiency leads to an ethical problem.

In the case around which chapter 15 is built, management at "Pit Stop" recognizes the role of team development in effective management. However, the skill to lead subordinates in teambuilding has yet to be developed. An ethical question surfaces as a result.

Thread #3: Personal Beliefs

Figure 3. Personal Belief Continuum

Personal Belief Continuum				
Unstructured				Well Defined
-10	-5	0	5	10

A manager's personal belief system may range from unstructured to well defined. A biblically based system, for instance, would be well defined in the pages of Scripture. The further the belief system has evolved and matured toward the well-defined end of the continuum, the more likely it is that ethical decisions and actions will result.

At "Oak Dale Bed and Breakfast" in chapter 7, Joanna is a young manager who has yet to develop her personal belief system in a structured way. As a result, she fails an ethical test precipitated by her attempt to adopt her superior's ethical system.

More mature managers in the "Decker and Associates" scenario of chapter 18 have a similar problem. In this case, an ethically and legally problematic situation develops because managers fail to develop a well-structured ethic.

The level of managerial knowledge and skill can affect the manager's location on the belief continuum. One manager may have a fairly well-defined belief system, but constantly become embroiled in unethical situations and actions because of poor managerial skill. While we would like to believe that adopting a Christian belief system would eliminate unethical practices in the business world, evidence refutes such a conclusion. A look at the comparative statistics between leaders in ministry and the general population reveals a striking similarity in areas such as adultery, divorce, abuse of power, and financial misconduct. It appears that this thread by itself is not a solution to unethical behavior in the personal and business arena.

However, without a well-defined ethical system, there is little chance for success in making ethical decisions as a manager. Throughout *Business Ethics*, therefore, the reader is encouraged to develop a personal statement of ethical position. We unashamedly believe the Christian worldview is superior to others. Hence, we encourage students to develop, adopt, and internalize the Christian worldview. This will assist them as they attempt to solve the ethical dilemmas of the case studies found in this textbook, as well as in their future interactions as entry or lower-level managers in the world of business.

Thread #4: Personal Motivation

Figure 4. Personal Motivation Continuum				

Personal Belief Continuum

Self centered   God centered

-10	-5	0	5	10

The personal motivation continuum separates self centered on one extreme from God centered on the other. Moving toward the God-centered pole of the continuum moves one closer to act with godly rather than selfish interests. One premise behind *Business Ethics* is that in the final analysis motivation will trigger the use of knowledge, skills, and beliefs to bring about either ethical or unethical decisions and actions.

"What would Jesus do?" While inadequate as a decision making rule, this popular question does encourage a process that involves establishing a motivational system based on God's will rather than human self-will. In chapter 16, "The Worker's Benefit Insurance" case describes a manager who has adequate knowledge, skills, and beliefs. His motivations, however, are not God-centered. The result is an ethical dilemma. Similarly, at "Dupont Men's Wear" in chapter 17, a business couple must consider their personal motivations after having worked out their stated belief system.

A personal motivation system provides the intangible element that often overrides knowledge, skills, and beliefs. While secular philosophies and theories tend either to encourage self-interest or set up rules by which to govern self-interest, *Business Ethics* attempts to guide readers in understanding what truly has value in directing actions—a God-centered eternal existence.

The Learning Process

We believe that active learning leads to action. Hence, active learning is a key element in the design of *Business Ethics*. We call upon the reader to apply higher-level cognitive processes of analysis, synthesis, and evaluation, as well as higher-level affective skills of valuing, organizing, and characterization. Unless the reader becomes an active learner, this book's content is nothing more than another collection of philosophies, theories, experiences, and opinions. However, when the reader is an active participant in learning, *Business Ethics* becomes a guide to self-knowledge and self-directed growth. We encourage personal analysis and reflection in conjunction with the analysis and selected adoption of philosophical, theoretical, and experiential elements.

Active learning elements of *Business Ethics* include case studies, interviews, ethical code formulation, self-analysis, and reflection activities. These activities help to define and refine the learner's belief and personal motivation systems, as well as to assist in the application of a systematic decision making process.

Core Areas of Learning

Business Ethics is designed to strengthen the student of business ethics in five core areas, with emphasis on their interrelatedness and the learner's ability not only to envision becoming a more ethical manager, but also to actualize the vision. A vision that does not initiate action is blind.

Gaining factual knowledge is the reader's first core area of learning. *Business Ethics* presents the basic elements of the five managerial functions: planning, controlling, organizing, staffing, and leading. This provides a refresher course or review for those familiar with business elements, as well as an introduction to newcomers to the formal study of business. Including substantive management information in an ethics textbook is a unique component of this integrated, ethical decision making process.

In addition to biblical principles, *Business Ethics* also includes a brief study of selected secular ethical philosophies and theories. This combination provides the reader with knowledge about how to act in situations that demand decisions. It also offers a basis for assessing and evaluating the merits of various approaches. Further, readers are encouraged to examine their personal views of ethical behavior in light of theoretical data.

Second, the authors believe that discerning students will learn from the experiences of others. Therefore, brief case studies or scenarios, as well as interviews with Christian business leaders, provide an integral part of the learning process. These case studies and interviews represent the real business world of entry- and mid-level managers and small-business entrepreneurs.

Third, the reader will engage in self-study. Evaluation questions include these:

- What does the reader already know about management and ethics?
- What does the reader believe about ethical conduct?
- On what basis has the reader made decisions in the past?
- What innermost desires comprise the reader's personal motivation?

These questions and more are embedded in the text, intended to become a part of the reader's learning process.

A fourth core area of learning is to gain analytical and process skills in self-reflection. Management skills and the critical analysis of personal belief and motivation systems, as reflected in past and present practices, do not develop by chance. They involve a deliberate process. The reader is challenged to become an active participant in that process.

Application to ethical decision making in management is the final core area of learning. The reader engages in a systematic approach to decision making, learning to recognize the interrelated elements that impact the ethics of a decision.

Style and Content

The authors have chosen words carefully for *Business Ethics*. The result is a very easy-to-read textbook. The authors believe that engaging the student in the topic is the first phase of a successful learning adventure. Therefore, we have made a conscious effort to draw the student into the subject of integrated Christian ethics by using a compelling writing style and real-life situations to which the student can relate.

 The first two chapters expose the reader to the normative philosophical understanding of ethics. Chapter 3 examines the relationship between ethics and the Christian faith. In chapter 4, the reader is instructed how to develop a personal statement of ethics. Armed with this preliminary position of personal business ethics, the reader tests that position in chapters 5 through 20 by exploring a series of situational studies. In each chapter, once the ethical dilemma has been established, the reader encounters "On Background" information, which provides the necessary management and ethics tools to help the reader analyze the situation appropriately.

 Each chapter also includes "Toward an Ethical Christian Worldview." This section examines a portion of Scripture and describes how the passage might relate to the relevant dilemma. "Toward an Ethical Christian Worldview" encourages the reader to develop the habit of applying biblical insight to managerial decisions, thus integrating faith and practice.

In "Ask the Pro," the reader encounters a business/management professional who already integrates faith and practice. The names of persons and businesses and their locations have been changed to protect their privacy, but a short biographical sketch is included to show that these professionals are people much like you, leading busy lives full of responsibilities. Each interview is designed to gain the practitioner's perspective on the situation at hand. Often, those interviewed offer strong practical insights into business ethics in general. Always, they provide tips on how a manager on the "front lines" might approach such a dilemma.

 Finally, chapters 5 through 20 ask the reader to become an ethical management consultant to the participants in the situational dilemma. A series of "You Be the Consultant" questions guides the reader in the process of providing an ethical solution to the circumstance at hand. These questions also encourage readers to examine their own statements of ethical position and to adjust them where necessary as they deal with the challenges of the real-life work world.

Endnotes

1. David Palmer, "Ethics course won't stop those who choose to do wrong," *Columbus Dispatch*, August 17, 2002: A11.
2. "Chick-fil-A Chief: Follow Bible Ethics," *Atlanta Journal-Constitution*, July 28, 2002:A19.
3. Dallen Peterson, *Rags, Riches, and Real Success* (Wheaton, IL: Tyndale, 2000).

An Ethical Framework

"Do your best to present yourself to God as one approved, a workman who does not need to be ashamed, and who correctly handles the word of truth."

(2 Timothy 2:15)

Chapter Challenges

A careful examination of Chapter 1 should enable the reader to:

- Identify the role of a Christian worldview in building a system of ethics.
- Define the term ethics.
- Explain the role of stakeholders in making ethical decisions.

The recent past may be characterized as the most serious period of ethical scandal on the part of business since the 1980's . . . The current period may be the worst ever for business ethics . . ."[1] These are the words of Archie Carroll, the Robert W. Scherer Professor of Management at the University of Georgia.

Perhaps the ethical problems of modern American business stem from the fact that managers are bombarded with pressures from all sides as they strive to balance the management equation in their everyday decision making:

Efficiency + Effectiveness = Profits

This equation represents the totality of management for many business leaders, even as they confront foreign competitors, new technologies, workforce demands, and a myriad of other challenges on a regular basis. How are managers to carry out their short- and long-term fiduciary responsibilities to owners and customers, as well as their human responsibilities to employees, their families, and themselves?

The Three E Equation

Many Christian business managers have added a variable to the manager's decision making equation. For them, the equation might be called the *"Three E Equation"*:

Efficiency + Effectiveness + Ethics = Profits + Long-Term Stability

Some Christian managers, however, continue to accept the belief that the business world's hunger for stronger and stronger bottom lines is incompatible with the addition of ethics as illustrated in the Three E Equation. As a result, Christians in business are often left with *cognitive dissonance*; that is, they hold two opposing views simultaneously. Their Christian beliefs maintain that certain principles are absolutes and contribute to the well-being of individuals and society. However, the business setting often utilizes an action system that honors higher profits above the well-being of individuals or moral values. In some cases, the well-being of an entire society is subordinated to profit. Managers at Enron and their accountants at Arthur Andersen are accused of utilizing just such an action system.[2]

Since many Christian business managers live in constant cognitive dissonance—believing the teachings of Jesus, but practicing business in ways that are completely opposed to those teachings—they experience a high level of stress and frustration. One has to wonder what impact this level of discord has on a Christian manager's self-image and resulting relationships with employees, family, and the community. Ironically, it is possible that this amount of frustration may foster an environment that leads to managerial ineffectiveness and reduced profits.

Therefore, it is imperative for Christian managers especially—and all managers generally—to have a well-established framework and a firm belief system to guide the decision making process. Without such a system, managers often will make decisions in an erratic fashion, decisions that are dictated either by the "squeaky wheel" or a blind desire to maximize profits at any cost. In order to gain the knowledge, skill, and motivation to develop and refine an ethics-based decision making framework and to operate it from a *Christian worldview*, it is necessary to "*study to show thyself approved*" (2 Timothy 2:15 KJV). Such study must focus on the secular world of ethical theory and business management practices, as well as on Christian principles, attitudes, and decision making skills. With these skills properly integrated, the Christian manager can formulate and begin to internalize a personal ethical position.

> *Christian worldview:* Those principles, attitudes and values that impact every area of life and grow out of a conviction that Jesus Christ is Lord.

The Common Sense Approach to Ethics

Ethics is a part of the fabric of American business. Imagine running a business where no one could be trusted. In such a world, the suppliers all would be liars, the bank would be out to steal businesses, and all employees would be loafing when the boss was not watching. Fortunately, most people do have a sense of right and wrong and follow some kind of moral code. They have at least an informal or common sense method of making decisions.

Common sense approaches to ethical decision making have been used in business and other areas of life for a long time. The process consists of asking a series of questions, such as these:

- Is this the right thing to do?
- Would I want my children to know what I am doing?
- Would I want this decision published with my name on the front page of the local newspaper?
- Is this the fair thing to do?
- Am I following the Golden Rule?

These questions represent a *Socratic model* of decision making. Named after the Athenian philosopher, Socrates, this model utilizes a series of questions that lead to a logical conclusion. When answered objectively, these generally lead business managers to ethical decisions. However, they also present some real problems for managers:

1. They do not encourage a causal analysis of the decision.
2. They do not examine the decision's extended consequences.
3. They do not identify the persons affected or the issues involved.
4. At least some common sense questions may be motivated out of fear or self-interest.

Further, the questions and the common sense method generally do not seek to discover God's will as revealed in Scripture or nature. Therefore, these questions exclude what many believe to be an important standard of what is right, just, fair, and/or proper. In short, the questions really are self-serving and utilize a non-scriptural source as their basis.

If the common sense approach to making ethical business decisions is too shallow, then how does one make sound decisions? The answer lies in understanding the nature of ethics. Ethics is a system of moral values that is applied in a consistent way to one's personal, social, and business life.[3] To apply this system of moral values effectively, one must understand the structural levels at which ethical dilemmas occur, who is involved in the dilemmas, and how a particular decision will affect them. In addition, one must consider how to formulate possible courses of action. Failing in any of these three areas may lead to an ineffective decision, resulting in more pain than cure.

> *ethics:* Science of moral values and responsibities.

The Ethical Dilemma

In business, as in other areas of life, an ethical dilemma occurs when a moral conduct issue is at stake, or when the economic needs or desires of a business or individuals conflict with their responsibility toward other people, the environment, or social institutions.[4] Formulating the proper decision to resolve the ethical dilemma involves many variables. One of the most compelling of these variables involves understanding whose needs are driving the demand for a decision. This requires careful analysis since people have a variety of needs, some of which are not expressed or obvious.

At the Personal Level

The first source of needs is at the *personal level*. Dilemmas at the personal level directly confront the decision makers themselves and require them to make individual decisions. A key question in this situation is, "What do I do to meet my needs?"

For example, suppose Byron has been passed over for a promotion. Instead, the promotion is given to a younger employee with fewer years of experience in the company. Should Byron file a complaint with a regulatory agency? The answer relates primarily to Byron's needs.

Or, suppose the husband of Tina's best friend has made sexual advances toward Tina. Should Tina tell her friend and risk ending their friendship or her friend's marriage? This is a personal issue that Tina must resolve herself.

At the Organizational Level

Organizations establish policies, systems, and structures to ensure that operations run smoothly and that organizational goals are attained. Therefore, at the second or *organizational level*, the manager makes decisions on behalf of the company or the organization with the purpose of meeting the needs of the organization. A manager operating at this level should ask, "Did this situation occur as the result of meeting a perceived organizational need through the formulation or application of a policy, procedure, system, structure, or goal?" That is, has the company created this moral dilemma while striving to meet other organizational needs? The manager's decision must balance the needs of the organization, as presented in the form of established policies, systems, structures, and goals, while attending to the company's responsibilities to others.

In Tina's case, the unwanted sexual advances could constitute sexual harassment if they occurred at work. In that case, the situation directly relates to the company's policy-making and legal responsibilities. The company managers want to resolve the situation not only to protect a fellow employee, but also to protect the company's assets and future. This is especially important because the design of the company's planning, controlling, and reward and punishment systems inadvertently may set the stage for unethical decision making to occur.

At the Societal Level

A third level of needs occurs at the *societal level*. Societies protect and advance their needs by adopting economic, legal, social, and political systems that determine how a business should operate within the culture. A key question to ask is "Are market forces, government regulations, laws, or political processes and ideologies that are outside my direct control dictating boundaries for my decision?" Here the issues that directly affect the success or even the survival of the company originate from systems outside the company. Conventional wisdom calls for managers to absolve themselves of personal responsibility at the societal level because the systems are outside their control. However, is it ethical to allow these systems to limit decisions, or is it ethical for these managers simply to comply with society's requirements? Don't Christian managers have a personal standard that overrides society's standard?

The Christian manager should ask this important question: "Is it possible in the short run to do the ethical thing—based on an ethical belief system grounded in both a Christian worldview and an understanding of ethical philosophy—while in the long run working for positive change in the economic, legal, social, and political systems?" For the Christian, such an approach could amount to being salt and light to the world (see Matthew 5:13-14).

At the Legal Level

Another societal system affecting the company is the law and its regulatory role in business. A major guiding principle for many business leaders is the belief that if it is legal, then it is ethical. This is based on the belief that in a democratic society the law represents the will of the people and, therefore, represents what is morally just in the society. Christian and other conscientious managers should analyze this belief by asking themselves a series of short questions. "Does the law really represent the will of the majority of the people in every situation or even the majority of situations?" "Do laws truly represent the changing moral values of society or the constant moral values of God?" "Are the forces and conditions that caused laws to be enacted the same or even similar years later?" "Is there consistency in the application of the law to all segments of society?"

Workplace law can provide examples of the pitfalls of using the law as the sole criteria of ethical behavior. The responsibility of employers to their employees is, by law, determined in some areas by the size of the company. For example, in the United States, while the employees of large companies receive health benefits, small businesses are legally exempt from offering affordable health benefits to their employees. If laws truly represent the will of the people, then the majority of Americans believe that only employees of large companies and their families deserve affordable health care. Some observers conclude that since this scenario is legal, it is also morally right. When the law is seen as the primary measure of right and wrong, morality is determined by a majority of people or a few individuals in the judiciary and not by God. All managers have the responsibility to obey the law of the land. They also have the responsibility to ask, "Do society's laws represent the final standard for my ethical decision making or are they the beginning point?"

At the Political Level

The political system in which the company exists is a second societal system that influences decision making. Yet, sometimes political systems send mixed signals. Let's examine a hypothetical example. A farmer in the Carolinas is considering the most effective use of his property. Should he plant tobacco or vegetables? Economic pressure tells him that to produce a strong bottom line, he should plant tobacco. The political system supports this decision by subsidizing tobacco farmers, providing low-cost loans and other financial aid for natural disasters, and artificially supporting the price of tobacco on the domestic trading market. However, at the same time, other sectors of the United States political system are banning the advertisement of tobacco products to certain markets, placing age requirements on the purchase of tobacco goods, and sponsoring health-related lawsuits against tobacco companies. The farmer very well may say that he has no control over the political system and its flaws and that he is free to plant tobacco. After all, both the political system and the legal system seem to agree and even encourage the planting.

> *stakeholders:* Individuals or groups who have
> a stake in a particular decision.

Stakeholders and Ethical Decision Making

Another key question for consideration in ethical decision making is "Who are the *stakeholders* in a given decision?" Typically, stakeholders in a company decision are employees, suppliers, customers, stockholders, and the community at large.[5] For example, in deciding whether to raise tobacco or vegetables, the hypothetical farmer may consider his employees' need for jobs, his family's need for security, or his community's need for economic stability. However, other important stakeholders also are involved in the farmer's decision. These include the consumers who may contract cancer, or the state's taxpayers who support the healthcare and welfare systems for cancer patents. When these latter stakeholders are taken into consideration, the decision to grow tobacco or vegetables becomes an ethical issue with enlarged dimensions.

A business manager must weigh several options when considering people's needs in the decision making process. For instance, the manager must anticipate the needs of all stakeholders affected by the decision, policy statement, or new structure. Sometimes the aggregate effect on larger, more remote groups of stakeholders—such those living in the community where a company is located—is more important than the effect on stakeholders within the organization.

Stakeholder consideration is especially important to those who believe that people are made in God's image. However, the consideration of people alone does not provide the moral standard for a decision. It is also important to think through how God's creation will be affected, and for the Christian manager, the appropriate standard comes from God's moral system.

Ethical Decisions Don't Ensure a Perfect World

Often, ethical decisions harm some stakeholders while helping others. One manager switched suppliers in order to obtain cheaper raw materials. She made this decision for the purpose of keeping her business viable and to protect the owners, employees, and community in which the business was located. As a result, however, the supplier's business failed, harming its owners and employees—in the same community.

Some decisions have extended results that are difficult to anticipate. A manager may resolve a dilemma for an immediate time frame and set in motion an unexpected extended consequence. That was the case for the New Orleans chef who created a blackened redfish entrée. He had no idea that his business innovation and nutritional dish would become so popular worldwide that it would endanger the world's redfish population.

While not all unexpected results of ethical decisions are as far reaching, they can be just as undesirable. On his first day on the job, one middle manager sent a morning memo to all lower level managers and staff. He believed he was doing the right thing by providing employees with up-to-date information for optimum job performance. However, before 10 a.m., he received a call from the corporation's main office. The CEO demanded to know how on his first day the new manager had made his staff so angry that they were threatening a walkout. What the manager did not know was that his predecessor also had a daily morning memo, which he had used to discipline and embarrass subordinate managers and employees. People feared that their new boss was using the same approach. The middle manager's motives were ethical and his openness in sharing information eventually led to positive long-term outcomes, but the short-term results were nearly catastrophic.

This example also illustrates another facet of ethical decision making. Decisions always involve personal implications. Decisions may trigger the company's reward or punishment systems, strengthen a manager's relationship with God, or otherwise affect the manager's personal life. However, the results of *not* making the ethical decisions usually are much more costly.

When applying a sound ethical decision making process to a dilemma, managers will find many solid solutions with varying degrees of acceptability. A simple yes or no answer will seldom suffice. In the short run, there is additional expenditure of energy and time involved in weighing the pros and cons of various acceptable solutions. In the long run, however, managers generally save costly time and energy in damage control and corrective actions by using a sound process for ethical decision making.

Recommended Websites

These websites have been selected because of their applicability to topics presented in this book. It should be noted that articles change frequently and some websites are not continued on the web. Also, additional websites can be found by doing a Yahoo or Google search for ethics websites.

1. Issues and Bioethics. http://www.accessexcellence.org/AB/IE (accessed May 2007).
2. Issues and Bioethics. http://www.bioethics.com (accessed May 2007).

3. American Marketing Association. http://www.ama.org/about/ama/ethcode.asp (accessed May 2007).
4. Markkula Center for Applied Ethics. http://www.scu.edu/ethics (accessed May 2007).
5. International Business Institute. http://www.business-ethics.org (accessed May 2007).
6. Institute for Global Ethics. http://www.globalethics.org (accessed May 2007).
7. Ethics Resource Center. http://www.ethics.org (accessed May 2007).
8. US Office of Government Ethics. http://www.usoge.gov (accessed May 2007).
9. Council for Ethics in Economics. http://www.businessethics.org (accessed May 2007).
10. Research Net. http://www.wsrn.com (accessed May 2007).
11. Federal Trade Commission. http://www.ftc.gov (accessed May 2007).
12. Title VIX. http://www.vix.com/pub/men/harass/harass.html (accessed May 2007).
13. Minority Information Service. http://www.finaid.org/otheraid/minority.phtml (accessed May 2007).
14. American Bar Association. http://www.abanet.org (accessed May 2007).
15. Occupational Safety and Health Association. http://www.osha.gov (accessed May 2007).
16. National Institute for Occupational Safety and Health. http://www.cdc.gov/niosh/homepage.html (accessed May 2007).

Questions ⍰ Discussion

1. Describe a situation in which you or an acquaintance, acting in a managerial role, used the Three E Equation to resolve an operational or manufacturing problem at work.

    a. What were the results of this approach?

    b. How would the results have differed if only effectiveness and efficiency had been considered?

    c. What if only efficiency had been considered?

2. Describe an ethical dilemma that occurred at the organizational level and the managerial decision to resolve it.

    a. Who were the relevant stakeholders?

b. Which stakeholders benefited from the actions taken to resolve the dilemma? How did they benefit?

c. Which stakeholders either did not benefit or were harmed by the action taken? How?

d. Did the issue directly relate to the enforcement of a company policy or procedure? Which one(s)?

e. Can you think of another action to resolve the dilemma that would have produced fewer and/or less severe negative outcomes for stakeholders?

Endnotes

1. Archie B. Carroll, "Business Ethics in the Current Environment of Fraud and Corruption: Will Our Moral Compass Fail?" *Vital Speeches of the Day* 69, no. 17, June 15, 2003, 529.
2. Wendy Zellner, Stephanie Anderson Forest, and others, "The Fall of Enron," *Business Week*, December 17, 2001.
3. *Webster's Ninth New Collegiate Dictionary* (Springfield, MA: Merriam-Webster, 1989), 426.
4. LaRue Tone Hosmer, *The Ethics of Management*, 3rd ed. (Chicago: Irwin, 1996), 136.
5. R. Edward Freeman, *Strategic Management: A Stakeholder Approach* (Boston: Pitman, 1984), 25.

2

Four Ethical Systems

"The sum of thy word is truth; and every one of thy
righteous ordinances endures for ever."

(Psalm 119:16 RSV)

Chapter Challenges

A careful examination of Chapter 2 should enable the reader to:

- Identify the primary components of four major ethical systems.
- Recognize the strengths of each of the four major ethical systems.
- Understand the weaknesses of each of the four major ethical systems

The search for what is right, just, and proper has fueled civilized societies since ancient times. Often these efforts have been based on a society's drive to understand and apply God's Word or His natural revelation. This search also has focused on finding a system that does not depend on God at all. The guiding forces in these latter attempts have ranged from serious application of logic and philosophy to personal fulfillment of an individual's basest desires. This chapter will introduce and explain four prominent ethical systems.

Utilitarianism

An early vehicle in the search for an ethical position is *utilitarianism*. A basic principle of utilitarianism is that the end result is important, not the motivation or the means by which the end is achieved. As a philosophy, utilitarianism became more refined in England in the nineteenth century, but this system has roots in the earlier Greek system, *hedonism*. Hedonism emphasized the end results of maximizing pleasure and minimizing pain.[1] In utilitarianism, managers seek to identify the positive end results of an action as well as the negative ones. If the positives outweigh the negatives, then the decision is considered to be an ethical decision.[2]

For example, a colleague took over the presidency of a failing college. An in-depth study of the college's affairs revealed that due to overstaffing some academic departments were seriously draining the institution's limited resources. The decision was made to reduce the workforce substantially in those areas. The tenets of utilitarianism qualify this as an ethical decision. The rationale, according to utilitarianism, is that it is better for some of the staff to lose their jobs than for the college to be forced to close. Closing the college would have a negative impact on all employees and students, as well as on the college's creditors and the surrounding community.

Utilitarianism and the Stakeholder

In order to apply utilitarianism effectively, managers must consider the impact of their decisions on all stakeholders involved. We generally think of people when we refer to stakeholders, but stakeholders can include the earth and its ecosystems, as we saw in chapter 1's example of the New Orleans chef. In the case of the college president, the more obvious stakeholders were the college's faculty, staff, students, and creditors, as well as the community into which the college contributed culturally and economically. Less obvious but no less important stakeholders included the families of the faculty and staff, the college's alumni, the college's donor base, the state's academic community as a whole, and future generations of students hoping to attend a college with the same kind of ethos as the one that had been closed. When a decision has to be made, a skill of mature decision making is the ability to identify key stakeholders, whether or not they appear to have the most at stake.

What Price Harm?

Utilitarianism is not concerned simply with the number of stakeholders potentially benefited or harmed by a decision, but also with the degree or amount of benefit versus the amount of harm. In general, if the amount of harm to the few is severe and the amount of benefit to the many is slight, then the right, just, and proper thing to do according to utilitarianism is to make the decision that protects the few from severe harm.

For example, when viewed through utilitarianism's ethical lens, one would have to question whether a state lottery is ethical. The vast majority of people who play the lottery lose, which is why the lottery makes so much money. The overwhelming majority of these lottery losers are lower income working people or people on welfare. The money they lose in the lottery translates into food, clothing, and other necessities and services that they or their families will not receive. Most citizens benefit from the lottery's payments to the state through reductions in their taxes. However, the reduced taxes are a very small percentage of the average citizen's total income. The loss of lottery-generated tax breaks would, in most cases, not reduce the level of basic needs available to those individuals and their families. In this case, utilitarianism would determine the state lottery to be unethical because the negative effects on the poor and their children are significantly greater than the tax reduction benefits to the general public.

The Negative Harm Principle

A specialized and unique application of utilitarianism, the *Negative Harm Principle*, generally is applied to questions about the rights related to safety and health. Its key element refers to whether a manager's decision has caused or avoided physical harm to stakeholders. Harm to the health of the stakeholders overrides other non-health benefits of a manager's decision.[3]

> *negative harm principle:* Specialized application of utilitarianism where stakeholders health and safety is impacted.

For many years the federal government, through its school lunch subsidy program, offered peanut butter to the nation's school children. This provided hundreds of millions of children with a good source of protein and zero cholesterol fat, two essentials for the human diet. However, a small percentage of children are born with an allergy to peanut products. This allergy can be so severe that a teaspoon of peanut butter may cause death in some children. Many school lunchrooms have stopped offering peanut butter despite its known benefits (to the many) because of its devastatingly harmful potential (to a few). This is an example of the Negative Harm Principle at work. The same principle also can apply in business to issues related to worker safety, product safety, environmental safety, or to any issue involving physical harm to people.

Utilitarianism's strength is in its impartiality. The stakeholders are considered both as subgroups and as a whole. An individual's self-interests, such as those of the manager, an employee, or a customer, are not an overriding consideration. Decisions based only on friendship, family relations, or political allegiances do not stand the utilitarian ethical test. Many aspects of the American legislative and judicial systems reflect this ethical philosophy.[4]

The Flaws of Utilitarianism

Utilitarianism also has several weaknesses. The first weakness is operational; it is often difficult to identify the relevant stakeholders.[5] This is caused in part by a manager's inability to completely set aside personal emotions and look for all relevant stakeholders. It is especially true when the manager or business entity must make decisions while under attack by one or more stakeholder groups, or when relevant stakeholders enter the picture late.

For example, the United States Food and Drug Administration (USDA) has approved and then later withdrawn medicines or food products from the marketplace because the products later were discovered to cause birth defects. Unborn babies were not considered important stakeholders in the original decisions to approve these products.

The second weakness also is operational; it is almost impossible to accurately weigh the results of decisions on the various stakeholder groups.[6] The results may be more than just economic. They also may be psychological, social, or political.

Perhaps the most profound weakness of utilitarianism is its indifference to the needs of individuals or smaller stakeholder groups when weighed against the needs of a larger set of stakeholders.[7] In the example of the financially struggling college, the individual needs of those being released were set aside in favor of the needs of the larger stakeholder groups.

Other examples of utilitarianism are more insidious. Voting laws in eastern states disenfranchised first-generation American citizens who had immigrated from Ireland and Middle and Eastern Europe. This was done in order to keep in power the established political systems that represented the majority of citizens. Like other nations, America's past includes the terrible institution of slavery. Slavery oppressed the few for the benefit of the many. At its worst, utilitarianism demonstrates that the benefit to the majority can become evil totalitarianism to the minority.

Ethical Egoism

One dictionary defines egoism as "the habit of valuing everything only in reference to one's personal interests."[8] When applied to ethical behavior, egoism states that the ethicality of a decision is determined by the decision maker's self-interest. Thus, the person who works hard and sets aside short-term gratifications in order to attend college and then graduate school because of perceived future psychological, social, and economic benefits operates from the position of *ethical egoism*. The department manager who makes decisions designed to improve the department's efficiency so that it appears to be more effective in the eyes of upper management also is applying ethical egoism.

Strengths and Weaknesses

Ethical egoism's primary strength is that it can be an effective motivational tool. Sales representatives or production managers who consistently make decisions to improve their departments' performance in order to gain large bonuses, to protect their jobs, or to be known as the best, fit this model.

However, the ethical egoism model for decision making also can reflect ethical, operational, and organizational weaknesses. For instance, it tends to put emphasis on the short term at the expense of the long term. One acquaintance, known as a highly successful insurance salesman, offers an example of ethical egoism's weaknesses. In his desire to maintain his position as the division's top salesperson, along with the accompanying financial rewards, he made the decision to write policies with larger and larger benefits without weighing the policyholder's ability to pay or the long-term effects on the company's financial health. In the short run, this practice gained him larger commissions and salesperson-of-the-month bonuses. In the long run, these oversold policyholders were unable to continue to pay. This caused them to lose their coverage, the company to lose money, and ultimately the agent to lose both his job and his lavish lifestyle.

A second weakness is that this approach to decision making leads to the dissolution of organizational vision. When decisions are based solely on the best interest of an individual or a department, the company's mission, goals, other departments, and systems become secondary.

Consider, for example, a university basketball team with a starting lineup of five high-scoring individual stars. They become the highest scoring team in the league and possibly in the college's history. Yet, they barely have a winning season. That is because each person's desire to pad his personal scoring average takes precedence over the team goal of winning games. Five highly motivated individuals do not automatically make a team. A team requires putting aside personal interests for the good of the group.

A third weakness of ethical egoism involves the lack of an effective mechanism to settle disputes between various self-interests. Every manager acts in his or her own best interest. This position says that self-interest, even at the expense of others, is the right thing to do. The inevitable result of ethical egoism is anarchy, which is characterized by undercutting, backbiting, and other negative effects on the company's general health.[9]

Kantian Ethics

Immanuel Kant established a set of ethical decision making principles called *imperatives* that form the basis of Kantian ethics. Examples of imperatives include always telling the truth and never stealing. In his quest to develop a usable ethical system, Kant developed what is called the *categorical imperative*. This is an important standard meant to guide behavior, a standard that should never be broken. The categorical imperative is composed of two formulations. The first states, "Act only on that maxim through which you can at the same time will that it should become a universal law."[10] Kant's second formulation of the categorical imperative states, "Act in such a way that you always treat humanity, whether in your own person or the person of any other, never simply as a means, but always at the same time as an end."[11]

> *categorical imperative:* Two standards that must be satisfied according to Kantian ethics. The first is act only on a maxim that you would be willing to become universal law. The second is to treat others as an end not a means.

You should be able immediately to see how this model differs from the first two ethical decision making positions. Kant's system emphasizes impartiality to individuals and groups. It is built around obligations and duties. When one person has duties, Kantian ethics automatically implies that others have rights. If these duties are obligatory, personal desires alone no longer control decision making. Unlike utilitarianism and ethical egoism, the end result and personal desire do not determine ethical behavior. Instead, the fulfillment of moral obligations or absolutes in the form of the categorical imperative defines the ethics of managerial actions.

Two Sides of the Kantian Coin

Let's look again at the two formulations of Kant's categorical imperative. Formulation one states, "Act only on that maxim through which you can at the same time will that it should become a universal law." This formulation is built on several primary principles, including the use of reason in ethical decision making, obligation to duty, and what Kant termed the principles of universalizability and reversibility. In effect, before enacting a decision a manager must ask, "Would I want all other managers in a similar situation to make the same decision (universalizability)?" A second question is, "If I were the person being affected by this decision, would I want my manager to make the same decision that I am considering (reversibility)?"[12] In a sense a manager has the obligation to help define the high moral ground for an entire industry through ethical decision making. It is a matter of duty.

Formulation two states, "Act in such a way that you always treat humanity, whether in your own person or in the person of any other, never simply as a means, but always at the same time as an end." This axiom recognizes the rights of others and the manager's duty toward them, as well as to him/herself. This prohibits the manager from manipulating or using people only as a means to gain a goal. Duties-based ethical systems do recognize that all members of an organization contribute value toward meeting the organizational goals. But Kantian ethics asserts that each person is an individual with needs, talents, and goals, all of which must be respected. Creating a workplace culture that balances the means-and-ends equation is a foundation stone of many modern models for effective business.

Kantian Strengths

Kantian ethics as a whole passes the test of logical consistency. The categorical imperative teaches that some things are right in every situation. It acts as an anchor to keep managers from being swayed by either changing emotions or the outcomes of decisions.

The United States Supreme Court adhered to the Kantian principles of consistency and universality (universalizability) in denying the requested vote recounts in the 2000 presidential election. The justices received scathing denouncements by individuals caught up in the emotions of the time, exacerbated by their lack of knowledge of the electoral process and the United States Constitution. Kant would say that, in the short run, the justices had to take the heat by doing the right thing for the benefit gained in the long run.

A second strength of Kantian ethics is its ability to bring about the recognition of right and wrong. This involves duties based on unchanging principles, called imperatives, which are universal rules. Additionally, right and wrong responses are based on the rules, not on an individual's personal wishes, emotions, or circumstances. Kantian ethics counteracts the human tendency to rationalize that a certain behavior—because of some personal reason—is wrong for one person, but right for another.

A third strength of Kantian ethics involves rationality. There are as many definitions of what is rational as there are principal stakeholders in a given ethical dilemma. However, a decision that can be rationally supported is still better than one that cannot be rationally supported.

Kantian Weaknesses

Kant's concept of imperatives includes weaknesses. First, duties may conflict. Some duties may be more important than others, leading to internal conflict. The rule never to lie may conflict with the rule to protect the lives of individuals. Corrie ten Boom was a Christian who lived in German-occupied Holland during World War 2. When Nazi officers repeatedly questioned her about whether or not her family was harboring Jews, she faced a terrible dilemma: either tell the truth and send people to their deaths, or lie to the Nazis in order to save the Jews.

A second weakness in Kantian ethics is that circumstances cannot always be ignored if we have real concern for people. Miss ten Boom looked at the implications of telling the truth. In this situation, rational logic was broken down by human need. In contrast, the United States Supreme Court decision for the 2000 presidential election was less complicated. The emotional circumstances surrounding the election debacle were charged, but not life threatening. The decision resulted in protecting the integrity of the electoral process as a whole. That decision was positive, although not popular with people who felt that a group of voters' rights had been ignored. Knowing which circumstances cannot be ignored and which are less pressing is a key leadership skill—one that effective leaders continue to hone on a daily basis.

Cultural Relativism

The American business community has experienced two major cultural impacts in the past fifty years. First, the combination of liberalized immigration policies with the decline of the "melting pot" emphasis of earlier American history has made the United States a very diverse and pluralistic society. As a result, if a small mid-western business located in an Anglo community expands its operation to another region of the country—for example, South Texas, portions of California, or the Northeast—it may find itself doing business with local suppliers that approach labor, values, and decision making from a different cultural perspective.

The second major cultural impact is the "one-world movement" characterized by an exploding number of multinational companies and worldwide markets. Practically every upper-level business manager or business owner is faced in some way with the task of operating efficiently, effectively, and ethically in this culturally, politically, and economically diverse global business world.

A New Business Frontier

This new business frontier includes several key components. The most obvious is the concept of diversity. Diversity is not just about color and race, language and technological sophistication, or climatic and political environments. Fundamental diversity reaches deeply into the ethics, morals, and values we honor and uphold.

A second key characteristic of this modern business climate is that each cultural group believes that its ethics, morals, and values are the correct ones. The mid-western small-town business noted earlier may encounter a very bumpy and potentially treacherous road when it embarks on its new venture. As its management establishes partnerships and supplier relationships, its conservative Judeo-Christian value system may conflict with businesses whose management embraces a different set of beliefs about the right and wrong ways to make decisions and to do business.

When in Rome

How can a business avoid conflicts, establish lasting relationships, and make reasonable profit margins in this culturally diverse business world? The answer for many is found in *cultural relativism*. This system says simply, "When in Rome, do as the Romans do." Cultural relativism maintains that the basis of judgment is relative, differing according to events, persons, and other circumstances. Cultural Relativism is based upon three important concepts:

1. Different cultures have different values.
2. There is no absolute set of values or truth; therefore, one culture cannot say that its values are right and another culture's values are wrong.
3. Approving one system over another is intolerant and ethnocentric.

The Strengths of Cultural Relativism

Cultural relativism can cause a business owner to analyze his or her ethical system to determine if it is based on unchanging principles or simply on the current "mood" of the community and culture.

Cultural relativism also can expose *ethnocentrism*. Ethnocentrism is the belief that one's own culture is superior to all others. It includes the notion that one culture's view of right and wrong is automatically superior to another's. In his fourteen years as a business leader in Latin America, co-author Ted Batson saw many North American and European business leaders confuse culture for ethics.

> *ethnocentrism:* Belief that one's culture is superior to all others.

Finally, cultural relativism can cause the business leader to examine the concept that power is ethics. This translates into the belief that "our way" is the only way because we are economically, militarily, technologically, or culturally more powerful or advanced than another culture. The idea of power can be applied to time and tradition. Some believe a practice "has to be right" because "we have always done it this way." Such an attitude can confuse habit with principles of truth.

The Weaknesses of Cultural Relativism

A major flaw in any system based on cultural norms is that if the culture determines what is right and wrong, the culture becomes a god. Therefore, since there are hundreds of cultures, there are hundreds of equal gods. Right and wrong, then, depend on the will of the gods at any given time. This idea is clearly illustrated in Stanley Grenz's statement about relativism and truth, "Truth is relative to the community in which a person participates. And since there are many human communities, there are necessarily many different truths."[13]

Josh McDowell and Bob Hostetler note that the problem does not end with a philosophical notion of the nature of truth. They believe that the practice of relativism in American culture has led to what they label the "new tolerance." They observe, "Not only does everyone have an equal right to his beliefs, but all beliefs are equal. All values are equal. All lifestyles are equal. All truth claims are equal."[14]

Another key weakness involves the contradiction between two key elements of cultural relativism:

1. There are no absolute truths.

2. Intolerance is always absolutely wrong.

In the everyday workings of the political and business arenas, individuals who do not bow to the god of tolerance are often denounced as politically incorrect. This system of totally accepting various beliefs of right and wrong breaks down and becomes one of intolerance when it confronts ethical and moral positions built on absolutes. Business or government policies and procedures built on or administered under cultural relativism can lead to oppression of persons or groups that do not accept as universally correct the dominant group's idea of what is right, just, and fair.

In his best-seller, *Persecution*, David Limbaugh makes a parallel and very striking point.[15] He declares that since Christians believe in absolutes, they are the only group in America for whom the norm of tolerance does not apply. He provides evidence of a growing intolerance toward evangelical Christians in an American society driven by relativism.

Another example of acceptable intolerance is seen in the confirmation process for United States federal judges. The "tolerance test" seems to be the key. Receiving a passing mark from the Senate Judiciary Subcommittee hinges upon whether a nominee believes that tolerance (relativism) or the Constitution represents a baseline (absolute standard) for determining if laws and procedures are right, just, and fair.[16]

While cultural relativism is gaining strength in America and is the ethic of choice among some managers, Christians face a new dilemma. As McDowell and Hostetler point out, the Bible clearly teaches that "all values, beliefs, lifestyles, and truth claims are not equal. It teaches that the God of the Bible is the true God (Jeremiah 10:10), that all his words are true (Psalm 119:160), and that if something is not right in God's sight, it is wrong (Deuteronomy 6:18)."[17] We will look at systems of ethics based upon God's revelation in the next chapter.

Ethical Systems Comparison Chart

As a means of synthesizing the key concepts of the four ethical systems, fill in the cells in the Ethical Systems Comparison Chart below.

Ethical Philosophy or Theory	Main Characteristics	Strengths	Weaknesses
Utilitarianism			
Egoism			
Kant's Imperatives			
Cultural Relativism			

Questions Discussion

Using your comparison chart as a guide, respond to the following questions.

1. Which position comes closest to integrating Christian values and principles? Defend your response by clearly identifying the Christian values and principles and how they relate to specific elements of the chosen ethical position.

2. With which position do you feel most comfortable? Explain your answer, giving specific reasons that reflect your beliefs and the key elements of the ethical position.

3. Which position is most prevalent in your workplace? Provide examples.

4. Is any one of the positions described in this chapter sufficient to guide a manager in making ethical decisions? Explain your answer and give examples.

Endnotes

1. John R. Boatright, *Ethics and the Conduct of Business*, 2nd ed. (Upper Saddle River, NJ: Prentice Hall, 1997), 36.
2. Ibid., 39.
3. Ibid., 383.
4. Joseph W. Weiss, *Business Ethics: A Managerial, Stakeholder Approach* (Belmont, CA: Wadsworth, 1994), 66.
5. Manuel G. Velasquez, *Business Ethics: Concepts and Cases*, 4th ed. (Upper Saddle River, NJ: Prentice Hall, 1998), 76.
6. Ibid., 76.
7. Weiss, 67.
8. Jess Stein, ed., *The Random House Dictionary of the English Language* (New York: Random House, 1966).
9. Scott B. Rae and Kenman L. Wong, eds., *Beyond Integrity: A Judeo-Christian Approach to Business Ethics* (Grand Rapids, MI: Zondervan, 1996), 29.
10. Immanuel Kant, *Groundwork of the Metaphysics of Morals*, trans. H. J. Paton (New York: Harper and Row, 1964), 61.
11. Ibid., 96.
12. Velasquez, 95.
13. Stanley J. Grenz, *A Primer to Postmodernism* (Grand Rapids, MI: Eerdmans, 1996), 4.
14. Josh McDowell and Bob Hostetler, *The New Tolerance: How a Cultural Movement Threatens to Destroy You, Your Faith, and Your Children* (Wheaton, IL: Tyndale, 1998).
15. David Limbaugh, *Persecution: How Liberals Are Waging War Against Christianity* (Washington, D.C.: Regnery, 2003).
16. Lynn Vincent, "Tyranny of the Minority," *World*, June 7, 2003.
17. McDowell and Hostetler, 20.

3

Christianity and Ethics

"Show me your ways, O Lord, teach me your paths;
guide me in your truth and teach me."

(Psalms 25:4, 5a)

Chapter Challenges

A careful examination of Chapter 3 should enable the reader to:

- Define the term natural law.
- Explain the principles of Old Testament ethics.
- Understand the basics of New Testament ethics.

"There's no such thing as business ethics," declares leadership expert John
C. Maxwell in his provocative little book by the same title.[1] Maxwell
contends that all ethics are personal and suggests that ethics boil down to one
simple maxim, the Golden Rule. "So in everything, do to others what you
would have them do to you" (Matthew 7:12). That, according to Maxwell, is the
sum and substance of business ethics and of ethics in general.

Someone may argue that the Golden Rule is a Christian principle and
therefore has no appeal or applicability to those of other religious faiths.
Maxwell demonstrates, however, that some version of the Golden Rule exists
in nearly every culture and in every major religion of the world. His research

uncovered passages strikingly similar to the Christian Golden Rule in the holy writ of several faiths, including Islam, Judaism, Buddhism, Hinduism, Zoroastrianism, Confucianism, and Bahai.[2]

Natural Law

Without using the term, Maxwell has declared the Golden Rule to be a part of *natural law*. Natural law is sometimes referred to as eternal law or even human nature. "Natural law is regarded by its supporters as transcending custom and the laws of particular societies because some aspects of human nature are the same for all human beings."[3] Natural law suggests that right and wrong are written on the hearts of human beings by nature itself. It is the belief in a moral standard independent of a particular society's customs or rules of law.

The great thirteenth-century theologian and philosopher Thomas Aquinas is credited with developing the concept of natural law. This approach was also foundational to the thinking of French philosopher John Locke. In America, Thomas Jefferson expressed natural law's strong influence on him when he penned these words in the Declaration of Independence: "We hold these truths to be self-evident, that all men are created equal, that they are endowed by their Creator with certain unalienable Rights . . ."

Two Emphases

Today the term natural law is used primarily in two ways. Scott B. Rae explains the first context of natural law:

> First, it refers to general, objective, and widely shared moral values that are not specifically tied to the special revelation of Scripture. Values such as justice, fairness, respect for an individual's dignity, the obligation not to harm another, truth telling, and the respect for life in prohibitions against killing are some examples of virtually universal values whose origins predate Scripture.[4]

While many moral standards are culturally derived, those that exist across cultural boundaries, according to this understanding, are derived from natural law. Proponents of this view maintain that certain values exist in enough different cultures to warrant the belief that these truths are written naturally on the hearts of individuals. These adherents argue that where differences exist in morality between cultures these differences are derived from something other than natural law.

Second, the term natural law sometimes refers to what occurs naturally in creation. Environmentalists adopt natural law thinking when they declare pristine wilderness to be superior in any and every case to development. The Roman Catholic Church has utilized a natural law argument in its traditional opposition to birth control. Contraception, the Catholic Church suggests, interrupts the natural created order and, thus, is morally wrong.

Conservatives who attended the General Convention of the Episcopal Church were appalled at the election of Gene Robinson, a self-avowed, practicing homosexual, to the episcopacy in the summer of 2003.[5] Their arguments were based to a large degree on their interpretation of Scripture, but also on natural law. They believe that homosexuality denies the natural creation of human beings and, thus, is morally wrong.

Nearly Derailed

According to Rae's analysis, natural law also played a significant role in the Clarence Thomas confirmation hearings in October 1991. Rae believes Thomas' belief in natural law nearly derailed his confirmation as a justice of the United States Supreme Court.[6] He suggests that the mood of the hearings and the attitude of many members of the Senate Judiciary Committee shifted when Thomas vocalized this belief.[7]

Rae theorizes that the media and other liberal observers found Thomas's belief in natural law frightening for two important reasons. First, natural law has been used too frequently to oppress minorities and women. Ultra-conservatives, for example, have argued that superior male leadership qualities exist in nature, and have offered that as a basis for keeping women out of decision making roles. Others have suggested that Whites are superior to Blacks in the natural state. As a result of these historic misuses of natural law, some members of those groups found Thomas's advocacy of natural law unacceptable.

A second reason many found Thomas's belief in natural law unacceptable is that natural law represents a God-centered ethic. The existence of a universal right and wrong presupposes the existence of a higher authority—a higher authority that has declared that standard. In its rush to secularism, modern America has become much more comfortable with man-centered rather than God-centered ethics.

Most Christians would agree with Judge Thomas's opponents on the first point. If Thomas intended to use natural law to suppress women and members of his own race, few would find his ethic acceptable. On the second point, however, orthodox Christians overwhelmingly would find themselves in agreement with Thomas and natural law. (By orthodox, we refer to the biblical Christian church worldwide, not specifically to the Eastern Orthodox Church.) Most Christians agree that right and wrong are correctly understood in God-centered rather than human-centered ethics. Further, Christians believe that while God has written right and wrong on the hearts of human beings, as understood by natural law, He also has revealed His ethic in another way. Believers look to God's special revelation of moral right and wrong in the Old and New Testaments.

Old Testament Ethics and Holiness

The ethics articulated in the Old Testament and foundational to Judaism and Christianity are based upon the principle that human beings are created in the image of God. "So God created man in his own image, in the image of God he created him; male and female he created them" (Genesis 1:27). That we are created in the image of God explains why life preservation is so central to Judaism and orthodox Christianity. One does not destroy that which has been created in God's image.

Being created in the image of God also emphasizes a godly lifestyle. To be ethical, according to the Old Testament writers, is to be godly. And since *holiness* is an attribute unique to God as revealed in Old Testament literature, it follows that to be more like God is to be holy. God's command to the people of Israel in Leviticus 11:44 sums up Old Testament ethics: "I am the Lord your God; consecrate yourselves and be holy, because I am holy."

Theologian Allan Coppedge writes, "Never has the Christian Church needed to place a greater emphasis on holiness of character than in our day. But human holiness cannot be understood without reference to divine holiness."[8] Perhaps the insurgence of less ethical behavior in today's culture can be linked to its inability or unwillingness to understand God's holiness and His requirement to be like Him.

While the Old Testament outlines many characteristics of the holy life, three emerge as foundational to the study of ethics as applied to business and management: justice, equality, and integrity.

Justice: God's Measuring Line

The Old Testament declares that the holiness of God issues in *justice*. Accordingly, God's true (ethical) followers are people of justice. We probably think first of its punitive aspects when we think of the word *justice*. But justice involves a standard for both punishment and reward. Isaiah refers to justice as God's "measuring line" (28:17), a way to correct imbalances. The concept of justice as applied to business and management today can best be understood when broken down into three component aspects.

Contractual Justice

Contractual justice occurs when an exchange of promises creates a special relationship or contract. The Old Testament demonstrates contractual justice when God deals with the people of Israel in a special way in exchange for their agreement to follow Him. God demonstrates contractual justice through a covenant with Israel: "Now if you obey me fully and keep my covenant, then out of all nations you will be my treasured possession. Although the whole earth is mine, you will be for me a kingdom of priests and a holy nation" (Exodus 19:5-6a).

> *contractual justice:* Justice that occurs when an exchange of promises creates a special relationship called a contract.

Contractual justice still exists today. Ethical business people believe that the terms of a contract are binding. To violate a contract is to be unjust and thus unethical. On the other hand, the court dockets are filled with cases involving principals who have violated or severed their contractual relationships. Contracts are thus not eternal in spite of their moral and ethical dimensions.

Distributive Justice

Questions of injustice surface when some people struggle to make ends meet, while others enjoy an abundance of the world's goods. This is a matter of *distributive justice*. God implies distributive justice when He gives these commands in Leviticus 19:9-10: "When you reap the harvest of your land, do not reap to the very edges of your field or gather the gleanings of your harvest. Do not go over your vineyard a second time or pick up the grapes that have fallen. Leave them for the poor and the alien. I am the Lord your God."

> *distributive justice:* Type of justice that emerges from questions regarding the distribution of wealth.

In modern economic philosophy, John Rawls of Harvard University has developed the theory of distributive justice. He believes that societies form around systems of wealth distribution. While these distribution systems have very different components and rules, all ultimately are unjust according to Rawls—except the theoretical "natural state," which hypothetically existed at the beginning of time and prior to the establishment of social organizations.[9]

One form of this position is evident among those who defend the actions of the September 11 hijackers. They base their position on the injustice of what they see as an outrageous imbalance of wealth distribution; that is, that the terrorists were angry at having so little wealth in comparison to the average American. Others refute that argument by pointing to the abundance of oil in the Middle East and claiming that the proponents of Islamic fundamentalism direct their hatred at all non-Muslims—whether or not the issue has anything to do with distributive justice.

Compensatory Justice

The rubric of justice also includes compensatory justice. God often negatively or positively compensates certain people or people groups for their behaviors. For example, the Egyptians received harsh treatment at God's hands for enslaving God's chosen people. "Then I will lay my hand on Egypt and with mighty acts of judgment I will bring out my divisions, my people the Israelites" (Exodus 7:4). God authorized compensatory judgment when He instructed the people of Israel to ask the Egyptians for gold and silver articles prior to their exodus from Egypt (see Exodus 12:35-36).

> *compensatory justice:* Type of long term justice that emerges from compensation for injustices of the past.

In an interesting twist on the concept of compensatory justice, a modern-day Egyptian attorney, Nabil Hilmi, plans to sue the world's Jews for that ancient plunder.[10] Apparently, the suit will focus on whether compensation of modern Egyptians is due in light of ancient compensatory plunder by the Israelites. Such are the thorny questions of justice.

Closer to home and more recent in their focus are arguments about affirmative action programs in America. These arguments essentially stem from a variety of views on compensatory judgment. Some argue that it is unethical to give preferential treatment on the basis of race when hiring or offering opportunities in higher education. Others contend that preferred treatment is ethical and necessary in order to compensate for the injustices of the past. The latter group sees social ethics as mandating compensatory justice. The former group sees unqualified equality as the most just and most ethical basis of behavior.

Equality: The Heart of the Matter

A second characteristic of God's holiness and the holy life is *equality*. Throughout Scripture God encourages His people to deal equally with one another. A classic Old Testament account poignantly reveals this truth. According to God's instruction, the prophet Samuel was to search for the next king of Israel among the sons of a man named Jesse (1 Samuel 16). Samuel nearly overlooked the youngest son, David. But in reality, David was God's choice to succeed Saul. The principle of equality is summarized in God's explanation to Samuel: "Do not consider his appearance or his height, for I have rejected him [Eliab, David's older brother]. The Lord does not look at the things man looks at. Man looks at the outward appearance, but the Lord looks at the heart" (v. 7). That is to say, God viewed all of the sons of Jesse equally. He did not treat the firstborn son with more deference than the youngest son, as was the custom of that time.

God not only judges the hearts of humans rather than their outward appearance and circumstances, but He also demands that His followers treat others with equity. While many Old Testament passages command equality among God's chosen, this command also extends to foreigners, the oppressed, and the needy. These commands include helping those in need (Proverbs 21:13), protecting the helpless (Proverbs 31:8-9), feeding the poor (Leviticus 19:9), and not oppressing the vulnerable (Deuteronomy 27:19).

Integrity: Walking in Truth

A third attribute of God's holiness as demonstrated in Old Testament literature is *integrity*. God reveals Himself throughout Scripture in terms of honesty and truth. Psalm 33:4 captures the essence of God's integrity. "the word of the Lord is right and true; he is faithful in all he does."

As with justice and equality, this aspect of God's holiness is expected of His followers who aspire to ethical behavior. Hence, the Psalmist prayed, "Show me your ways, O Lord, teach me your paths; guide me in your truth and teach me" (Psalm 25:4, 5a). The prophet Zechariah summarizes this when he announces, "This is what the Lord Almighty says: '. . . These are the things you are to do: Speak the truth to each other, and render true and sound judgment in your courts; do not plot evil against your neighbor, and do not love to swear falsely. I hate all this,' declares the Lord" (Zechariah 8:14, 16-17).

Absolute v. Relative Truth

Since modern American culture increasingly denies absolute truth, this ethical quality has been minimized in favor of relative truth. Truth no longer is seen as an issue that is black or white, yes or no, heads or tails. Instead, truth depends on the situation. Thus, if the situation varies, then truth may vary from one situation to another.

In the area of Christian ethics, many modern students trace the popularizing of "Christian" moral relativism to the 1966 publication of Joseph Fletcher's *Situation Ethics: The New Morality*. Fletcher presents the argument that there are three approaches to ethical decision making. On the one hand is legalism with its social and biblical absolutes, intolerance, and lack of love, and on the other extreme is antinomianism (literally meaning "against law") which is the absence of any absolutes. In this school of thought, every situation is approached as unique, and the ethical decision is made without the use of any established set of rules or principles. Fletcher supports the middle ground between these two extremes. He says that Christian *situation ethics* is the proper course. This is an ethic that states that what is ethical concerning a specific action may very well vary from situation to situation and individual to individual provided that ethical consistency is provided by the unwavering application of biblical agape love. This love always seeks the best for the individual that is the target of its attention. Therefore, love is the guiding principle that always seeks the good for the individual even if it negates absolutes such as thou shall not kill or steal.[11] This system of ethical thought is similar to the ethics of virtue, which requires the decision maker to act in ways that will improve the virtue of the stakeholders involved. Thus, building character or adding virtue to another is the driving ethical force.

> *situation ethics:* Ethic developed by Joseph Fletcher stating that the ethical decision will vary from situation to situation.

In a more recent example of situational ethics, Jayson Blair was forced to resign his position with the *New York Times* after admitting that he made up stories and then passed them off as his own journalistic endeavors.[12] In a world devoid of truth, how Mr. Blair gleaned his "facts" seemed irrelevant to many. In an ironic twist, *Esquire* hired Blair to write a review for *Shattered Glass*, a film about Stephen Glass, who made up stories for the *New Republic*. David Granger, *Esquire* editor-in-chief, reportedly justified hiring Blair, saying, "We thought it was a clever way to do a movie review, to have the most famous fabricator review another infamous fabricator."[13] Looking at integrity through the lens of holiness, we know that "clever" and "ethical" are not necessarily synonymous.

Business ethics in twenty-first-century America has departed radically from Old Testament ethics. While the former focuses on situations from a human perspective, the latter exemplifies God's perspective. And God's holiness recognizes justice, equality, and integrity as the standards by which people should live.

New Testament Ethics and Holiness

The difference between Old Testament ethics and New Testament ethics is a shift in emphasis rather than overall approach. "As in Judaism, so in the New Testament, the imitation of God (or Christ) is seen as the fundamental basis of ethics."[14] Christ, the second Person of the Trinity, maintains the holiness inherent in the Godhead, and continues to demand holiness in His followers as the appropriate response of commitment to Him.

Living a Life of Love

To the principles of justice, equality, and integrity, Jesus and the early church add a strong emphasis on love as a standard of ethical behavior. Paul also insists that in light of Christ's coming, love is an important aspect of becoming more godly. "Be imitators of God, therefore, as dearly loved children and live a life of love, just as Christ loved us and gave himself up for us . . ." (Ephesians 5:1-2). In his epistles, John concurs and spells out the necessity of loving other human beings as a response to God's character. He writes, "Dear friends, since God so loved us, we also ought to love one another" (1 John 4:11).

The New Testament writers understood this new emphasis on love as a component of ethical, holy behavior in response to Jesus' specific commands. In what must have been considered shocking in its time, Jesus even went so far as to suggest that love must be extended to one's enemies. In His most famous sermon, He taught, "You have heard that it was said, 'Love your neighbor and hate your enemy.' But I tell you: Love your enemies and pray for those who persecute you" (Matthew 5:43-44).

Empowered by the Holy Spirit

Besides emphasizing love as a component of holiness, the New Testament introduces for the first time the presence and power of the Holy Spirit indwelling the believer on a continuous basis. While in the Old Testament, the Holy Spirit empowered one or more of God's people from time to time, in the New Testament the Holy Spirit is a continual presence in every believer. This presence makes it possible for disciples to achieve ethical purity and holiness of heart and life.

Jesus had made a promise to His small band of eager followers. "But when he, the Spirit of truth, comes, he will guide you into all truth" (John 16:13a). On the day of Pentecost, that promise was fulfilled. Immediately and boldly, the disciples began to demonstrate holy and ethical behavior. Acts 4:33-35 summarizes some of the characteristics of the early church:

> With great power the apostles continued to testify to the resurrection of the Lord Jesus, and much grace was upon them all. There were no needy persons among them. For from time to time those who owned lands or houses sold them, brought the money from the sales and put it at the apostles' feet, and it was distributed to anyone as he had need.

In looking at this passage from an ethical point of view, we can say that the disciples

- spoke *truth* about the Resurrection;
- ministered *justice* to those in need;
- attempted to facilitate *equality* among the brethren;
- acted with *love* towards others.

A central truth of the New Testament is that once followers of Jesus Christ are empowered by the Holy Spirit, they can become godly in their ethic. This happens because the Spirit enables them to live a life of holiness as demonstrated in ethical justice, equality, integrity, and love.

Facing Moral Dilemmas

Clearly, for the Christian—including today's Christian business manager—the Spirit-filled life is necessary to initiate a lifestyle that demonstrates ethical behavior. Yet, evidence abounds that Spirit-filled living is not the only quality essential for ethical behavior. Two different Spirit-empowered believers can come to strikingly different solutions for identical moral dilemmas. Further, the same two Christian managers can seek to interpret the same biblical truths, yet reach vastly different conclusions.

For example, one entry-level supervisor sought to act lovingly and justly toward an employee who was a single mother. He agreed to punch her time card, giving her the extra twenty minutes she needed to get her child to an important dentist appointment. Upper management saw the matter differently, interpreting the supervisor's act as disregard for integrity (disobeying the rules), as well as undercutting equality (showing favoritism). The supervisor was disciplined for unethical behavior.

A Christian manager also can experience inner conflict when faced with a number of different scenarios. Should he emphasize love over justice in one situation, and equality over truth in another? What if his decision in the first scenario ethically contradicts his decision in the second scenario? Managers who wait until they are faced with such choices have waited too long. They must develop in advance a clear ethical position designed to encompass as many situations as possible. How to develop such a personal position is the subject of chapter 4.

Questions Discussion

1. Do you believe in the existence of natural law? Give evidence to support your answer.

2. What problems do you foresee in attempting to apply biblical ethics to a management dilemma? How can these problems be overcome?

3. Is it possible to be ethical without being a Christian? Support your answer with evidence.

Endnotes

1. John C. Maxwell, *There's No Such Thing as "Business Ethics" : There's Only One Rule for Making Decisions* (New York: Warner, 2003), Preface.
2. Ibid., 22.
3. Robert N. Van Wyk, *Introduction to Ethics* (New York: St. Martins, 1990), 57.
4. Scott B. Rae, *Moral Choices: An Introduction to Ethics,* 2nd ed. (Grand Rapids, MI: Zondervan, 2000), 37.
5. Edward E. Plowman, "Formally Heretical," *World*, August 16, 2003, 22-23.
6. Rae, 36.
7. For a review of the facts surrounding the confirmation hearings see: Gloria Borger and Ted Gest, with Jeannye Thornton, "The Untold Story," *U. S. News and World Report*, October 12, 1992, 28-32. Or see Orrin Hatch, *Square Peg: Confessions of a Citizen Senator* (New York: Basic, 2002), 141-62.
8. Allan Coppedge, *Portraits of God: A Biblical Theology of Holiness* (Downers Grove, IL: InterVarsity, 2001), 16.
9. John Rawls, *A Theory of Justice*, rev. ed. (Cambridge, MA: Belknap/Harvard, 1999), originally published 1971.
10. "What About 400 Years of Slavery?" *World*, September 27, 2003, 8.
11. Joseph Fletcher, *Situation Ethics: The New Morality* (Philadelphia: Westminster, 1966), 17-39.
12. Seth Mnookin, "The Times Bomb," *Newsweek*, May 26, 2003, 40-51.
13. "It Takes One to Review One," *World*, August 9, 2003, 12.
14. Van Wyk, 38.

4

Developing a Personal Statement of Ethics

"But be ye doers of the word, and not hearers only,
deceiving your own selves."

(James 1:22 KJV)

Chapter Challenges

A careful examination of Chapter 4 should enable the reader to:

- Differentiate between three views for interpreting Scripture.
- Begin developing a personal statement of ethics.

To Be a Better Man

In the spring of 2003, reports surfaced that political pundit Bill Bennett had lost as much as $8 million over several years in high stakes gambling.[1] As the summer heated up, so did the ethical questions surrounding Bennett's lifestyle. There were mixed reactions from conservative loyalists. On the one hand, Bennett's followers expected the former drug czar and editor of the best-selling *The Book of Virtues* to live above reproach. They believed their self-appointed hero of morality should have avoided such arguably unethical behavior.

On the other hand, many concluded that Bennett's personal life was his business alone. No one doubted that Bennett's income could support a gambling habit. He was never accused of illegal behavior. Hence, many took the position that no one really had been hurt by this aspect of his lifestyle. Bennett himself responded to the debate with a concise analysis. Referring to his Roman Catholic belief system, he said simply, "Gambling's not a sin in my church."[2]

Within a few weeks, however, Bennett vowed that he was "now done with gambling. Period."[3] Cynics argued that his change of heart was strictly a result of his eagerness to reenter public life free from the baggage of national scandal. Bennett himself declared the change to be the result of deep introspection and the development of a personal ethic that apparently went beyond that of the church. "I stopped a lot of the usual action in my life and have done a kind of inventory of myself . . . and that's been good for me. The task is, and put this in capital letters, to become a better man."[4]

What Changed?

In looking at Bennett's decision to give up gambling, we can consider factors surrounding his decision.

- The church's position had not changed.
- Scripture had not changed.
- The acceptability of gambling had not changed.
- The legality of gambling had not changed.
- Bill Bennett's family circumstances had not changed.
- Only Bill Bennett's personal ethic had changed.

Bill Bennett's review of his own life and his announcement of an updated personal ethic gained unusual national attention. However, an ethical review is not an unusual activity. Leaders consistently discover the need to develop and perform according to a personal ethic. They find it necessary from time to time to review and update their own ethical position. As John Maxwell wrote, "Ethics is never a business issue or a social issue or a political issue. It is always a personal issue."[5]

Scripture Only

Such was the case for Ethan, a Christian who owned and operated a retail business. Ethan maintained that his personal ethic was based simply on "Scripture only." He declared, "Along with the rest of my independent church, I believe the Bible. That's all the ethic I need."

On many issues Ethan's approach worked satisfactorily. However, ultimately he was faced with a dilemma for which his "Scripture only" position was inadequate. Ethan had hired Jason, a teen from a troubled family, to work as a clerk in his business. He believed that he would have an opportunity to exert a positive Christian influence on Jason. The problem arose because Jason arrived late for work at least four days a week. Although the tardiness amounted to ten minutes or less, it clearly was a pattern. Ethan had repeatedly warned Jason about the importance of punctuality. Obviously, he needed to follow up on his warnings. The matter no longer involved Jason alone. Other employees were forced to cover for him in his absence.

Ethan faced an ethical dilemma. On one hand, the scriptural position was one of mercy and grace. On the other hand, there definitely were godly standards about the use of time. Further, there was the issue of fairness to other employees. Ethan asked himself, "Should I fire Jason or forgive him, so that I can continue to work toward his rehabilitation?"

Ethan's "Scripture only" ethic left him without a clear moral choice in this matter. He was forced to develop a more comprehensive ethical system. Many Christian managers faced with ethical dilemmas have developed such a system by first creating a personal statement of ethics. One of the purposes of this text, as we explained in the introduction, is to help the reader develop a personal statement of ethical position.

Building the Foundation

Before exploring the components of a personal statement of ethics, we need to examine the keystone upon which all Christian ethical positions are based—Scripture. However, the "Scripture only" ethic is not the same as a scriptural ethic. A "Scripture only" ethic sees the Bible as the beginning and end of ethical thought. A scriptural ethic builds upon Scripture as its foundation, but may include reason, experience, and tradition to structure a solid ethical position. It is important to remember that even a completely developed scriptural ethic does not answer every question because Scripture can be interpreted in many ways. In addition, scriptural passages can be adapted to real-world scenarios in a number of ways.

Three Views of Scripture

Allen Verhey suggests three possible ways to use a scriptural ethic for real-world choices.[6]

Fundamentalist View

A *fundamentalist view* teaches that the biblical ethic is normative for today's culture, except for those passages originally intended to be temporary. Of course, debate arises from determining just which passages were intended to be temporary. For example, some strict fundamentalists maintain that Paul's indication to the Corinthian church that women should be silent (1 Corinthians 14:34-35) is normative for today's culture. Some even see this passage as a general prohibition against any and all female leadership.

Some see issues other than this prohibition as Paul's primary focus in the Corinthian church. Therefore, they reason that the prohibition against women in leadership is applicable only to that situation. Obviously, even among those who hold to the fundamentalist view, there is diversity and a need for an expanded personal ethic.

Liberal View

Verhey identifies a second or *liberal view*. According to this position, a teaching is applicable to today's moral choices only if it is the Word of God as opposed to the human writer's viewpoint. Paul clearly identifies his own opinion in at least one passage (1 Corinthians 7:10). Determining how much of the writer's opinion colors God's Word, as well as its overall applicability to today's ethical choices, is a springboard for much discussion among those who hold to the liberal view.[7]

Interpretive View

Finally, Verhey identifies what might be called an *interpretive view*. In this view, the Christian engaged in applying scriptural truth to moral choices must first determine the original intent of the passage. The intent, as opposed to the literal words, is then applied to any contemporary ethical decision.[8] However, as with the fundamentalist and liberal views, debates rage over the original intent of any number of scriptural passages. For example, the command "You shall not murder" (Exodus 20:13) is interpreted by some to apply at the moment of conception. Others interpret this command as applicable from the moment of birth. Thus, it is still necessary for one who holds to the interpretive view to consider and construct a personal ethical viewpoint.

Developing a Statement of Personal Ethics

Clearly, regardless of one's view of Scripture, the Christian business leader or manager must develop a personal ethic—a statement of personal ethical intent. This statement is built on an individual's understanding of Scripture, and purports to anticipate ethical dilemmas that may arise in life. Correctly structured, it contains an appropriate anticipatory response to these dilemmas. Scripture and faith can and should be foundational to the Christian's personal ethic, but each person must build upon the foundation in order to determine the appropriate response in any given situation.

Evidence indicates that today's business managers eagerly accept the challenge to develop a statement of personal ethics. If there was a time when business and professional leaders managed their organizations according to the explicit dictates of a church's teachings and rules, that day is past. Today's business leaders "want fact and freedom simultaneously. They respect the teachings of their religious traditions, but they want to be active participants in interpreting, applying, and sometimes redefining the rules meant to guide them."[9]

Increasingly, business managers and students of business are discovering the advantages of writing out their personal statements of ethics in advance of any moral dilemma. That way, when issues arise, they have given prior thought to what they believe and how they intend to behave.

No On-the-Job Philosophizing

As a supervisor in a small manufacturing plant, Chris took his faith seriously. He also felt it necessary to think through his ethical belief system in advance. He learned from experience that the day-to-day rush of planning and supervising the work of his eighteen employees left little time for on-the-job philosophizing over ethics. He also discovered that as he revisited his personal statement of ethics from time to time, it required a bit of updating and fine-tuning in light of things he discovered in his work. In time, however, he was satisfied that the statement adequately reflected his personal beliefs. He also was confident that when implemented in the real world in which he operated, the statement made him a more ethical Christian manager. Chris's well-thought-out and fine-tuned statement appears in Figure 4.1.

Figure 4.1. A Statement of Personal Ethics

Chris Ault

As a disciple of Jesus Christ, I believe that everything I do reflects Him and His kingdom. Therefore, I will endeavor to make decisions on the basis of the key question, "What would Jesus do?"

Often I will find the answer to this question in the Scriptures, which is God's Word of truth. Therefore, I must be a regular student of the Bible in order to be an ethical manager.

Sometimes the answer is not spelled out in Scripture. Then I must ask myself a series of follow-up questions:

1. Which decision would do the most good for the most people?
2. How would I want to be treated if someone else were making the decision?
3. Have I already made statements or in any other way given an indication of my decision that others may be counting on?
4. Recognizing that I will stand before Christ some day to be judged, what decision should I make?

Even utilizing these probing questions is no guarantee that I will always perform ethically. Therefore, I will revisit this statement at least every three months to ensure that it is still leading me to ethical decision making. I also will pray regularly for my employees, suppliers, customers, and coworkers that God will prevent me from making decisions that will harm them.

A Personal Top Ten

Scripture is a key ingredient in Chris's statement, yet his position does not reflect interpretations of any particular passage. By contrast, another Christian manager incorporates interpretations of particular scriptural passages into her statement of personal ethics. Alison's statement appears in Figure 4.2.

Figure 4.2. A Statement of Personal Ethics

Alison Stewart

These are my top ten ethical guidelines:

1. Make every decision remembering that Jesus is watching.
2. Remember that Christian people are to be holy, just, and truthful.
3. Submit to your employer unless to do so would violate God's law.
4. Obey the government unless to do so would violate God's law.
5. Treat others as you wish to be treated.
6. Realize that all people are created in the image of God.
7. Recognize that since the fall all human beings are born in sin.
8. Be honest and above reproach in all things.
9. Treat the environment as a specially created gift from God.
10. God first, others second, self last.

Alison's statement of personal ethics has been refined over several years of management experience. Initially, however, it was the result of an in-depth scriptural study, as well as the study of several important topics related to ethics.

Writing a Statement of Personal Ethics

Formulate a first-draft statement of personal ethics by first identifying what ethical concepts are important to you (e.g., truth, discernment, fairness), and then prayerfully considering various scriptural passages to glean insight and information. Many resources are available to help you with this topical study. These include the concordance in your Bible, a good Bible dictionary, many Christian websites, the opinion of secular as well as Christian ethicists, and your own personal experiences.

Give special attention to those areas of life in which you are often tested. For example, one manager frequently lost his temper. He knew that he needed to be more patient. He resolved to include patience as both a personal goal of self-development and a component of his personal statement of ethics. To incorporate patience into his statement, he first will conducted a topical in-depth study of Scripture to find what God's Word said about patience. Then he wrote the specific truths he learned in his personal statement of ethics.

A Sample Topical Search

Effective managers will be committed to the idea that a statement of personal ethics must be practical as well as philosophically consistent. As a result, reviewing a series of scriptural passages relating more directly to employer-employee relationships will prove fruitful. Read the following Scriptures with an eye to how they could be instrumental in developing a personal statement of ethics. Beside each Scripture, write a summary statement that explains how that passage relates to business ethics.

Your summary statements might include a reference to *respect* for coworkers, employees, and employers. This is important, as 1 Timothy 6:1 points out, because when we are disrespectful, we slander God's name. Your search also might have found *sincerity* and *wholehearted service* to be important attributes in employee-employer relationships. To incorporate these findings into a personal statement of ethics, you would focus on these qualities in your first draft. A sample wording might include some of these thoughts:

> "I will put my all into my job and give my employer a full day's work for a full day's pay. I will perform even the mundane tasks with sincerity and thoroughness, and I will be busy at all times—not just when my employer is looking in my direction. I will treat everyone I come into contact with respectfully, even when they do not reciprocate."

Summary of Biblical Investigation in Ethical Behavior

Selected Scriptures	Key Insights
Leviticus 19:1	
Deuteronomy 24:14	
Malachi 3:8	

Selected Scriptures	Key Insights
Matthew 20:1-15	
Ephesians 6:5-9	
Colossians 3:22	
Colossians 4:1	
1 Timothy 5:8	
1 Timothy 6:1	
Titus 2:9	
1 Peter 2:18-20	

Integrating Faith and Practice

Having studied relevant Scriptures and reviewed the ethical positions of important philosophies, such as those presented in chapter 2, a manager is ready to write a first-draft statement of personal ethics. From time to time, most managers review their position in light of some ethical dilemma or moral choice they face in the workplace. Sometimes they simply perform a periodic review of the statement to assess how recent spiritual or emotional development has impacted their personal ethical position. Over time the statement becomes a vital part of who an individual is as a manager.

Of most importance, a statement of personal ethics can significantly impact a manager's day-to-day faith. That alone causes those who make the effort to contrast sharply with many of their Christian colleagues. "Most business managers acknowledge that religion played an important role in their moral upbringing. Yet few say that religion significantly affects their daily business decisions."[10] Managers who develop a personal statement of ethics effectively integrate faith and practice. They become "doers of the word, and not hearers only" (James 1:22 KJV).

Questions Discussion

1. What are the strongest points in Chris Ault's statement of business ethics? What are the weakest?

2. What are the key elements with which you agree in Alison Stewart's statement of personal ethics? With what points do you disagree?

3. What is the role of secular philosophies and theories of ethics in the formation of a personal code of ethics?

4. How does one's view of the value of people affect the adoption of secular and biblical principles in the development of a code of ethics?

Endnotes

1. Jonathan Alter and Joshua Green, "Bennett: Virtue Is as Virtue Does?" *Newsweek*, May 12, 2003, 6.
2. Editors, "To Become a Better Man," *World*, August 9, 2003, 24-25.
3. Ibid.
4. Ibid.
5. John Maxwell, *There's No Such Thing as "Business Ethics"* (New York: Warner, 2003), 13.
6. Allen Verhey, *The Great Reversal: Ethics and the New Testament* (Grand Rapids, MI: Eerdmans, 1984), 170.
7. Ibid.
8. Ibid.
9. Alan Wolfe, *Moral Freedom: The Search for Virtue in a World of Choice* (New York: W. W. Norton, 2001).
10. Edward D. Zinbarg, *Faith, Morals, and Money: What the World's Religions Tell Us about Money in the Marketplace* (New York: Continuum, 2001).

Assignment: First Draft

Review the ethical systems of Chapter 2. What particular aspects of any of these philosophies can you apply to your personal statement of ethics? Then examine the Scriptures below and write a summary statement after each verse describing how that verse relates to business ethics. Be sure to include the Scriptures we highlighted in the sample topical search above. To assist you, we have chosen three concepts essential to a personal statement of ethics and listed relevant Scriptures. If you choose to develop additional concepts or qualities, support them with Scripture.

Use the space at the end of this chapter to write the first draft of your personal statement of business ethics. Be sure to include any important truths you have already discovered as a business manager or in your everyday interactions. Remember that this is a first-draft statement. Later in this text, you will be given opportunities to review and refine your statement. Chapters 5-20 are designed with that end in mind.

My Personal Statement of Ethics will include the quality of justice:

- Exodus 23:1-8
- Ecclesiastes 5:8
- Ecclesiastes 7:7
- Isaiah 1:17
- Isaiah 5:14
- Isaiah 56:1
- Lamentations 3:35-36
- John 7:24
- Romans 14:17
- 1 Corinthians 6:12
- 1 Corinthians 13:6

Are there any other Scriptures you wish to include on justice as it relates to ethics?

Review justice as it was presented in Chapter 3. What aspects are applicable to your personal statement of ethics?

My personal statement of ethics will include the quality of holiness:

- Genesis 17:1
- Exodus 19:6
- Leviticus 11:44
- Psalm 32:2
- Psalm 73:1
- Psalm 119:1
- Proverbs 21:8
- Isaiah 4:3
- Zechariah 14:20
- Luke 6:45
- 1 Timothy 5:22
- 1 Peter 2:1
- 1 John 3:3

Are there any other Scriptures that you wish to include on holiness as it relates to ethics?

Review holiness as it was presented in Chapter 3. What aspects are applicable to your personal statement of ethics?

My personal statement of ethics will include the quality of integrity:

- Exodus 20:16
- Exodus 23:21
- Deuteronomy 25:13
- Psalm 119:29
- Psalm 120:2
- Proverbs 3:3
- Proverbs 11:1
- Matthew 15:19
- 2 Corinthians 8:21
- 1 Thessalonians 4:12
- 1 Thessalonians 5:22

Are there any other Scriptures that you wish to include on integrity as it relates to ethics?

Review integrity as it was presented in chapter 3. What aspects are applicable to your personal statement of ethics?

Statement of Personal Ethics

Name _____   Date _____

5

The Christian Manager as Ethical Decision Maker

"... if you call out for insight and cry aloud for understanding ... then you will understand what is right and just and fair—every good path."

(Proverbs 2:3, 9)

Chapter Challenges

A careful examination of Chapter 5 should enable the reader to:

- Differentiate between issues of fact, value and policy.
- Understand criteria for ethical decision making.

Case Study

Sunset Manor Retirement Center

Ever since earning her nursing license over fifteen years ago, Julie Fredericks has worked at Sunset Manor Retirement Center. In addition to providing traditional nursing home care, Sunset Manor serves the housing needs of those retirees who select from among a variety of available independent living arrangements. Julie has always preferred working in the Alzheimer's unit, where she supervises a staff of five nursing assistants on the day shift. Together, they care for fifteen patients.

Of necessity, the patient-to-caregiver ratio is high, since the needs of the people are great. Sunset Manor has a fine reputation among both clients and competitors for providing above-average care. The commitment to quality is one reason Julie finds her work so rewarding. "The residents are so sweet, and there is just the right combination of nursing and administration. I love my job," Julie told a friend recently.

A Difficult Decision

Today, however, Julie is not so sure. She has just received word that she must release one of her five assistants. The memo from the front office indicates that after careful budget review and analysis, administrators have determined that employee costs are simply too high in the Alzheimer's unit. Asked to reduce the staff by one member, each shift supervisor has been instructed to submit the name of one employee to the Personnel Department.

Julie loathes the idea. "Those administration types simply don't understand the heavy demands of working with our special needs people, "Julie complains to her second shift counterpart. "Our responsibilities take more time and energy than those in other areas of Sunset Manor."

"I refuse to do it," her colleague responds. "I'm convinced it is morally wrong to understaff this area. I won't participate in the hatchet job. If they intend to lay off any of my people, they will do it without my help."

"Disobeying orders doesn't seem like the correct approach," Julie argues. "I don't think I have much choice, although I certainly wish for the residents' sake that we had some alternatives."

Later, Julie sits with personnel files spread before her, trying to decide which of her five nursing assistants should be let go. She wants to be fair both to the employees and to the residents. The decision proves to be extremely difficult.

The Personalities Involved

Sally Chambers has been with Sunset Manor nearly as long as Julie and plans to retire in about three years. She demonstrates careful efficiency in her approach to the workload and seems to accomplish more than other staff members. However, Sally sometimes becomes obsessed with the need to meet specific goals. Forging ahead with government-mandated paperwork, she can be abrupt, even rude, to residents and their families. Even so, Julie appreciates Sally's attention to detail, since Julie has never enjoyed these kinds of mundane tasks.

Janice Robinson is the complete opposite of Sally. She loves the people in the Alzheimer's unit almost to the exclusion of administrative responsibilities. She could sit for hours and visit with residents or their families. Family members often comment positively on her caring attitude. "It is about people work, not paperwork," Janice loves to say. As a single mom with two elementary-age children, Janice depends on her salary at Sunset Manor to make ends meet.

Angie Franklin, the newest member of Julie's staff, joined the team as a replacement only a few months ago. Already Julie has come to depend heavily on Angie's knowledge and ability. She attends school at night, and needs less than a year to complete her nursing degree. Julie routinely gives her more responsibility than she does the other assistants. In fact, she encourages Angie to practice her nursing skills within the limits of propriety and the law.

Jake Minor, the only male member of the staff, has played a unique role during his five years at Sunset Manor. The others depend on Jake to lift patients or perform other strenuous tasks. Jake came to Sunset Manor after his conversion to Christianity and several subsequent months of drug rehabilitation. With no family and few outside interests, he wanted to lead a more productive life. He pours his heart and soul into his work at Sunset Manor. More than once he has commented to Julie that few places would have offered him the second chance he needed. "I owe my life to Sunset Manor," he explains.

Regina Munson rounds out Julie's staff. Perhaps better than anyone else at Sunset Manor, Regina understands the needs of the elderly—and the residents love her. In addition to her work at Sunset Manor, she cares for her own aging mother at home. Some believe she has heavy financial responsibilities. Others call her a workaholic. For whatever reason, Regina has proved to be an extremely dependable employee. In fact, records indicate that she has not missed a single day of work in the nearly five years since she was hired.

What Is Right?

Complicating Julie's decision, Sunset Manor does not have a union. In addition, company history provides very little precedent for decision making in workforce reduction. Julie goes over the files again and again, trying to decide which staff member to release. The more she thinks about it, the more her second shift counterpart's idea of refusing the task appeals to her. Julie even wonders if she should offer to quit, basing her decision on being asked to do something she finds unconscionable.

"I just don't know what is right," she declares. "I don't even know *how to decide* what is right."

On Background

Criteria for Ethical Decision Making

Julie acknowledges that not only must she make a difficult decision, but also that she feels inadequate for the task. She joins a large segment of managers who find constant decision making to be one of the most difficult aspects of their jobs.

As Julie wrestles with the options available to her, she will certainly consider both the ethics of her dilemma and the ethics of decision making in general. To this end she may want to consider six criteria for ethical decision making.

1. Ethical decision makers recognize that all decisions are not the same.

Her current dilemma may prove to be one of the most agonizing in Julie's managerial career. Through a ripple effect, her decision stands to impact the lives of many others. To be an ethical decision maker, Julie needs to acknowledge the seriousness of the situation and carefully weigh all options. This means she will have to devote more time and emotional energy to this decision than to less critical issues, such as choosing a supplier for a particular product, or scheduling employee days off.

To better understand the differences in decisions, view them as involving three types of issues:

- fact
- value
- policy

Ethical decision makers readily recognize the differences in these three types of issues. Further, they recognize the need to deal differently with decisions involving issues of fact than with those involving value or policy.

Decisions Based on Fact

Because they consider the truth or falsity of an assertion, decisions surrounding issues of fact are generally the easiest to make. Most managers find it relatively simple to collect the data and then make a decision based on issues of fact. For example, a manager who reviews product safety data recognizes that a particular product may be harmful to the consumer. She follows preset guidelines that assess the potential for and severity of injury. The product in question will either meet the guidelines or it will not. An issue of fact determines the product safety manager's course of action.

Decisions Based on Value

Decisions surrounding *issues of value* consider the relative worth or rightness of a particular course of action. In such questions, one manager's ethical and honest conclusion may differ from another manager's ethical and honest conclusion. Julie's second shift counterpart has decided that it is morally wrong to lay off an employee in her unit. She has made a decision of value not to participate. Julie instead has determined that it is morally wrong to violate the instructions of an employer. She is proceeding with the layoff, having come to a different conclusion on the question of value.

Making decisions on value should not be confused with the modern pseudo-normative ethical theory, Emotivism. The emotivist believes that one's personal feelings are the only determiners of what is ethical. If a person strongly believes that a course of action is ethical, it is ethical, even if the belief is not based in facts, biblical principles, or reason. In contrast, the Christian who allows his or her conscience to guide decision making utilizes biblical principles as the plumb line to insure that what is felt is from the Holy Spirit and not from personal biases.

Decisions Based on Policy

Decisions of policy usually involve the word "should." They focus on which course of action *should* be taken. This contrasts to decisions that *must* be taken (related to questions of fact) or decisions *determined* to be superior to an alternative course (related to questions of value). For example, a manager who buys a higher-priced, lower-quality item from one supplier may do so based on a policy decision. The manager may be willing to pay the higher price and accept the lower quality because of issues of loyalty, commitment, or customer service. In short, he concludes, "In this case I should pay more because . . ."

2. Ethical decision makers analyze a situation from many points of view.

Since Julie's decision potentially will impact a host of people, she will want to examine the position of as many stakeholders as possible in the analysis phase of decision making. She must consider her own superiors at Sunset Manor, her five staff members, the staff members' families, and her counterpart on the other shift. Julie's decision even includes her counterpart's employees, who will see Julie taking managerial responsibility while their own supervisor fails to act. Certainly and perhaps most importantly, Julie will have to take into account the effect of her decision on the clients in the Alzheimer's unit. While it would be easier if she limited the analysis phase to her own needs and wants, such self-centered behavior must never be an option for the ethical Christian manager.

> *issue of fact:* Decisions that consider the truth or falsity of an assertion.
>
> *issue of policy:* Decisions that consider what course of action should or should not be taken.
>
> *issue of value:* Decisions that consider the relative worth or rightness of an issue.

3. Ethical decision makers are action oriented.

The ethical decision maker must make decisions in a timely fashion. Julie would be acting irresponsibly if she made a snap decision or simply flipped a coin. However, because of the many perspectives she has to consider, Julie also is in danger of becoming so enmeshed in the analysis that she fails to make a timely decision. Managers are ultimately paid for decisions, not analysis. Ethical decision makers avoid the "paralysis of analysis." To drag the decision out beyond the point of reasonable analysis also challenges ethical standards. Delaying necessary decisions yields unethical results through the unproductive use of time.

a. Every day that Julie does not announce her decision is another day that one employee cannot prepare for termination.

b. Every hour that Julie spends in the decision process is an hour that she cannot give to her employer in other profitable endeavors.

c.   Every minute of doubt translates into a less productive minute across the entire organization, since Julie's employees are focusing attention on the future layoff rather than current job issues.

4. Ethical decision makers acknowledge emotional bias.

A young man declared to his latest romantic infatuation, "I'll always love you. I know because I've never felt this way before about anyone." Decision making on the basis of feelings may prove adequate in puppy love. However, it seldom provides a solid basis for sound managerial decisions.

In the decision making process, Julie must attempt to the best of her ability to distance herself from her emotional involvement with her employees. Since Julie is human, some emotion is bound to be present. It must therefore be accepted and acknowledged in order for Julie to make an ethical decision.

Emotional bias can creep into managerial decisions in various forms. One manager found it difficult to discipline employees in a certain age group because they reminded him of his own parents. Another made poor decisions regarding employee time off because of her own unacknowledged guilt about the amount of time she spent away from home and family. Yet another manager found it difficult to be objective concerning a policy on tuition reimbursement. She had worked long hours and made significant sacrifices for her own education without the convenience of that benefit.

These managers will move toward more ethical decision making when they recognize their own emotional involvement in these areas. They may find it useful to think of personal emotion as one of the many perspectives included in appropriate analysis. Then, having acknowledged their biases, they can move on to more objective analysis through other points of view.

5. Ethical decision makers view results realistically.

Few circumstances dictate either 100 percent negative or 100 percent positive outcomes. Yet some managers seem to insist on seeing the future as exclusively one or the other.

A fund-raising executive for a nonprofit corporation insisted on avoiding goal setting. "A goal only limits my thinking," he argued. "Without it we have the potential to raise unlimited resources." Such a rose-colored view denies reality. Another manager refused even to consider a product price increase, saying, "If we decide to raise prices, we'll never sell another unit." Such thinking undoubtedly overstates potentially negative outcomes.

Ethical decision makers routinely examine potentially positive and negative outcomes. They recognize that in actuality they probably will realize some combination of both.

6. Ethical decision makers search for causal links.

- A basketball coach declares, "The last time we played zone defense, we lost; therefore, we will never play zone again."
- An investor states, "Every time I sell on Friday, the market opens higher on Monday. I'll never sell again on Friday."
- A sales representative reasons, "Whenever I stay away from the home office for longer than one week, I lose sales. I'm not taking two-week trips anymore."

In each situation, these managers have made a fatal error in decision making. They have examined two independent pieces of information and assumed a causal link. The coach lost because of injury to his key scorer. The investor's small holdout had no real impact on the total market. The sales representative failed to factor in that he usually doesn't take Friday afternoon phone orders when he is out of the office.

Failing to discover correct causal links leads to faulty decision making. The ethical decision maker researches and analyzes information carefully, searching for the correct links and, subsequently, the correct course of action.

Julie faces a complex situation and must make a very difficult decision. She may have developed her own approach to such problems, or she may seek the advice of other managers for input into her analysis and decision making. In either event, as she wrestles with her judgment, she should utilize the six criteria above in order to reach an ethical decision.

A Guide for Ethical Decision Making

This simple seven-step decision making process is helpful in the organization of the data and the exercising of thought process needed to make an ethical decision.

Step One

Most business decisions have human consequences. Identify the relevant stakeholders by asking yourself, "Who stands to benefit, and who will probably be harmed by the decision that I am about to make?"

Step Two

Since most business ethical dilemmas involve economic needs or desires, identify them. Again a question is good to guide your search. Ask yourself, "Who stands to gain economically, and who stands to lose economically as a result of my decision?"

Step Three

As a manager, you have a responsibility to the laws of the land and the policies of your company. A third question to pose is, "Have any laws or company policies been broken, and will my intended resolution of the dilemma break any?"

Step Four

You now have gathered sufficient data to develop a short list of possible courses of action (decisions) that you can take to resolve the business dilemma at hand.

Step Five

Conduct a Christian Worldview analysis. Ask yourself, "Are the courses of actions that I am considering supported or prohibited in God's written and revealed revelation?"

Step Six

Conduct a secular ethical philosophy analysis. Ask yourself, "Are the courses of actions that I am considering supported or prohibited by sound secular ethical thought?"

Step Seven

Utilizing the results of your analysis, you should select the best decision from your short list.

Toward an Ethical Christian Worldview

Ephesians 6:5-9

Slaves, obey your earthly masters with respect and fear, and with sincerity of heart, just as you would obey Christ. Obey them not only to win their favor when their eye is on you, but like slaves of Christ, doing the will of God from your heart. Serve wholeheartedly, as if you were serving the Lord, not men, because you know that the Lord will reward everyone for whatever good he does, whether he is slave or free (Ephesians 6:5-9).

It is estimated that at the time Paul penned these words to the Church at Ephesus, nearly fifty percent of the 120 million people living in the Roman Empire were slaves. The master-slave relationship was an obvious way for Paul to teach on the subject of obedience.

Although it never directly attacked the institution of slavery, Christianity effectively broke the fetters of the slave by lifting the servant to a higher plane. Christianity consistently taught the slave about spiritual freedom in the midst of physical servitude. Romans 16 demonstrates that early on many of those who were slaves came to a saving faith in Jesus Christ. Influenced by the witness of changed lives, their masters often became Christians as well.

The Characteristics of Christian Obedience

In the Western world today, the institution of slavery has been destroyed. The clear teaching of obedience within appropriate limits lives on, however. Such teaching lies at the heart of a solution to Julie Fredericks' dilemma. Paul says that the servant or employee must be obedient to the master or employer. Based on Ephesians 6:5-9, he identifies four characteristics of obedience. The Christian obeys

1.   "with respect and fear" (v. 5)

     Paul uses this same phrase in 1 Corinthians 2:3, 2 Corinthians 7:15, and Philippians 2:12. This favorite expression of the apostle does not imply cringing before the master, as the wording of the King James Version might imply ("fear and trembling"). Instead, it commands a respect or reverence for those who are in authority.

2. "in sincerity of heart" (v. 5)

The word translated "sincerity" and "singleness," is found throughout Paul's writings (e.g., Romans 12:8; Colossians 3:22). The original Greek word literally means without hypocrisy or divided loyalties. Sincerity of heart stands in direct contrast to double-mindedness. The employee should be focused and unswerving in his or her loyalty to the employer.

3. not just "when their eye is on you" (v. 6)

The older English translations use the expression "*not with eyeservice*" (e.g., KJV). This is the flip side of singleness of heart. Obedience is not something that the employee should turn on and off as the situation warrants. It is a quality that is internalized, a sincere seeking after the employer's best interest. Watching the clock or looking busy when the boss is around reflects hypocrisy and double-mindedness.

4. "wholeheartedly" (v. 7)

Paul demands Christian love even in the servant-master relationship. How much more would he insist on such wholehearted goodwill in the modern employee-employer context? The idea in this word choice is that the service must be enthusiastic, not grudging. An employer has a right to expect dedicated enthusiasm in the workplace.

Summarizing Ephesians 6:5-9 reveals that Paul believes an employer has the right to expect three things from employees:

1. Respect
2. Loyalty
3. Enthusiasm

While this is the nature of obedience, it is important to remember that obedience to an earthly employer has limits. Paul says slaves must obey their earthly masters. However, he implies that a higher master takes precedence. The older translations are instructive in this phrasing: "Servants, be obedient to them that are your masters according to the flesh" (KJV). There is a limit to obedience in the workplace. The commands of God in the spiritual realm are never to be disobeyed in the name of obedience to an earthly authority. For example, no one would expect an employee to murder or steal because an employer gave instructions to do so. One might respond to such a suggestion by saying, "Well, of course not! It is against the law of the land."

Paul would respond, "There is a better reason. Such behavior is against God's law."

This biblical teaching stands in stark contrast to what Alex C. Michales refers to as the "loyal agent's argument" which basically says that a manager's duty is to serve the employer in whatever way is possible to advance the employer's self-interest.[1] This is a type of exchanging of one's moral code for blind loyalty and in the process becoming the property of the company. It is ironic that this modern attempt to deny the appropriateness of stressing ethics in the workplace actually reduces managers to a type of slave relationship with employers.

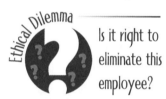

Is it right to eliminate this employee?

Julie Fredericks must decide whether or not eliminating an employee from her staff will be a violation of God's moral law. If she feels that such a change will seriously threaten the care and well-being of patients in the Alzheimer's unit, she has an ethical obligation to refuse the instruction of her superior. If the matter is not quite that serious, she has an ethical obligation to serve her employer with obedience.

Ask the Pro

John Carmichael is Executive Vice President of an international missions organization. Following graduation from college, he began a career as a missionary to Haiti. He later served as field director for the missionary effort in that country. For nearly twenty years, he has held a variety of administrative and management positions in the organization's home office. His responsibilities as executive vice president include serving as chief operating officer.

The authors asked John for his input on the dilemma facing Julie Fredericks at Sunset Manor. His candid assessment follows:

Q: What is your take on the Sunset Manor case? Who should Julie let go?

Carmichael: This is a tough situation. I believe we must address two issues before we even consider whom to let go. First, Julie found fulfillment in her job because of the quality care Sunset Manor provides. I wonder if she can cut staff and still be true to herself? But more importantly, can she cut one person and still provide adequate care for the patients who depend upon it and deserve it?

Q: But the company is already saying to let someone go. Doesn't she have an ethical responsibility to her employer?

Carmichael: Of course, but the greater moral issue involves providing adequate care for the patients. I first would try to find a way to manage through a restructure to do an adequate job. In that case, I would recommend terminating the person who had been there for only a few months. However, if I believed Sunset Manor could not provide adequate care for its clients, it then would become morally wrong to try to operate with one less person. In that case, I would go to my supervisor and say, "I can't be true to myself and do this. I recommend I be the one you let go."

Q: What about providing for her family, paying her bills, etc.? Julie probably needs this job. Should she quit over the company's understaffing problems?

Carmichael: I have to stand before God one day. He is the One I ultimately have to answer to. One of my guiding principles is, "It is never wrong to do what is right." In this case, that means if I lose my job because of a moral issue, then I have thrown myself back upon God—and He will take care of me.

Q: You spent seventeen years in Haiti, and have been exposed to a variety of cultures around the world. How much of ethics is culture based? Is there a universal right and wrong?

Carmichael: There are some things that never change, but culture has a great deal of impact. For example, when I first arrived in Haiti, there were things I labeled as bribery, things I would not do. After I had been there long enough to learn the culture, I did not use that term at all. I did those things.

Q: Can you be specific?

Carmichael: Suppose you are stopped by a policeman for some minor infraction. Haitians will give the policeman three or four dollars. He gives them back their licenses and they go on. I used to think that was wrong. It was bribing a policeman. Today, I see it differently. That policeman, if he gets paid at all, is three or four months behind in his salary. If I go downtown to follow procedures, it costs me a half a day of work, in addition to the $10 or $15 fine that will go into the pockets of those sitting in the office. That night, however, the policeman's kids would still be hungry.

Q: Would you try to slip a policeman in Miami a few dollars?

Carmichael: There is no way I would even consider doing that here in the United States.

Q: So, are all ethics culturally based, or are there universal limits?

Carmichael: For me the limits are found in Scripture. I would not violate the Bible, as I understand it. I would not steal, though many Haitians find stealing acceptable. Similarly, I would not lie in any culture. I won't cheat someone. Those scriptural standards are universal.

You Be the Consultant

Help Julie decide on the most appropriate course of action by responding to these key questions:

1. Is the second shift supervisor's decision to refuse to dismiss an employee an ethical decision? Why or why not? Under what circumstances would refusing the order of a supervisor be ethical?

2. Is Sunset Manor's management being ethical by requesting Julie to make the layoff decision? Why or why not?

3. What procedure do you think Julie should follow to make her decision?

4. How would a follower of Utilitarianism make this decision? Defend your answer.

5. How should the person to be dismissed be informed of the decision? How should the rest of the work group find out about the decision?

6. Whom would you dismiss? Why? What impact does your statement of ethical position have on your decision?

Endnotes

1. Alex C. Michales, *A Pragmatic Approach to Business Ethics* (Thousand Oaks, CA: Sage Publications, 1995), 44-53.

6

The Christian Manager as Ethical Planner

"May he give you the desire of your heart and make all your plans succeed."

(Psalm 20:4)

Chapter Challenges

A careful examination of Chapter 6 should enable the reader to:

- Recognize and identify the two components of a business plan.
- Define core values.
- Explain the elements and purpose of a mission statement.
- Identify the importance of planning in ethics.

Case Study

Hur Ministries

Allen Ford slipped wearily into his chair in the interview room at Hur Ministries. He had lost count of how many hours he had spent in this chair through the week. Yesterday he had interviewed candidates until 10:00 p.m. The three previous days, he hadn't finished until after 9:00 p.m. It was now 7:45 a.m. and the first candidate of the day would arrive shortly.

Allen sipped from his coffee mug and closed his eyes in contemplation. Ironically, the heavy demands and long hours evidenced the tremendous success of Hur Ministries. Yet, the demand for candidates far outweighed the number Allen could match with clients. When he had established Hur Ministries three years ago, he could not have dreamed of such phenomenal success. But his success had come at a price. The tremendous pressure of his job and his increasing fatigue were signs that the last few years undoubtedly had been the single most difficult time in his fifty years of life.

Lost in the Battle

It began with the divorce. In retrospect there was no one to blame but himself. He and Joan simply drifted apart. She developed interests of her own while he worked sixty and seventy hours a week at the plant. She appealed again and again for more of his time. He called it nagging. Eventually she met "someone who appreciates me," as she put it. She filed for divorce a few months later.

Joan and Allen battled fiercely both in and out of the courtroom, primarily over property issues. Allen's twenty-year history of very lucrative positions, coupled with their frugal lifestyle, yielded significant assets.

Somehow, in the midst of the battle, no one had noticed that the couple's only child, seventeen-year-old Steven, had distanced himself from the family chaos and withdrawn into a private world of drugs. When he died of a drug overdose, the authorities ruled his death suicide. Both Joan and Allen that they had missed the warning signs of Steven's drug abuse. Although Steven's death temporarily brought them closer, there had been too much damage to their relationship. Joan left town with her new husband. Allen new only that she had divorced him a few months later. He had no idea where she now lived.

Lifting Up Hands to the Lord

Allen reacted differently than his wife to the upheaval caused by his divorce and the death of his son. He returned to the faith of his childhood. He found a strong church, recommitted his life to Christ, and set out to help other families who still had time to avoid the mistakes he had made. He wanted his life to make a difference.

One Sunday Pastor James preached from Exodus 17:8-15. In this passage, Aaron and Hur held up the hands of Moses while the Israelities battled the Amalekites. As long as Moses held his hands high, the Israelites gained on the enemy. When Moses lowered his arms to rest, the Amalekites began to dominate. "Aaron and Hur held his hands up—one on one side, one on the other—so that his hands remained steady till sunset. So Joshua overcame the Amalekite army with the sword" (vv. 12, 13).

Allen wept bitterly when he realized that had someone been there to hold up Steven, he would still be alive today. If only someone had listened to Steven, counseled with him, and become a friend when he needed one. That marked the beginning of Hur Ministries.

Managing Growth

Shortly after that Sunday, Allen founded Hur Ministries. The focus of the ministry was to act as a clearinghouse, matching Christian young adults with elementary and high school students whose parents were in the process of divorcing. As mentors, the young adults would hold the kids up during this difficult period.

In the first six months, Hur Ministries was a one-man operation—Allen Ford managed everything. Later, as courts and social agencies began to refer clients to Hur Ministries, Allen found it necessary to hire a recruiter whose job was to locate mentors. He also hired a staff to help with administrative work. Soon after, he hired a trainer to teach volunteers the techniques of peer counseling, proactive listening, and friendship evangelism.

Still, only Allen Ford selected mentors. The selection process included reading a detailed application and conducting a personal interview. As a way to lighten his workload, the staff had encouraged him to hire an interviewer. However, Allen was convinced that he was the most qualified person to select a mentor—the kind of mentor who would have made a difference in Steven's life. "I can't teach what it is that I'm looking for," he argued. "But I know it when I see it."

Last year Hur Ministries had matched more than 3,000 young people with suitable mentors. Unfortunately, another 2,500 had been turned away because there was inadequate time to conduct the candidate interviews. Now, a social service agency in a distant city had offered Hur Ministries a contract to expand to their area. Allen had explored the possibility of traveling one day each week in order to conduct the interviews. It seemed too promising an opportunity for the ministry to turn down.

A church friend who operated his own business offered some advice. "Allen," he said, "you have to decide where you intend the ministry to be in the future. If you want to continue growing, you will have to develop different procedures."

"It's not my business," Allen responded. "The Lord will send us the right clients, the right mentors, and the right opportunities. I intend to remain faithful and do this work the right way."

A knock at the door jolted Allen back to reality. "Mr. Ford," the receptionist announced, "your first interview is here."

On Background

The Business Plan

On the surface it appears that Allen Ford's problems involve time and procedures. Using current operational procedures, there simply are not enough hours in the day to foster Hur Ministries' growth. The efficient, effective, and ethical management of a business, church, or a family does not occur by chance. It requires planning by those involved. A business will have several types of plans. The plan that gives direction to the organization is the *business plan*. Nickels, McHugh, and McHugh define business plan as "a detailed written statement that describes the nature of the business, the target market, the advantages the business will have in relation to competition, and the resources and qualifications of the owner(s)."[1] The business plan is fleshed out through two other plans, the strategic plan and the operational plan.

> *business plan:* Detailed written statement of a business that is comprised of a strategic plan and an operational plan.
>
> *strategic plan:* Process of identifying major goals, policies and strategies for an organization.
>
> *operation plan:* Comprised of short term and specific goals of an organization designed to meet the strategic plan over time.

Careful inspection of Hur Ministries' operations reveals a deeper problem than lack of time. Allen has no business plan. He doesn't know where Hur Ministries is headed. He continues to make business decisions with long-term implications without the benefit of a strategic plan. It is the authors' belief that this both adversely affects the meeting of important goals, and it very well may set the stage for unethical decisions to be made. When managers are in new terrain, lack clear well-though-out direction, and are under extreme pressure from various stakeholders, the situation is ripe for panicky or hasty decisions that are more reactionary and protective than rational and proactive.

The Strategic Plan

Ethical managers agree that the absence of a strategic plan usually yields ineffective decision making on a day-to-day basis. In addition, many realize that such a deficiency sets the stage for possible unethical decision making.

Consider the case of a small computer programming business that hired a programmer. The new employee was excellent with computer work, but seriously lacked social skills. "No problem," concluded the business owner. "All we need this employee to do is program. He never has to meet the public."

Two years later, an unexpected downturn in business made it necessary for management to combine positions. The programmer now had to serve as a telephone receptionist during a portion of the day. Ultimately, the programmer was released because he lacked even basic skills in dealing with the public. Many criticized the dismissal as unethical. The company's management believed it had no other choice. An effective strategic plan would have allowed management to anticipate the business turn and avoid the ethical dilemma.

The strategic (long-range) plan is defined as, "the process of determining the major goals of the organization and the policies and strategies for obtaining and using resources to achieve those goals."[2] Strategic planning is a first step in fleshing out the business plan. Experts use a variety of tools to develop a strategic plan. Most approaches employ at least four elements:

1. A statement of core values,

2. A mission statement,

3. A vision statement, and

4. A statement of operational goals.

An effective strategic plan provides direction for reaching identified company goals and objectives, and also anticipates barriers to their realization.

Core Values: The Heart of the Organization

Core values are those principles around which a business is established and maintained. They serve as the compass to guide managerial decision making in five basic managerial functions. For example, a business might make a commitment to "never sacrifice quality for price." Other core values might include: "integrity at every level," "customer satisfaction," "lowest cost," "fastest growing," or "low employee turnover." Since the core values of a business become the basis for its future plans, it is essential to invest sufficient time and gather broad-scale input from key stakeholders in order to identify the core values that will best exemplify the attributes of the company.

The Mission Statement: A Guiding Light

The *mission statement* provides the stakeholders with a succinct statement of the fundamental purposes of the company. An organization's mission statement should be brief enough to be known by all members of the team. One industrial facility adopted this mission statement: "Come, grow with us." Every employee knew the statement and recognized that personal growth and business were the heart and soul of the organization.

> *mission statement:* Succinct statement of the fundamental purpose of the company which becomes the guiding light for every organizational decision.

The mission statement also should be comprehensive enough to provide a clear, thorough guiding light for every organizational decision. For example, the authors adopted a mission statement early in the research/writing process of this textbook:

To seek ways to bring about positive, ethical changes in the structures, functions, and cultures of American businesses by challenging managers to grow cognitively and spiritually.

The mission statement gives team members an easily remembered summary of the organization's core values—its reason for being.

The Vision Statement: An Eye to the Future

A *vision statement* usually expands upon the organization's mission. It seeks to answer the strategic question, "How will we know whether or not we have accomplished our mission, our reason for existing as a company?" Planners develop a vision statement with an eye to the future: "as an organization, where are we trying to go?" A three-year or five-year vision is common in many businesses. Some believe that a vision statement, like the mission statement, should comprise only a sentence or two. However, most believe that at the very least a one-page statement more adequately allows for vision explanation and development.

A vision is an important ethical statement of the company's perceived, achievable, and measurable future. It is in striking contrast to a dream, which represents where a company's leaders might like to be in three years, but have no realistic hope of seeing realized.

For example, the manager of a fledgling used car lot declared to the local bank that the company's vision was to be the largest dealership in the county within five years. The bank refused to participate in the venture, explaining that the company instead should adopt a more modest, yet realistic business plan of 7-10 percent growth per year.

Vision keeps its feet on the ground, melding the "what might be" with the "how to." At the same time it reinforces why the company exists by translating the core values into measurable goals for the employees, managers, and other stakeholders to see. It gives stakeholders a yardstick to evaluate a company's fit with their goals and aspirations. A breeding ground for potential unethical decision making occurs when there is no clearly defined operational plan for the attainment of the company's strategic plan.

Operational Goals: Steps on the Path

Once an organization establishes an ethical vision that reflects its core values and implements its mission, the management team is ready to establish *operational goals*. Operational goals break the long-term vision into short-term specific plans.

For example, one company divided its five-year plan into manageable goals for each of the five years. The CEO declared, "This is what we must accomplish this year in order to achieve our vision in five years." Another firm referred to its operational goals as "Quarterly Aims." The shorter duration of the operational goals forced the management team to revisit the vision statement more frequently in order to determine its validity in light of current trends and market conditions.

Operational goals are fleshed out in the operational *plan* that not only gives day-to-day direction for the meeting of the operational goals but also defines the rewards and punishments system that provides for the effective and efficient implementation of the operational and strategic plans.

Experienced managers sometimes develop their own approach to strategic planning. Some may use different names for the basic elements of the plan. Others may expand upon the four components. Nevertheless, an ethical manager always has a strategic plan. At a minimum, that plan should include statements of core values, mission, vision, and operational goals. The ethical manager also reduces the opportunity for unethical decision making by management and employees by aligning the strategic plan, the operational plan, and the rewards and punishments system of the company.

Toward an Ethical Christian Worldview

Luke 14:28-30

Suppose one of you wants to build a tower. Will he not first sit down and estimate the cost to see if he has enough money to complete it? For if he lays the foundation and is not able to finish it, everyone who sees it will ridicule him, saying, "This fellow began to build and was not able to finish" (Luke 14:28-30).

Counting the Cost

Before making this analogy, Jesus tells the crowd that there is a cost to discipleship and that the cost is extraordinarily high. Jesus notes that discipleship may preempt business activity, family joys, or other pleasures. He then offers a parable designed to encourage His listeners to carefully consider these high costs. The parable assumes the importance of planning.

Often wealthy landowners built a tower at the corner of the vineyards or other estate lands. As a defense mechanism, the tower could be used for observation, giving the landowner an advantage over an approaching enemy. Building such a tower required enormous resources in material and labor. Imagine the embarrassment—not to mention the financial loss—that a landowner might endure were he to run short of resources prior to completing the tower. As a matter of good business, the landowner certainly would want to plan his project carefully.

In a more recent example, a development company began to build a large motel complex along a busy interstate highway. Before the project reached completion, it became obvious that the company could not withstand the cost overruns. As a result, the company declared bankruptcy. Subsequent development of that particular interchange proceeded at a very slow rate, primarily because of the eyesore known as the "ghost motel." Part of planning ahead includes counting the cost.

Planning Ahead

> *Or suppose a king is about to go to war against another king. Will he not first sit down and consider whether he is able with ten thousand men to oppose the one coming against him with twenty thousand? If he is not able, he will send a delegation while the other is still a long way off and will ask for terms of peace* (Luke 14:31-32).

Here Jesus uses the threat of war to make the same point about the cost of discipleship. He stresses common-sense planning and advance analysis. A military leader who fails to prepare adequately for battle can create a deadly disaster with lasting implications.

While historians disagree about the circumstances surrounding the defeat of George A. Custer at the Battle of Little Big Horn, at least one viable theory involves the possibility that Custer failed to estimate adequately the size of the Indian force. Inadequate planning may account for Custer's "last stand" and the deaths of more than 200 of his men.

Within God's Will

> *Now listen, you who say, "Today or tomorrow we will go to this or that city, spend a year there, carry on business and make money." Why, you do not even know what will happen tomorrow. What is your life? You are a mist that appears for a little while and then vanishes. Instead, you ought to say, "If it is the Lord's will, we will live and do this or that"* (James 4:13-15).

One Christian businessman failed to develop the business plan recommended by consultants. He argued that it was a spiritual matter. Since planning, as he saw it, limited the real work of the Holy Spirit, the serious Christian should avoid it. He viewed trusting the Lord to be in direct opposition to planning. He even backed up his argument with the above scriptural passage from James.

Should Allen Ford of Hur Ministries adopt a business model?

However, A. F. Harper notes, "The sin of these men was not in planning for the future, but in failing to consider God in their plans."[3] The tower builder in Jesus' parable, who plans yet ignores God's clear teaching, is undoubtedly worse off than his non-planning counterpart. James teaches that Christians should plan with a careful eye to the will of God. He uses the metaphor of mist or fog to make his point, noting that life is brief like a fog under the influence of the morning sun. In only a moment, all the best of earthly plans can come to naught. Therefore, the wise manager plans both for the temporal world and the eternal world.

Ask the Pro

Mike Dates has served as Executive Director of a Family YMCA for twelve years. He brings more than twenty-five years of leadership in nonprofit corporations to this position, having served as athletic director, dean of men, principal, and marketing director for a variety of Christian institutions and organizations. Mike holds degrees from three colleges and universities, earning the M.A. degree twenty-five years ago. He has been active in his community and church and has served on the church board and as a Sunday school teacher.

The authors asked Mike to apply his many years of management experience in the nonprofit sector to the Hur Ministries case. He agreed to sit down in his office for the following interview:

Q: Before we get to Hur Ministries, let's just take a moment to discuss ethics in general. How would you define ethics?

Dates: Ethics means deciding ahead of time what you are going to do in a given situation. I believe there must be a few really firm rules. They are your non-negotiables.

Q: What are they for you personally?

Dates: I have to be honest and fair. I can't cheat, lie, or steal. Actually, I guess the Ten Commandments are a good place to start. I don't struggle in those non-negotiables. They are fixed. But the gray areas are much harder.

Q: Can you think of an example?

Dates: Sometime ago, our board here at the Y decided to get a license to operate a bingo hall to raise money. I don't personally play bingo. I don't gamble. I didn't really want to do it, but I wouldn't leave my job because of it. Maybe someone who felt more strongly than I did about gambling would see it differently. In fact, we had a board member resign over the issue. It ended up that we never used the license, and I was glad. For me, that was a gray area.

Q: Given your definition of ethics, what ethical issues do you see in the Hur Ministries case?

Dates: Allen's refusal to adopt a business model is unethical in itself.

Q: Explain what you mean.

Dates: He is unrealistic in his expectations. It is good to depend on the Lord, but there are business techniques that could help Allen. He seems oblivious to that. He reminds me of Moses trying to do everything. His father-in-law said to him, "Look, you need to appoint a management organization rather than kill yourself by continuing to do it all."

Q: What about Allen's opinion that if he doesn't do it, it won't be done right?

Dates: That is clearly unrealistic and demonstrates inexperience in management. He needs to hire some interviewers to take notes. He can still make the decisions, but someone else could lead the effort to implement those decisions. His attitude leads to the kind of ineffectiveness which is far too common in nonprofits. In the business world, if you don't make a profit, you're gone. Nonprofits sometimes limp along for years without being effective. Hur Ministries is not nearly as effective as it could be if he adopted some sound business practices. Twenty-five hundred potential customers are not being served because he won't do it right. I believe he will have to answer for that one day. It is not about being proud that we ministered to three thousand; it is about accepting responsibility for the ones we failed to serve.

Q: How can a nonprofit manager avoid that pitfall?

Dates: There are a lot of times when I could just go ahead and do something, but I have decided to take it to the board for approval. I choose voluntarily to be accountable. Allen needs a board to establish some policies and protect him from his own ego. I see him as selfish and egotistical, reflecting this attitude, "I'm the only one who can do the job well."

You Be the Consultant

Help resolve the problems at Hur Ministries by answering the following questions:

1. Hur Ministries operates without a strategic plan. Why? What ethical problems have developed as a result?

2. Suppose Allen Ford hired you to serve as a planning consultant. What core values and mission would you suggest for Hur Ministries?

3. One advisor suggested that Hur Ministries adopt the mission, "Supporting our City's Youth." Another liked the phrase, "Mentoring the Next Generation." How would the differences in these missions impact the vision of Hur Ministries?

4. Suppose that the three-year vision Hur Ministries adopts includes expanding to match mentors with 12,000 at-risk clients each year. What operational goals would you suggest for the first six months?

5. Aside from the lack of planning, what ethical problems do you see at Hur Ministries? What is the best way to address them?

6. In what ways does your statement of ethics reveal the need for adequate planning? Are weaknesses evident?

7. Is Allen Ford most likely operating from utilitarianism, ethical egoism, Kant's categorical imperative, or cultural relativism? Why do you think so?

Endnotes

1. Williams G. Nickels, James M. McHugh, and Susan M. McHugh, *Understanding Business*, 5th ed. (Boston: McGraw-Hill, 1999), G2.
2. Ibid., G17.
3. A.F. Harper, *Beacon Bible Commentary*, vol. 10 (Kansas City: Beacon Hill Press, 1967), 236.

7

The Christian Manager as Ethical Implementer

"Serve wholeheartedly, as if you were
serving the Lord, not men..."

(Ephesians 6:7)

Chapter Challenges

A careful examination of Chapter 7 should enable the reader to:

- Distinguish between ethical and unethical goals.
- Recognize the ethical limitations of implementing some operational goals.

Case Study

Oak Dale Bed and Breakfast

Joanna Williamson smiled with satisfaction as she signed her name to the employment agreement. Even her new title—Oak Dale Innkeeper—carried a satisfying ring. The responsibilities matched her abilities perfectly.

Mr. Fred Keller, owner of Oak Dale, agreed that the new relationship held great promise. Oak Dale had been Fred's boyhood home. Recently, he had remodeled the ground floor of the old farmhouse to create a quaint five-unit bed and breakfast facility. The lower level provided a newly redecorated apartment for the innkeeper.

Solid Christian Principles

Fred viewed Joanna's interest in the position as an answer to prayer. He wanted his innkeeper to share his Christian faith, someone who could adjust readily to the demanding schedule of a small bed and breakfast. He met Joanna after explaining his need to the admissions director of a nearby evangelical seminary. Both Joanna and her husband Roy were students at the school.

In exchange for scheduling, cleaning, and cooking a hearty breakfast for the guests, the employment package provided Joanna and her husband the apartment and utilities. In addition, Joanna earned 10 percent of the gross revenue. The agreement enabled Joanna and Roy to stay in school until graduation, and gave Fred the Christian innkeeper he was looking for.

Fred proved to be well organized. From the earliest days of the business, he had carefully crafted the ethical framework of Oak Dale Bed and Breakfast. "The mission of Oak Dale is to provide a quality bed and breakfast operated on solid Christian principles," he declared. "I know we can't exclude all non-Christians, but I intend for our clientele to be exposed to the gospel, even if they don't know Christ when they arrive. Further, one of our operational goals is to refuse to rent to unmarried couples. There will be no "shacking up" on my property."

A Special Offer

Joanna started to raise a question, then thought better of it. Fred continued, "I'm sure the occupancy rate will be low at first. But, we will do plenty of advertising and build up some repeat business over time. This area has a good number of summer visitors due to the nearby lakes. The winter months may be more of a struggle."

"What we really need is a winter promotional incentive," Joanna enthusiastically offered. "Something to encourage people to come during the off-season."

"Excellent idea!" Fred responded. "How about a discount for pastors, missionaries, and others in full-time Christian service? We could make that discount apply only in the winter months."

After some discussion, the pair agreed on a thirty percent ministry discount during December, January, and February. The arrangement promised to provide some additional cash flow during those months, and also offer an inexpensive time of renewal for those in Christian ministry. During the first month as innkeeper, Joanna drafted the following letter:

OAK DALE BED AND BREAKFAST
100 Four Seasons Drive
Middleville, Indiana

Dear Ministry Professional:

At Oak Dale Bed and Breakfast, we recognize that the demands of your ministry allow little time for personal rest and relaxation. However, during the slower winter months, we have an offer that should allow you that opportunity.

During December, January, or February, you are invited to stay at Oak Dale with a 30 percent discount off our regular rates. Of course, these rates include spacious rooms with private baths, as well as a full breakfast.

Even if you cannot join us at Oak Dale this season, we hope you will spread the word of this great opportunity. I encourage you to pass this letter on to another ministry professional in your community.

The enclosed brochure includes a detailed description of the facilities, a map of our location, and our e-mail address and phone number to assist you in making reservations. I hope to hear from you very soon.

In Christ's service,

Joanna Williamson

Joanna Williamson
Innkeeper

Joanna used phone books and denominational district directories to develop a mailing list. Soon callers began mentioning the letter, and occupancy dramatically improved. By late February, Joanna was feeling comfortable in her new role.

An Unexpected Contingency

On one particular Friday, she glanced at the schedule and realized that for the first time during the winter, all five rooms were booked on the same night. Three of the rooms would be occupied by repeat customers who had visited during the fall season. The occupant of room four, Reverend Gary Grossman, had mentioned the promotional letter that a colleague had given him. This entitled him to the Christian service discount. Room five had been reserved for a Jerry and Norma Heitmyer. Norma had called to make the reservation, saying that they were celebrating their first anniversary.

"Completely full," Joanna said with satisfaction. She called Fred to share her excitement. "That's marvelous," Fred responded. "I never dreamed Oak Dale would take off so quickly. God has indeed been good to us and to the business. Implementing our basic Christian mission has been the key, Joanna. And you are doing a great job as innkeeper."

Joanna hung up the phone with Fred's words of praise still ringing in her ears. The bell rang indicating that guests had already begun to arrive. Two women and a man, all strangers, stood on the front steps.

"Hello," the man said. "I'm Rabbi Grossman. I have a reservation for your inn. A Protestant minister in my home community shared a ministry discount letter with me. And," he said, turning to the two women, "this is Norma and Jeri. We all just met as we came up the walk."

"Hi, I'm Norma Heitmyer," one of the women said, extending a hand. "This is Jeri."

Joanna stammered, "Reverend . . . I mean Rabbi . . . Norma and Jerry . . . ah, Jeri . . . Oh my!"

On Background

Implementation

Joanna has just confronted a hard reality that managers often face. She and Fred Keller have developed operational goals consistent with the vision and mission of Oak Dale. However, in implementing one of those operational goals, they have encountered an unexpected snag.

The ethics of implementation revolves primarily around two key issues: (1) ethical limits, and (2) unethical goals.

The Ethical Limits of Implementation

A manager must decide beforehand the ethical limits of implementation. Sometimes ethical operational goals cannot be effectively implemented aside from unethical processes and procedures. Suppose, for example, that a firm decides to increase its female representation at the upper levels of management. The goal—to more accurately reflect the diversity of the culture at large—is itself ethical. However, firing male senior managers in order to implement the goal would certainly stretch ethical limits.

In another example, a nonprofit organization establishes the operational goal of increasing membership by five percent during a particular fiscal year. Nothing appears unethical about this plan. By year's end, the CEO offers cash incentives to current members who recruit others. That practice directly violates the organization's charter. Hence, we see an unethical implementation of an ethical goal.

Unethical Goals

The second area of concern surrounds implementing operational goals that are themselves unethical. This is of special importance since "the managerial systems for planning, control, and motivation are inter-related within a company, both conceptually and pragmatically."[1] It is easy to see how the rewards and punishments for success or lack of success in carrying out the organization's strategic and operational goals can lead to the development of unethical operational goals or unethical implementation practices of sound operational goals. Since lower level managers charged with implementation of the operational plan often have little input in the development of operational goals, this scenario occurs with some degree of regularity.

For example, a sales representative for a particular company believes that one item in the company's product line could prove to be unsafe to consumers. He feels ethically justified in not pushing that particular item. Because of his superior sales ability, he still excels in overall sales. A problem develops when the company makes the item in question the focal point of a massive sales appeal for one quarter. At that point, the sales representative is forced to consider the ethical limits associated with implementing what he views as an unethical goal.

Constitutional Dilemma

Many will view the dilemma Joanna faces as fitting into this second category of ethical concern. In their view, excluding non-Christians or those with particular sexual practices from Oak Dale is unethical. They will suggest that an ethical innkeeper would not implement the Oak Dale operational goals because to do so would deny the belief that all humans are created by God and therefore have value and deserve fair and just treatment.

Before you decide how to advise Joanna in this matter, you should be aware that the Fair Housing Act (Title VIII of the Civil Rights Act of 1968) prohibits any discrimination on the basis of race, color, national origin, religion, gender, familial status, and handicap. These groups of people, sometimes labeled *protected classes*, have the same rights to purchase or lease property as all others have.

> *protected classes:* Groups protected by the civil rights act of 1968 including race, color, national origin, religion, gender, familial status and handicap.

However, the Constitution clearly mandates freedom of religion as a fundamental American right. Fred Keller has a guaranteed right as an American citizen to practice his faith as he sees fit. Still, courts are divided on the question of whether religious freedom or freedom from discrimination takes precedence.

In the landmark case of *Thomas v. City of Anchorage et al.*, the Ninth Circuit Court of Appeal ruled in favor of two landlords who refused to rent a house to an unmarried couple. The owners justified this decision because they believed that cohabitation outside of marriage violated their religious beliefs. The couple sued, claiming violation of their civil rights. The court sided with the landlords' claim that enforcement of housing laws violated their religious rights.

However, this opinion was not popular with everyone, and in a number of states such as California, Illinois, and even conservative Georgia, movements developed to pass state laws that will close what many view as an unjust loophole in the Fair Housing Act.

Therefore, it would appear that Joanna and Mr. Keller face ethical questions not definitively answered by the law. Further, ethical Christians may disagree about whether Oak Dale's leadership should revise its operational goals or forge ahead with implementation. Managers should not view vision, mission, core values, and operational goals as eternally fixed. Effective managers revisit these from time to time in an attempt to maximize business performance. Moreover, they should review these business plans as they relate to ethical implementation.

Toward an Ethical Christian Worldview

James 2:1-4

> *My brothers, as believers in our glorious Lord Jesus Christ, don't show favoritism. Suppose a man comes into your meeting wearing a gold ring and fine clothes, and a poor man in shabby clothes also comes in. If you show special attention to the man wearing fine clothes and say, "Here's a good seat for you," but say to the poor man, "You stand there" or "Sit on the floor by my feet," have you not discriminated among yourselves and become judges with evil thoughts?* (James 2:1-4)

On the surface, the words of the Apostle James seem to contradict the behaviors of Oak Dale's management. He clearly exhorts believers to avoid favoritism. James goes on to illustrate this principle by offering an analogy.

Two visitors appear at the same meeting. One man is obviously wealthy and is given a choice seat. The poor man is told to sit on the floor. Discrimination toward other humans is a practice that Scriptures discourage. God has reserved the right to be the judge of a person's actions. How these biblical teachings fit with the belief that Christians should not support the unholy acts of humans is one that all believers struggle with at some time in their lives. As you develop and refine your ethical Christian worldview, you will want to examine multiple Scriptures related to interpersonal relations so that you synthesize the underlying principles and concepts. Is Joanna caught between an operational goal and biblical teaching related to the treatment of humans? Should we then conclude that Joanna should give these visitors a room for the night?

A Matter of Justice?

To better understand this scriptural passage, we need to look at the original Greek word for "meeting." In the original language, it is used of a type of assembly held in a Jewish synagogue. However, this word typically describes assembling for the purpose of handing out justice, not worshiping. It would parallel more closely an American court of law than a church meeting for worship. The teaching dictates impartiality in matters of justice.

This clear call to justice compels us to re-examine the Oak Dale practice of giving preferential treatment to Christians. One could argue that such a practice violates the command against favoritism. This person might reason, "To do business as they do at Oak Dale is simply unjust."

A Matter of Judgment?

By their fruit you will recognize them. Do people pick grapes from thornbushes, or figs from thistles? Likewise every good tree bears good fruit, but a bad tree bears bad fruit. A good tree cannot bear bad fruit, and a bad tree cannot bear good fruit. Every tree that does not bear good fruit is cut down and thrown into the fire. Thus, by their fruit you will recognize them (Matthew 7:16-20).

In contrast, Fred Keller undoubtedly justifies his business action on the basis that he is supporting his sisters and brothers in the faith. He may argue that making such distinctions reflects verses like those found in Matthew 7.

Fred might interpret the phrase "by their fruit you shall know them" as a command to practice distinction and show appropriate favoritism.

In these verses Jesus uses the analogy of a fruit tree. He notes that if the tree is good, the fruit will be good. The converse is also true. A tree that does not bear good fruit is cast into the fire. Clearly, the church has been given authority to judge the productive behaviors of its members. Does it follow, then, that it is acceptable to reward productivity with a business discount?

As Joanna seeks to incorporate her faith into every area of her life, is she not privileged—perhaps even obligated—to inspect fruit and make a clear distinction between Christians and those who are not, according to Matthew 7?

How can Joanna determine the proper decision?

Or is the passage in James more applicable, prohibiting her from showing favoritism? Joanna must decide quickly which verses apply to this situation. Up to this time, she has implemented the vision of her boss, Fred Keller. Now **she** must decide the role of faith in her own life and practice.

Ask the Pro

Julie Barns is broker/owner of a local franchise of a national realty company in a Midwestern manufacturing city of 30,000. She has operated this business with two partners for the past three years, and has a total of fourteen years of experience in real estate sales.

Prior to developing her career in real estate, she worked in the automobile parts manufacturing industry for nearly twenty years. The last six years in manufacturing, she served as a production line supervisor, overseeing the work of more than 100 production employees.

Julie attends a Missionary Baptist Church where she is involved in women's ministries. Through a Saturday morning prayer meeting via conference call, she also stays in close contact with her five brothers and sisters, who are now scattered across the eastern United States. The authors caught up with Julie over lunch and asked her to comment on the Oak Dale case.

Q: I suspect that as a real estate professional you have some strong opinions as to what is happening at Oak Dale.

Barns: I certainly do. I don't care what the owner's religious beliefs are; he cannot discriminate.

Q: Isn't it true that because Oak Dale is such a small operation, it may be legal for him to exclude certain people from the dwelling?

Barns: I think he would not be exempt because he has too many rooms, and because he isn't living on the premises. Regardless, I would not want to be associated with him or his business.

Q: It is really Joanna Williamson, the innkeeper, who has a dilemma. She is just trying to keep a good job. Her employer made the rules. What should she do?

Barns: In my opinion, she should quit and report him.

Q: You not only would give up the job, but turn him in as well?

Barns: Yes, it takes people who are willing to take a stand. She should have walked away from this job to start with.

Q: Does that mean when you make one unethical decision, it leads to having to make more?

Barns: The lack of ethics tends to create more problems—a snowball effect.

Q: What about his right to his religious beliefs? After all, it is his property.

Barns: He has a right to hold those beliefs. In fact, I personally agree with his positions. Cohabitation is not biblical. But, when you choose to work with the public, you agree not to force your faith on others. For example, I can't preach in the office or to my clients. I worship as I choose, but in the marketplace I sometimes must overlook other lifestyles.

Q: At what point do you say, "Enough. As a Christian I refuse to be involved"? Obviously for you it is not cohabitation. What about the homosexual couple?

Barns: Same thing. In fact, I have sold property to homosexual couples. I disagree with their lifestyle, but as a professional I must get beyond that and provide the best service possible.

You Be the Consultant

Help to resolve Joanna's dilemma at Oak Dale by answering these questions:

1. Do you believe the Oak Dale decision to offer lodging discounts to Christians in ministry is an ethical one? Why or why not?

2. Do you believe the decision to exclude unmarried couples is ethical? Why or why not?

3. What should Joanna immediately do in response to Rabbi Grossman, Norma Heitmyer, and Jeri? What should she do in the days and weeks following?

4. How would your response to Norma and Jeri differ if they were an unmarried heterosexual couple (Norma and Jerry)? Why?

5. How would a follower of ethical egoism deal with Joanna's dilemma? Cultural relativism? Utilitarianism?

6. Do the two statements of business ethics developed by Chris Ault and Alison Stewart in chapter 4 provide an adequate framework for responding to Joanna's dilemma? Explain.

7. How might the personal statement you developed at the end of chapter 4 be applied to the dilemma facing Joanna?

Endnotes

1. LaRue Tone Hosmer, *The Ethics of Management*, 3rd ed. (Chicago: Irwin, 1996), 146.

8

The Christian Manager as Ethical Organizer

"I guide you in the way of wisdom and
lead you along straight paths."

(Proverbs 4:11)

Chapter Challenges

A careful examination of Chapter 8 should enable the reader to:

- Recognize the importance of an organizational chart
- Identify various forms of organization from their organizational chart.
- Understand the relationship between organizational structure and ethical decision making.

Case Study

Pirrman's Lawn Care

"Stacy, I have a special project for you," Dick Pirrman announced to his office manager, Stacy Schafer. The request seemed a little unusual, since for the most part

Dick distanced himself from the office. In fact, he had turned over almost all the office aspects of his business, Pirrman's Lawn Care, to Stacy. Her duties included payroll, taxes, purchasing, billing, and anything else that required paperwork. "I'm into growing things," Dick once quipped, "and papers and pencils don't grow."

The business unofficially began during Dick's high school years when he mowed the lawns of several elderly people in his small hometown. Dick tried college for one semester, but dropped out. He relocated in a thriving city with a growing number of retirees and went back to mowing. During the next six years business grew "faster than grass in the springtime," as Dick liked to say.

Today, Pirrman's Lawn Care has four separate crews of residential and commercial mowers. In addition, two trucks deliver and apply chemicals twelve hours a day during the summer months. Still another crew works strictly on landscaping jobs, which Dick bids and assigns. He manages it all from his pickup truck and often pitches in on one task or the other, doing the physical labor he enjoys so much.

The Special Project

"Hildebrand Nursery is for sale," Dick continued. "As you know, that is the best greenhouse and nursery in this area, and I intend to buy it."

"That's great," Stacy responded. "I know you've talked for a long time about eliminating the middleman in the landscaping work."

"More than that," Dick said. "Their retail sales appear to be very strong. It seems to me like a natural growth area for Pirrman's Lawn Care."

"I think so too," Stacy agreed. "But what does that have to do with me and this special project?"

Dick propped an elbow on the counter and adjusted his glasses. "I talked to the bank yesterday about the money to buy out Hildebrand. They seem to view it as a strong possibility, but before they go to their board for loan approval, they want to see an organizational chart, along with a policies and procedures book. Draw me up something quick, will you?"

"I don't know about that, Dick," Stacy answered cautiously. "It's been a long time since my college class in organizational development. I'm not sure where to begin."

"Just make it look fancy," he said, chuckling. "Those people at the bank don't know anything about the lawn care business anyway. Once I get the loan, I'll run the expanded version of Pirrman's Lawn Care just like I always have."

"There *is* a purpose to those organizational tools," Stacy continued. "The bank people know that adding Hildebrand Nursery will double your number of employees and gross income. They simply want to know how you plan to manage it all."

"I guess I'll need some more business heads like you in the store, but my plan is to manage Hildebrand the way I do the rest of the business. I'll just do what makes sense at the time." He turned to the door as if to leave.

"The more you acquire, the more risky that approach becomes," Stacy pressed, rising from her chair and approaching the counter. "You need a clear chain of command to effectively handle that many more people and increased volume."

Opening the door, Dick paused and looked over his shoulder. "I guess you may be right," he agreed reluctantly. "So, draw me up an organizational chart and sell me on it. I will in turn present the structure to the bank."

Later that day Stacy looked over the basic data as it related to employee count. She came up with the following list:

1. Eight employees on four teams for mowing

2. Two drivers with trucks on application

3. Two Lawn Doctor landscapers

4. The owner and one office manager

5. Four additional Hildebrand landscapers

6. Seven people in the store at Hildebrand

Additionally, she recognized that Mr. Hildebrand had operated a very hands-off business in contrast to Dick Pirrman's strong central command at Pirrman's Lawn Care. Hildebrand had appointed one of his landscapers as manager of that division. He also included a store manager and a purchasing agent in the employee count for the store. These three were the only ones who reported directly to him.

"This won't be easy," she mused. "Especially with Dick likely to continue to make all the day-to-day decisions himself."

On Background

Organizational Structure

A proper *organizational chart* for Pirrman's Lawn Care encompasses more than just lines and boxes. Stacy has correctly advised Dick Pirrman that the structure of his business may become vitally important as the business expands and develops because the effective operation of a business greatly depends on the quality of its organizational design. Nickels, McHugh, and McHugh define organizational design as, "The structuring of workers so that they can best accomplish the firm's goals."[1] A function of the organizational design is to define the span of control, or "the number of subordinates reporting directly to a given manager."[2] In addition to its economic impact, the correct structure for a particular business sets the stage for sound ethical decisions in the future. Similarly, the absence of organizational structure may facilitate inefficient, ineffective or unethical decision making that may lead to ethical dilemmas for employees and the business as a whole.

When Structure Is Missing

One company hired a new secretary/receptionist to accommodate its growing workload. The new employee immediately became overwhelmed with demanding special projects assigned by all six of the firm's key managers. She resigned in frustration after only a few weeks. This company failed to remember the important principle that every employee deserves to report to a single supervisor in a clear chain of command.

In another example, an industrial firm was barraged with questions from the press after the arrest of an employee in the workplace. The organizational structure failed to indicate who was to handle public relations in such a matter. As a result, several different managers gave conflicting reports to the media. This company discovered an important principle the hard way: an adequate organizational structure delineating corresponding responsibilities must take into account potential contingences as well as regular organizational expectations. Failure to do so may set the stage for ethical dilemmas to arise.

> *organizational chart:* Visual representation of an organization's structure.

The Organizational Chart

An organizational chart visually represents a company's organizational design. It is "a diagram of an organization's structures, showing the functions, departments, or positions of the organization and how they are related."[3] This management tool shows at a glance the division of work, the various departments within the company, the reporting structure, lines of communication and chain of command, the coordination of functions, what groups or individuals bear responsibility for the various aspects of the organization's performance, etc. A well-designed chart is a useful management tool for the company's superiors and subordinates and a guide for interaction for those outside the organization.

Flat Organizational Structures

A flat organizational structure has few levels of management. It typically describes an organization that has decentralized management, and in which there are broadly defined jobs and general job descriptions. Decentralized or flat organizational structures might use cross-functional teams to utilize employee expertise from different parts of the organization to solve problems or develop new products or services. Employees might be cross-trained to facilitate sharing of knowledge, tasks, and responsibilities in order to assure smoother operation of the company.

This organizational structure is often found in smaller organizations where cross-training allows for maximum use of the talents and skills of a limited workforce. Larger organizations striving to meet the demands of a more competitive marketplace may use this structure to improve efficiency. Eliminating levels of middle management cuts costs and decreases the time required to get innovations from the idea stage to the customer.

Flexibility and speed in decision making are typically strengths of flat organizational structures. However, there are some disadvantages. Employees must be trained to multi-task, an often expensive venture. Because this approach to organization seems to place more confidence in workers' abilities to produce and to manage themselves honestly and with a high level of accountability, the ratio of managers to employees is much smaller, thus possibly reducing the frequency of communication between the workers and management. A flat organizational structure is found in Figure 8.1.

A Flat Organizational Structure

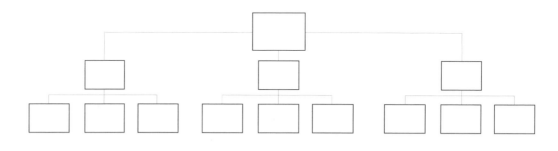

Tall Organizational Structures

Organizations such as the armed forces, diversified companies, and large corporations often utilize the more top-down management structure approach known as the bureaucratic or tall organizational structure. This structure features highly specialized jobs and narrow job descriptions with many levels of management.

Benefits of a tall structure include:

- a high degree of skill development in employees in a department,
- advancement structures based on level of skill development,
- utilization of the principle of economies of scale (due to concentration of materials and skilled individuals within the department),
- good coordination within departments,
- stronger control of the company's operations by top management.

In general, the weaknesses of the tall organization are the advantages of the flat one—flexibility and speedy decision making. The amount of time and expenditure of energy necessary to overcome the inertia within each level of management often make it difficult to quickly change poor policies, institute new initiatives, or to efficiently adapt to a changing business environment. This weakness was graphically illustrated in the armed forces during the war in Iraq. Early on, it was apparent that many of the vehicles transporting United States troops lacked proper armor. It took months for officials at the Pentagon to decide on the proper decision making structure to handle equipment complaints from Iraq before they began planning and implementing corrective action. During that lag time, many field officers took their vehicles to Iraqi metal shops to have the doors fitted with armor. The smaller structure on the battle field overcame inertia and resolved the problem while in Washington, the taller structure with its territory and rank issues was still trying to work out the protocol for problem resolution.[4] Figure 8.2 demonstrates a tall or bureaucratic organizational structure.

Figure 8.2. A Tall or Bureaucratic Organizational Structure

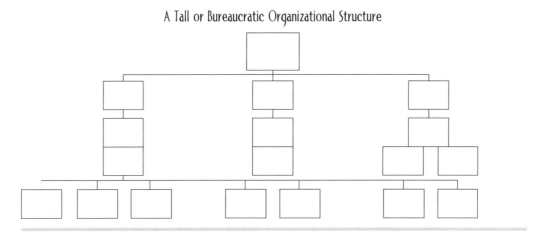

A Tall or Bureaucratic Organizational Structure

Managers have long recognized that an appropriate organizational structure sets the stage for effective organizational operations. Similarly, a structure that aligns the day-to-day operations of the company with operational goals that reflect the company's mission, core values, and vision will limit inconsistencies in the functioning of the staffing, planning, controlling, and rewards and punishments systems within the company that can foster unethical decisions, processes, and practices. Stacy will need to be certain that she portrays the company's scope of operations and management philosophy accurately. Additionally, she will want to propose a structure that facilitates ethical as well as effective day-to-day operations by reflecting the interdependence of the various aspects of the business.

Toward an Ethical Christian Worldview

Exodus 18:13-23

The next day Moses took his seat to serve as judge for the people, and they stood around him from morning till evening. When his father-in-law saw all that Moses was doing for the people, he said, "What is this you are doing for the people? Why do you alone sit as judge, while all these people stand around you from morning till evening?"

Moses answered him, "Because the people come to me to seek God's will. Whenever they have a dispute, it is brought to me, and I decide between the parties and inform them of God's decrees and laws."

Moses' father-in-law replied, "What you are doing is not good. You and these people who come to you will only wear yourselves out. The work is too heavy for you; you cannot handle it alone. Listen now to me and I will give you some advice, and may God be with you. You must be the people's representative before God and bring their disputes to him. Teach them the decrees and laws, and show them the way to live and the duties they are to perform. But select capable men from all the people— —men who fear God, trustworthy men who hate dishonest gain——and appoint them as officials over thousands, hundreds, fifties and tens. Have them serve as judges for the people at all times, but have them bring every difficult case to you; the simple cases they can decide themselves. That will make your load lighter, because they will share it with you. If you do this and God so commands, you will be able to stand the strain, and all these people will go home satisfied" (Exodus 18:13-23).

The issue in Exodus 18, like the situation at Pirrman's Lawn Care, concerns organizational structure. Apparently, because Moses was in direct communication with God, he rationalized that he was to assume total responsibility as judge for the more than two million people of Israel.

Jethro, Moses' father-in-law, correctly points out that this lack of organizational structure will lead to negative results. "What you are doing is not good," he says, quickly assessing the situation. The practice is neither efficient nor effective. There promises to be a serious impact upon Moses personally. Further, the people have to wait for justice, from morning until evening (vv. 13-14). The lack of adequate organizational structure delays justice and thus, is unethical.

Upon Jethro's advice, a structure is established in which judges preside over thousands, hundreds, fifties, and tens. The text does not indicate whether the numbers refer to family units or individuals. Either way, judgment is now meted out more swiftly. Presumably, a system of appeals is included, with Moses acting as a final arbiter and receiving only the "difficult cases" (v. 22).

This organizational structure expands to include the appointment of captains and officers in Deuteronomy 1. Thus, ethical organization moves from a strictly "courtroom" interpretation to influence other areas of Israelite life. Moses and the people learned that the lack of organization is itself a type of structure—all too often an unethical one. Although these examples deal mostly with the concepts of speed of action and due process, it is important to understand that Moses was forced to recognize the capabilities of the people under his control and to utilize those individuals in the most appropriate ways. Here we see the interrelatedness between the managerial functions of staffing and controlling and the organization's structure. The lack of properly functioning managerial functions sets the stage for possible neglect or mistreatment of people under the manager's control.

As Pirrman's Lawn Care expands, implementing a clear organizational structure will help meet the growing demands of the business, and will provide a structure for fair and adequate decision making in the areas of staffing and training, resource allocation, planning, control systems, and capital investment. As the

How can one handle the lack of ethical organization?

presence of a well-developed organizational structure provides guidance for the managerial decisions in these areas, it reduces indecision and reactionary decision making that often unethically affects employees, suppliers, and customers.

Ask the Pro

Dr. Mary Jeter is a vice president of one of the fasting growing small colleges in the United States. During her ten years of service the enrollment has increased nearly 400 percent. After completing her undergraduate work at a southern Bible and liberal arts college, she obtained a doctorate in higher education administration from West Virginia University.

Dr. Jeter has been in her present position for 12 years. During that time, the enrollment of the university has more than tripled. In addition to the responsibilities of her position at the university, she teaches in the Master of Business Administration and the Master of Education programs. In the past, she worked in administrative and pastoral capacities in a variety of organizations and churches, including five years in nursing home administration.

In light of the rapid expansion of Dr. Jeter's university, the authors asked Dr. Jeter to discuss the Pirrman's Lawn Care case and provide insight into the structures necessary as businesses undergo expansion.

Q: There seems to be both managerial and ethical issues at work at Pirrman's Lawn Care. Would you agree?

Jeter: The ethical issues immediately caught my attention in this case. In order to obtain a loan, this business owner will have to sign that what he represents about the organization is true. He is trying to fabricate a model for the organization that will never be used. This will be a misrepresentation of the business to the bank. That is a criminal offense. If the business has been a one-man show and he suddenly has four vice presidents show up on an organizational chart, there is misrepresentation.

Q: Do you see any managerial flaws in the case?

Jeter: Yes! He is asking an employee to be involved in a situation that is very unethical. If I were Stacy, I would question the manager's request.

Q: How should she handle the situation?

Jeter: If I were Stacy, I would say to Dick in private, "Dick, you know we cannot take false information to a bank. We need to represent the organization accurately." I would also document my conversation if I were Stacy. I would put right principles above my job.

Q: Might that cost her a job?

Jeter: If it meant losing my job, I would still confront him. It is unethical for the owner to put an employee in that situation.

Q: How realistic is this scenario?

Jeter: This happens every day, but it still is not right. Let me give you a real-life example. My father worked for a company for 30 years. One day his supervisor, the president of the company, asked him to do something which my father's ethical standards would not allow him to do. So he said to the president, "You know I really appreciate you. You are a great president. I would do almost anything for you, but I can't do that."

The president responded angrily, but later my father was promoted to vice president. On his deathbed, that president looked at his son and said about my father, "Son, I would willingly give this man the keys to the company because I know that he is a man of principle."

My father had four children, but he took a stand on an issue even if it meant he would lose his job. It was more important for him to do the right thing. In reality, he didn't lose the job; he was rewarded with a promotion and the respect of the president of the company.

Q: And Stacy might get the same results?

Jeter: She might. I know I would like to see more employees take a stand for what is right.

Q: Does the organization's structure affect the degree of accountability that provides control over management decision making?

Jeter: Organizational structure definitely impacts accountability and managerial decisions. Organizational structure and accountability are correlated terms. I have found that, for senior executives and managers, good organizational structures and operating systems will often reduce pressure to compromise.

However, many small business owners view established structures and accompanying accountability for actions as a negative, for the very fact that structures bring more control into the organization. They often do not understand that structure deals with span of control and its inherent accountability which are necessary for the business to produce and sustain growth. The more that a manager can instill vision and the principles of accountability into the fabric of the organization the more they will bring a sense of professionalism to the organization and the more likely the organization will grow. Investors will want to see appropriate structures in place. Good managers will assure those structures are in place.

Q: Can freedom from structural control set the stage for unethical decision making?

Jeter: My philosophy is that I need the accountability to be an effective leader. Structure controls and safeguards my decision making by opening up my decision making to scrutiny which in turn makes or encourages me to be an ethical leader.

Q: You have seen your universty triple in size over the past eight years. What relationships have you seen between its structures and its rapid growth?

Jeter: As businesses experience rapid growth they need to constantly be monitoring their structures and accompanying systems to ensure that they have adequate span of control and accountability systems in place. In our university, we have changed our organizational structure several times over the past eight years in order to manage the present and also plan for future growth.

Q: Dr. Jeter, in your experience in leading small businesses through rapid growth, have you seen a relationship between the type of structures in place and the type of managerial philosophy embraced by management?

Jeter: There has been a definite shift in managerial philosophy in our university. Eight years ago when our organizational structures supported a student enrollment of 2,500 students, our management philosophy was concerned more with keeping details in line and empowering the top management. Over the years as our structures have adapted to serve a student enrollment of 7,000 and then 10,000 students, top management's philosophy has shifted to one of empowering others to manage their departments and serve our constituency.

You Be the Consultant

Help resolve Stacy's problem at Pirrman's Lawn Care by answering the following questions:

1. Dick Pirmann wants a mock organizational chart for the bank, yet he seems open to the idea of organizing Pirrman's Lawn Care in a new way. How should he proceed? Why?

2. What ethical problems may arise if the strong centralized leadership style of Dick Pirmann is applied to the Hildebrand organization?

3. What ethical problems would likely become apparent if Pirmann were to simply slide into Hildebrands's slot on the organizational chart?

4. Suggest an organizational chart for Stacy's proposal.

5. How would a Kantian ethicist view the issues surrounding the development of an organization chart? Would these views differ from a utilitarian or one who follows ethical egoism?

6. Would your statement of business ethics be adequate to accomplish Stacy Schafer's project at Pirrman's Lawn Care? Defend your answer.

Special Assignment

Personal Ethics Statement Update

Rewrite your personal statement of ethics on the pages provided. Be careful to integrate what you have learned in chapters 5 through 8. Make certain your position will meet the practical ethical tests which may arise while performing the managerial tasks of decision making, planning, implementing, and organizing.

Statement of Personal Ethics

Name _____   Date_____

Endnotes

1. Williams G. Nickels, James M. McHugh, and Susan M. McHugh, *Understanding Business*, 5th ed. (Boston: McGraw-Hill, 1999), G13.
2. James A. F. Stoner and R. Edward Freeman, *Management* 5th ed. (Englewood Cliffs, NJ: Simon and Schuster Company, 1992), 313.
3. Ibid.
4. Michael Moran, *Brave New World: America and the Post–911 World*, MSNBC. http://www.msnbc.msn.com/id/A731185 (accessed August 23, 2007).

9

The Christian Manager as Ethical Employer

"Masters, provide your slaves with what is right and fair,
because you know that you also have a Master in heaven."

(Colossians 4:1)

Chapter Challenges

A careful examination of Chapter 9 should enable the reader to:

- Recognize the elements of the managerial function of staffing.
- Establish ethical standards for staffing.

Case Study

White's Service Garage

Mickey White pored over the employment applications on the table in front of him. "Here we go again," he mused. "I have to find another new attendant."

For the past seven years, Mickey had owned and operated White's Service Garage, one of the few traditional service stations left in the city. Mickey serviced all automobile makes and models and offered full-service as well as self-service gasoline islands. A long-time fixture in the community, the garage was located on a busy intersection. Several chains had offered to buy him out and turn his place into a more modern convenience store, but Mickey enjoyed being a mechanic and assisting the public. However, he did not enjoy the problems associated with hiring and keeping quality help.

A One-Man Operation

For the most part, White's functioned as a one-man operation. Mickey did all the repair work himself, as well as purchasing inventory and supplies. Saturday afternoons and weekday evenings were reserved for record-keeping and other bookwork. He hired one employee to staff the "front end," as Mickey referred to it. That employee's job consisted of answering the phone, scheduling appointments in the repair bay, selling accessories, collecting money from the customers, and pumping gas and providing associated services for the occasional full-service customer.

Mickey paid minimum wage and expected his employee to work when the garage was open—8 a.m. until 8 p.m. Monday through Friday, and 8 a.m. until noon on Saturday. "That sixty-four-hour workweek means someone can earn a decent week's pay," Mickey reasoned.

Once again, for the fourth time in the last six months, the position was open. Mickey decided to select a new employee from the four applications he had passed over earlier. "After all," he thought, "the most recent one only lasted ten days. These four are probably still available."

Finding Decent Help

The first applicant was enrolled as a student at the local Bible college. He had held a similar position in his hometown during high school, and offered references from that job. Because he was taking classes, he needed a flexible work schedule. He also refused to work on Wednesday evenings because that was his church night.

The second applicant, a high school dropout, had never held a full-time job. He liked cars and seemed interested in mechanics. "I got no work record," he had written on the application, "cepting part-time, since I just quit school last month."

The third applicant had retired as a factory laborer three months earlier. He had explained when he dropped off the application that he could work only twelve hours per week without jeopardizing his pension from the plant. "I'll work around the clock, though, if you pay me cash with no taxes taken out," he offered.

The fourth applicant had recently been released from the county jail for possession of narcotics. His work record until a few years ago appeared normal. "The drug thing really messed me up," he had explained to Mickey. "That's over now. What I really need is a second chance."

"What a bunch of losers," Mickey grumbled as his wife Shirley entered the room. "Why can't I find decent help?"

"Applications again?" she asked. "I thought you hired someone to run the front end."

"I did, just a few days ago. I had to let him go, though. He turned out to be another moron."

"What this time?" Shirley inquired.

"You remember old Mrs. Shepherd?" Mickey asked. "She's a regular customer at the garage."

"Of course. She's that sweet little lady who always buys from the full-service island."

"That's her. Except she wasn't so sweet when the boy genius didn't wash her windshield, or even check under the hood. Guess he thought full service meant pumping her gas and taking her money."

"Did he give any reason for the oversight?" Shirley asked.

"Not really. He said he just didn't think about what we meant by full service. Said he had never heard of the idea before."

Turning to the applications in front of him, Mickey continued, "Any idea which one of these might not have to be told every move to make?"

On Background

Staffing

Mickey is involved in the important management function of staffing. Staffing is generally considered to be one of the basic managerial functions by many writers in the areas of human resource management and organizational management (including Hilgert and Leonard[1], Mathis and Jackson[2], and Robbins and Coulter).[3] It involves the three distinct tasks of recruiting, selecting, and training employees. Each of the three must be completed for the hiring process to be complete and ethical. However, it is evident that Mickey may not fully understand the principles of staffing. As a result, he has set himself up for disappointment again, and also set the stage for unethical behaviors.

> *recruiting:* Process of encouraging people to apply for an open or potentially open position.
>
> *selection:* The process of screening potential employees who have been recruited.
>
> *training:* The process of orienting employees to their job and its expectations.

Recruiting Employees

Recruiting involves encouraging people to apply for an open or potentially open position. Sometimes employers advertise a position, use word-of-mouth or professional recruiters. In other cases, managers may recruit through employment agencies or by networking with associates. Ethical managers recruit without regard to an applicant's race, nationality, gender, or age. They also take special care to avoid misrepresenting the company's values, mission, vision, and operational goals, or the position to be filled with its responsibilities, fit in the company structures, and accompanying compensations.

Mickey apparently has decided not to re-advertise the opening at White's Service Garage. As a result, he places himself at a recruitment disadvantage by limiting the pool of potential employees. He may have decided that time does not allow for adequate recruitment or that the cost of recruitment exceeds the benefits. However, according to most employers a larger pool of candidates more than compensates for the cost of recruitment.

Selecting Employees

The second phase of staffing is *selection*. Selecting employees involves screening applicants who have been recruited. Some situations will require a manager to conduct extensive interviews or administer written tests. In other situations, a review of applications may provide the employer with the information necessary to make an appropriate selection. Ethical managers screen in a manner that is open and fair to every applicant. They recognize their ethical obligation to select the candidate who represents the best possible match to the current opening and the company's ethos. The ethical manager also must be certain that the decision to reject any candidate is based on that candidate's inability to meet the job qualifications, and not on age or another discriminatory factor.

In one situation, a manager, (the principal of a large, grades 1-12, rural school campus), sought to fill the position of assistant principal for the elementary grades. The principal was criticized for rejecting an applicant he believed was overqualified for the position. The applicant had many years of experience as a principal of large urban schools as well as higher academic preparation than any administrator in the entire school corporation. Some believed the principal's ethical responsibility should have been to find the most highly qualified individual. However, he correctly argued the necessity of matching the candidate to the position and considering all potential outcomes of that match. This manager felt that an overqualified individual might become frustrated or divisive if the position required less than what the candidate had to offer.

Training Employees

The final phase of the hiring process is *training*. Although this phase involves additional time and expense, it pays rich dividends in improved employee performance, worker satisfaction, and employee longevity. As a result, ethical managers willingly accept their responsibility to provide quality training for a new employee. They realize that it is unethical to assume that employees understand expectations without first testing that assumption.

Training will vary from one position to the next. At a minimum, it must incorporate an orientation, which may take several minutes or take up the first few weeks of a new employee's time on the job. A comprehensive orientation should include an introduction to the work environment and coworkers, safety and quality control issues, and suggestions on how the employee can gain additional information when necessary. Depending on the complexities of the job or the frequency of new regulations by regulatory agencies, regularly scheduled continuing education may be a part of an ethical orientation system. A key underlying question is, "Is it ethical to expect a given level of performance from an employee without providing the tools necessary to do the job?" Having adequate knowledge to succeed is a key tool for success.

Mickey faces what has become an all-too-familiar task at his worksite—hiring a new employee. Before he proceeds, he would be well advised to test the ethics of his own hiring procedures. He should ask himself, "Have I been ethical and effective in recruiting potential candidates? What ethical standards should I employ in the selection process? How must I orient and train a new employee in order to maximize an employee's potential for success?"

Toward an Ethical Christian Worldview

Matthew 20:1-15

Jesus tells a story in Matthew 20, one that Mickey White may find interesting. It involves the employer/employee relationship, and some interesting things that can go wrong.

> *The kingdom of heaven is like a landowner who went out early in the morning to hire men to work in his vineyard. He agreed to pay them a denarius for the day and sent them into his vineyard.*
>
> *About the third hour he went out and saw others standing in the marketplace doing nothing. He told them, "You also go and work in my vineyard, and I will pay you whatever is right." So they went.*
>
> *He went out again about the sixth hour and the ninth hour and did the same thing. About the eleventh hour he went out and found still others standing around. He asked them, "Why have you been standing here all day long doing nothing?"*
>
> *"Because no one has hired us," they answered.*
>
> *He said to them, "You also go and work in my vineyard."*
>
> *When evening came, the owner of the vineyard said to his foreman, "Call the workers and pay them their wages, beginning with the last ones hired and going on to the first."*
>
> *The workers who were hired about the eleventh hour came and each*

received a denarius. So when those came who were hired first, they expected to receive more. But each one of them also received a denarius. When they received it, they began to grumble against the landowner. "These men who were hired last worked only one hour," they said, "and you have made them equal to us who have borne the burden of the work and the heat of the day."

But he answered one of them, "Friend, I am not being unfair to you. Didn't you agree to work for a denarius? Take your pay and go. I want to give the man who was hired last the same as I gave you. Don't I have the right to do what I want with my own money? Or are you envious because I am generous?" (Matthew 20:1-15)

A Matter of Expectations

At first glance, the early workers in Jesus' parable of the vineyard have a legitimate complaint. However, further examination of the passage reveals that each worker has been treated with ethical fairness.

The marketplace in ancient times was the central meeting place in every city. Here one could find the seat of judgment, men philosophizing, merchants buying and selling, and prospective employees willing to work. The employer in Jesus' story went to the marketplace early in the morning and hired all the workers he could find, agreeing to pay them a denarius, the going rate for a full day's work. He returned at 9 a.m., noon, and 3 p.m. and gathered up more workers, agreeing to pay them "whatever is right" for the partial day. Finally, at 5 p.m. he returned one more time, hired still more workers, and gave them the same promise.

The problem arose when he instructed the paymaster to give everyone a denarius, a full day's pay. Those who labored all day assumed they would receive more than that to which they had previously agreed. In short, they calculated a rate by the hour, while the employer paid each one according to his need for a day's pay.

Interestingly, the employer did not shortchange anyone. Ethically, he kept his original agreement. The dispute arose over the matter of expectations. Those hired first expected more than the agreed amount and became jealous and angry when others received the same for less work.

Ethical Dilemma

How can an employer's expectations reflect ethical principles?

The issue at White's Service Garage also may involve expectations. Ethical employers understand that employees expect reasonable hours, fair pay, and adequate training for the job. Mickey must decide whether he has provided adequately to meet these realistic expectations, or—like the early morning workers in the parable—whether his employees simply expect too much.

Ask the Pro

Ralph Lawrence is the owner and operator of Ralph's Car Wash. He holds a bachelor's degree in business from the University of Southern Mississippi, and has owned the car wash for ten years.

He and his wife, along with the couple's two children, worship at a nearby church. He has served on the church's administrative council, staff parish committee, finance committee, and has held other volunteer responsibilities.

Ralph's civic involvement includes service on the Board of the YMCA and occasional speaking engagements at local high schools on topics related to business and employment. Since he employs a staff of nearly thirty people (about half of which are part-time and entry-level employees), the authors asked him for advice on the White's Service Garage scenario. We visited his office at the car wash. The results of that conversation appear below:

Q: We specifically wanted you to look at this case, because you hire so many entry-level and part-time employees. How realistic is the White's Service Garage problem?

Lawrence: The service industry in general has a very high turnover rate. Whenever you have entry-level positions that pay at a lower pay scale, you automatically get a lot of transition. I have some hiring procedures that help, but it is a common occurrence.

Q: Would you tell us about the procedures that help?

Lawrence: I don't put a sign out front. I don't put an ad in the paper. I don't call the unemployment office. If someone drops in looking for work, I hand that person an application to take home and fill out. That's an initial screen to see if this person has the motivation to take it home, fill it out, and bring it back. I typically don't hire "off the street" because it doesn't work about 100 percent of the time.

Q: That's a pretty broad statement.

Lawrence: I have much better success when I either know the individual or that person's family. The other way I hire employees is to ask someone already working here if they know someone who needs a job and is willing to work. They don't recommend someone who is lazy, because they have to work beside that person. As a result, I have people who have been with me for ten years. I have others who have left and come back. In general, I think we are doing better than average.

Q: Are there other areas where Mickey White is using the wrong approach?

Lawrence: He's putting too much of a workload on one person at that pay scale. That many hours should be divided among two or three people. Of course, that leads to other problems: you have two sets of problems from home, two cars that won't start and two personalities to deal with. You compound the problems in some ways.

Q: What about his training program?

Lawrence: He certainly needs to write a job description and find a way to communicate it effectively. Perhaps a training video demonstrating how to do the job would help. He has to find some way to set policies and procedures and then abide by them. It is not ethical to expect performance that is not effectively taught and communicated.

You Be the Consultant

Answer the following questions to see if you can resolve Mickey's problem:

1. Mickey laments to you, "Why can't I get good help?" How would you respond?

2. How would you advise Mickey to recruit for the job opening? What ethical factors should he consider?

3. Examine each of the four current applicants for the job opening at White's Service Garage. What ethical considerations would surround the selection of each one? Which applicant would you select? Why?

4. Design an orientation/training process for Mickey to use with his new employee. What ethical aspects should be included in such a program?

5. How might one who follows cultural relativism view the employment scenario at White's? Would that differ from ethical egoism? How?

6. Explain how your ethical statement allows for effective, ethical staffing. Support your answer.

Endnotes

1. Raymond L. Hilgert and Edwin C. Leonard, *Supervision: Concepts and Practices*, 8th ed. (Belmont, CA: Thomson South-Western, 2001), ch. 12 and 13.
2. Robert L Mathis and John H. Jackson, *Human Resource Management,* 7th ed. (St. Paul, MN: West Publishing Corporation, 1994), ch. 8,9, and 10.
3. Stephen P. Robbins and Mary Coulter, *Management*, 7th ed. (Upper Saddle River, NJ: Prentice Hall, 1999), ch. 11.

Notes

10

The Christian Manager as Ethical Performance Appraiser

"Do not pervert justice; do not show partiality to the poor or favoritism to the great, but judge your neighbor fairly."

(Leviticus 19:15)

Chapter Challenges

A careful examination of Chapter 10 should enable the reader to:

- Recognize the importance of ethical employee performance appraisals.
- Identify various types of performance appraisals.
- Utilize ethical performance appraisal.

Case Study

Tipton Manufacturing, Ruill Plant

Wayne Phillips had been on the job for all of three months. It seemed like thirty years. When he signed with Tipton Manufacturing at a university senior job fair, the entry-level position seemed like a dream come true. Tipton offered a competitive salary and benefits. In addition, while other firms talked of training programs and a position as a production supervisor, Tipton offered Wayne the plant manager position at the Ruill, North Carolina facility.

Involving only twelve production workers and an office assistant, the plant manager position at Tipton Manufacturing—Ruill, more accurately compared to frontline supervision at larger companies. Yet, the company made a practice of moving plant managers every two to four years, usually to larger plants with more employees. The idea involved exposing people to the entire operation, leading up to more significant management opportunities.

Culture Shock

Right now Wayne doubted that he would last long enough even to visit other Tipton facilities. For one thing, Wayne and his wife Jean had not adjusted well to the move south. Raised and educated in Michigan, the pre-employment visit to Ruill was the first opportunity for either of them to experience the South. "Just another small town," they concluded. "They're all alike."

Now, three months later, they questioned the wisdom of that conclusion. People moved slowly, made decisions slowly, and even talked more slowly. They sometimes used words that Wayne and Jean did not even understand. The couple had become acquainted with very few of the town's folks, and still felt like outsiders at the local community church. Wayne did not feel much more comfortable at the plant. He had to dig for any information on operations. People simply did what he asked—nothing less and certainly nothing more.

The Ruill facility made men's uniform shirts. Each of the twelve production workers had a reputation as an accomplished seamstress and typically managed her own work. For example, some workers completed a garment from start to finish, then began another. Others chose to cut material for part of their shift, and then assemble for another block of time. The factory averaged a total of fifty shirts per day. Each week the completed garments were sent to the packaging division located in Nashville, Tennessee.

Disturbing Data

Over the last several days, Wayne had contemplated production wages. Headquarters had issued a memo announcing a four percent increase in dollars available for production workers. Wayne was instructed to distribute raises as he saw fit, and to make the increase effective in thirty days. As he investigated current salaries and his predecessor's recent history in handling such matters, Wayne discovered some disturbing data. Eight of the seamstress staff earned minimum wage. Historically, they had received increases only when mandated by the federal government. The other four workers earned nearly $1.50 per hour more, although they performed exactly the same work as the other eight.

Wayne's investigation revealed that no one on the production floor was supposed to know anyone else's wage. Further, his assistant in the office seemed reluctant to discuss the matter, but Wayne sensed she knew more than she cared to reveal about the wage discrepancies. He could not tell if she simply did not want to update the "new guy from up North," or if she was protecting her beloved former boss.

Rather than press the issue with her, Wayne asked her to prepare a table showing each production worker, her hire date, the number of units she produced the previous month, the number of workdays she missed last year, and her current wage rate. The results of that study are shown below in Table 10.1.

Figure 10.1, Tipton Manufacturing, Ruill, Employee Pay Scale

Tipton Manufacturing, Ruill, Employee Pay Scale

Employee	Hire Date	Monthly Production	Days Missed	Hourly Rate
1	6/22/87	87	12	$5.75
2	9/14/92	68	6	$5.75
3	8/12/94	66	22	$5.75
4	7/15/87	79	42	$7.23
5	6/10/99	83	30	$5.75
6	4/12/00	68	1	$7.23
7	2/14/01	85	5	$5.75
8	1/16/01	78	7	$5.75
9	3/31/01	74	25	$7.23
10	5/28/00	88	17	$5.75
11	7/2/01	76	22	$7.23
12	12/15/99	89	38	$5.75

Wayne saw absolutely no pattern to the pay scale inequities. His analysis of age and race factors indicated no evidence of illegal discrimination. Yet some explanation must surely exist for such a wide disparity in rate of pay.

An Unusual Business Practice

Finally, Wayne decided to phone George Jeffers, the recently retired plant manager. Wayne knew George as a local, well-respected member of the Ruill community. However, the corporate people who had hired Wayne had advised him not to rely too heavily on George's experience. "Not only is George anxious for retirement," Wayne's boss suggested, "but, frankly, his advice usually is not of much account. He was a 'good old boy' from that community down there who had some very unusual business practices."

George seemed genuinely willing to help when Wayne called. However, his advice left Wayne with additional questions about what course of action he should take.

"Well," George reported, "I always gave whatever raises were available to the same four. It truthfully was kind of a ministry for me, since those four attend the same church I do. I knew they were devout Christians and single mothers struggling to make ends meet. More importantly for you, those four are from families that have been in our community for a long time. They are people who can make you or break you in Ruill, son."

On Background

Legislation Governing Pay Practices

Wayne has uncovered a disparity in wage rates involving twelve production employees. He first must decide what to do about the current disparity. Then he must determine what to do with current and future additional funds allocated for employees. Several issues need to be a part of Wayne's thinking on this difficult ethical problem.

Checking for Discriminatory Behavior

Wayne seems to have dismissed the possibility of race or age discrimination in the disparity involving these twelve employees. His own research and George's comments seem to support that conclusion. Still, Tipton Manufacturing may be at risk with regard to Title VII of the 1964 Civil Rights Act. Some of the provisions of this act include the following:

- It prohibits employers, public or private, who employ fifteen or more persons from discriminating in any aspect of employment.
- It prohibits discrimination of persons on the basis of sex, race, religion, or national origin.
- The Age Discrimination in Employment Act of 1967 added persons, ages forty or older, to the list of protected individuals.

Establishing Performance Appraisals

In addition to solving the problem of possible discriminatory behavior against one or more employees, Wayne also must consider issues related to the need for adequate *performance appraisal.* Performance appraisal is the term applied to a systematic review of an employee's job-related strengths and weaknesses. The absence of an impartial performance appraisal process and its equitable application will provide opportunities for managers to make unethical decisions that an adequately functioning system could have eliminated.

> *performance appraisal:* Systematic review of an employee job-related strengths and weaknesses.

Firms often use performance appraisals to determine appropriate compensation for in-house job placement, for advancement determinations, or for discipline. An ethical performance appraisal system is required by law to ensure that procedures are used to evaluate persons without regard to race, sex, national origin, religion, or age. An ethical system goes beyond the categories required by law to ensure that performance appraisals and other tools that measure the employee's value to the company and its mission are used in confidential and impartial ways in identifying the degree of reward or punishment employees are to receive.

The most ethical performance appraisal systems avoid ratings on such non-quantifiable traits as dependability or attitude. Instead, raters evaluate employees on specific and measurable work dimensions. Often the process begins with a job analysis or job description. The rater then compares an employee's performance to clearly communicated standards of excellence. An appraisal system that fails to communicate expectations well in advance of evaluation would be considered less than ethical.

Types of Evaluation

Evaluation itself may take one or a combination of several forms. For instance, a rater may use a pre-approved checklist form, or may write a narrative essay on each employee. Regardless of the process, care must be taken to emphasize both the strengths and weaknesses of each employee. Some companies utilize a process of self-evaluation in conjunction with the performance appraisal. This approach allows an employee to develop some ownership in the process, and exercise a degree of control over what appears in the employment file.

Many firms also include an interview as an essential element of ethical appraisal. The interview allows for employee feedback to the appraisal and provides a measure of employee control over the process. Care must be taken that the performance appraisal interview provides only one of numerous steps in the feedback process. Feedback in a variety of forms is part of an ethical organization's evaluating process.

In other firms, goal-setting grows out of the performance appraisal process. This procedure works especially well with self-directed employees who have a share in the responsibility for their task development. Some companies tie compensation to performance appraisal. This connection helps establish a pay structure that is consistent, equitable, and ethical. The connection between performance appraisal and compensation works best in merit or incentive systems. Usually base wage systems reflect only the value of the work performed and fail to differentiate between various employee inputs.

With this information as a guide, Wayne must decide which course of action is most ethical in light of the current situation. Before taking action, he will want to gain as much insight as possible from others who may have faced similar problems.

Toward an Ethical Christian Worldview

A surprising amount of space in Scripture addresses the relationship between employers and employees. Several passages speak directly to the issue of wages. In each case these verses support the need to pay workers a fair wage for their labors. Consider the following, for example:

- *Woe to him who builds his palace by unrighteousness, his upper rooms by injustice, making his countrymen work for nothing, not paying them for their labor* (Jeremiah 22:13).

- *The worker is worth his keep* (Matthew 10:10).

- *For the Scripture says, "Do not muzzle the ox while it is treading out the grain," and "The worker deserves his wages"* (1 Timothy 5:18).

- *Look! The wages you failed to pay the workmen who mowed your fields are crying out against you. The cries of the harvesters have reached the ears of the Lord Almighty* (James 5:4).

Are Wage Distinctions Biblical?

Paying people appropriately does not completely answer the question facing Wayne Phillips at Tipton Manufacturing—Ruill. While his predecessor paid the workers, he reserved the highest wages for those who shared his faith. Deuteronomy 24:14 is instructive in this matter. It notes that there is to be no wage distinction between the children of Israel and the aliens living among them.

Do not take advantage of a hired man who is poor and needy, whether he is a brother Israelite or an alien living in one of your towns. Pay him his wages each day before sunset, because he is poor and is counting on it. Otherwise he may cry to the Lord against you, and you will be guilty of sin (Deuteronomy 24:14-15).

The term *alien* used in this passage refers to those from other ethnic groups or cultural backgrounds. Israel was also homogenous religiously. Still, no distinction

Ethical Dilemma

How can an employer exhibit fairness (in his business) for all employees?

in wages was to be made to those outside the Israelite community.

Sadly, all too often one person's unethical behavior creates an ethical dilemma for others. Wayne Phillips must now decide how to respond to the fact that through the actions of his predecessor his company historically has made a distinction in wages between those within the confines of a particular religious group and those outside those confines.

Ask the Pro

Ramona Brown is administrator of an urban Christian college preparatory school. The school serves a variety of Christian families with 342 students in kindergarten through grade 12.

Before assuming her present responsibilities, she served the school for two years as assistant administrator. She also has experience as a classroom teacher in a variety of educational settings in New Jersey, Iowa, and Indiana. She holds degrees from Asbury College in Wilmore, Kentucky, and Georgetown College in Georgetown, Kentucky. The latter institution awarded her the master's degree in education.

Along with her husband and their son, Ramona worships at a large church nearby. They have assisted with a host of ministries in a variety of settings. The authors sat down with Ramona Brown in her office to discuss the Tipton Manufacturing case. Here are the results of that interview:

Q: Obviously the manufacturing setting in this case is very different from your area of expertise. Were you able to find a point of reference?

Brown: Absolutely. In fact, this case is very similar to something we went through here at the school a few years ago. A disparity in teachers' salaries had developed in various subject areas. Certain subject areas were paid higher salaries in order to attract teachers in those areas. The reason was not unethical, like at Tipton Manufacturing, but over time it became unfair to other teachers who were making sacrifices to be here and contributing just as much.

Q: Was the issue addressed?

Brown: It's fixed. We established a base scale with increments for years of experience and professional development.

Q: In order to make that adjustment, did some get a cut in pay, or were you able to raise the pay for everyone?

Brown: Some took cuts, and some left. It was difficult, but it had to be addressed. Because our salaries are low anyway, there is always a temptation to pay a main breadwinner or a single parent more than others. But, that is not fair. Now, we offer all benefits and supplements to everyone, the same across the board.

Q: You implied that you think Tipton Manufacturing got into this wage disparity as a result of unethical behavior.

Brown: Absolutely. As Christians we have to stand for what is right. The Tipton Manufacturing thing really bothered me. Hourly rates were awarded inconsistently. There seems to be no established policy. A personal agenda guided the salary process. The fact that he [George] was paying people more because they attended the same church just screamed "unethical behavior and lack of integrity."

Q: How important is it for Christians to demonstrate ethical behavior?

Brown: It is absolutely essential. We try to teach this in disciplining students. We have worked hard to establish policy and include parents in student discipline. We guide students through a process of admitting when they are wrong and making things right—restitution. We have thought that through, and we guide every student the same way through that process. It is especially exciting when solid Christian parents resist the temptation to take a son or daughter's part and support the school as we attempt to teach accountability and integrity.

Q: So you see integrity as a key to management ethics?

Brown: I do. Recently the board's personnel committee and I had to dismiss an employee over a clear issue of integrity. That employee was involved in behaviors that violated the core values of our school. Many questioned our decision because we couldn't publicly say why the person was dismissed. On the other hand, if we didn't deal with the issue, what would it say to students? What would it say to other employees? We had to make a decision whether to let it ride or take a stand in favor of character and integrity. You just do what you need to do, and hope you have built enough trust with parents and other constituents that they believe you wouldn't take that kind of action unless it was absolutely necessary.

You Be the Consultant

Answer these questions as you consider the situation at Tipton Manufacturing:

1. Is the present wage scale at Tipton Manufacturing equitable? Is it ethical? Is it sound business practice?

2. George gave more than one reason for the disparity in wage scale. Are any of the reasons ethical? Why or why not?

3. Develop an ethical performance appraisal system for use at the Tipton Manufacturing plant at Ruill. Would such an appraisal differ if you were an ethical egoist? If you were a cultural relativist? Why?

4. To what extent is it ethical for Christians to care for one another in the workplace? At what point does such behavior become unethical? Would a Kantian agree with your answer? Would a utilitarian?

5. What immediate actions should Wayne take? What future actions?

6. How would a plant manager in Wayne's situation respond if that manager operated from these ethical systems?
   a. utilitarianism

b. Kant's categorical imperative

c. ethical egoism

d. cultural relativism

e. your statement of ethics

11

The Christian Manager
As Ethical Leader

"Whoever wants to be great among you
must be your servant."

(Matthew 20:26)

Chapter Challenges

A careful examination of Chapter 11 should enable the reader to:

- Differentiate between Theory X and Theory Y leadership styles.
- Explain the concept of servant leadership.
- Implement effective and ethical leadership styles in various circumstances.

Case Study

West Park Apartments

Twenty-four-year-old Karen Lane sat in the manager's office of West Park Apartments. Even after being on the job for three months, she still felt very much alone in her position as manager of the complex. She had been hired from a field of six applicants. The fact that she already held a real estate broker's license, required for property management by her state, had been a huge factor in her selection.

As manager of the West Park Apartments, Karen supervised the general operation of the 200-unit complex. She received a base salary, in addition to free rent on-site in a two-bedroom unit. In exchange, she kept the apartment complex as full as possible, collected rents, and supervised the work of an office manager and three maintenance technicians.

Seeking Respect

The maintenance area had proven to be Karen's greatest challenge. She had little understanding of maintenance and repair work, but as the apartment complex manager she felt responsible for properly leading the maintenance staff. Perhaps because of her lack of technical knowledge, or because all three male employees were older than Karen, their relationship had been strained almost from her first day on the job.

Sometimes a disagreement developed over whether to repair or replace an item. For example, the fan motor on the forced-air gas furnace in one unit had gone out last week. Joe Bowersox, the technician assigned to the job, recommended replacing the entire furnace. "Given the age of the unit and the high cost of replacement parts," he suggested, "I'd say just call the furnace people and have them install the whole unit."

Karen suspected Joe was thinking that if the whole furnace were replaced, the job would be contracted out. On the other hand, replacing the fan motor would be Joe's responsibility. "No," she insisted. "Buy the parts and repair it yourself. It's not that big a deal." Joe had milked the job an entire eight-hour shift, and still continued to grumble about Karen's "poor decisions."

Kenny Puegot, was even more outspoken in his assessment of Karen's leadership. Kenny had worked at West Park for several years since retiring from a nearby assembly plant where he had served as union steward. In addition to odd jobs, he landscaped and maintained the grounds. Residents often commented on the well-manicured lawns and weed-free flowerbeds at West Park.

Soon after taking the manager's position, Karen had asked Kenny to take an expanded role in painting vacant apartments for the next occupants. "I always help out on painting," Kenny responded, "as long as the mowing is caught up."

"This time the painting is a priority," Karen pressed. "It won't hurt to let the grass grow a few extra days in order to get these units ready and occupied."

"Kids running the show won't work," Kenny had growled under his breath. "Especially female kids." Karen had let his jab go, but she concluded that the real issue was not about lawns, but about Kenny's unwillingness to accept her leadership.

Now she faced a confrontation with the third member of the maintenance staff. At twenty-seven, Gary Kessler was the youngest of the three. He had not been particularly friendly to Karen, but had simply done what he was told, nothing more or less. At least that seemed to be his behavior pattern when he *came* to work. Over the last three months, Gary had missed eight days and had reported late for work six additional days. After the sixth absence, Karen had talked to Gary. "You simply have to come to work more regularly," she stated firmly. "We count on your being here."

"Well," Gary had started, "Ihave this problem that . . ."

"I agree, Gary," Karen interrupted. "You have a problem. One more missed day and it will be a bigger problem. I expect you on the job and on time every day. Any questions?"

"Nope," Gary mumbled, shrugging.

"That's all then," Karen said, dismissing Gary to return to work.

Karen was troubled as she prepared for today's confrontation with Gary. Her repeated warnings hadn't seemed to faze him. "Somehow I want to find a way to help these people understand that I am in charge here. They simply have no respect for my leadership," Karen thought.

On Background

Leadership Styles

As Karen contemplates what approach to use in dealing with Gary's attendance record, she may want to consider some leadership basics. In 1960, Douglas McGregor wrote a landmark book on leadership techniques. In *The Human Side of Enterprise*, McGregor outlines what became known as Theory X and Theory Y management.[1]

Much of what has been written in the decades since McGregor's monumental work builds upon the Theory X and Theory Y concepts. *Theory X* generally views people in a negative light. Employees are not motivated intrinsically by a commitment for doing quality work, loyalty to the company, or pride in being a part of an organization. Instead they are lazy, must be closely supervised, and are incapable of making decisions on their own or making contributions to the organization, processes, and improvements of their work responsibility. Theory Y tends to view employees as persons who are capable of self-management. They are thinking individuals who can contribute individually or as group members to improvements in their work areas. Theory Y employees respond to intrinsic motivations as well as extrinsic motivations such as pay incentives, company stock options, and promotion opportunities.

> ### McGregor's Leadership Theories
>
> *theory X:*   In theory X, employees are viewed as lazy and incapable. They must be closely supervised.
>
> *theory Y:*   In theory Y, employees are viewed as capable of self management and self motivation.

The structure of the company may be better suited to a particular leadership style. For instance, a company with a flatter organizational structure may work better with a less autocratic leader and a more Theory Y one. If this is true, is it unethical decision making to hire an autocratic leader for a flat organization or vice versa? When hiring a member of the leadership team, the owners should consider how the proper match of leadership style and organizational structure would affect all aspects of the organization and its fiduciary responsibilities. Karen seems to have equated leadership with Theory X management. Such an attitude negatively impacts performance, and may raise serious ethical implications as well.

The Christian Side of Leadership Style

Genesis 1:27 tells us that man is made in God's image. This imputes infinite value to humans, demonstrated by the price that God paid through the sacrificial death of His son to redeem mankind. Being created in God's image gives us the right to be treated with respect and dignity. It also means that human beings possess the godly attributes of creativity, trustworthiness, inspiration, initiative, and satisfaction in a job well done.

Jesus' leadership style in preparing his followers for the task of founding the Christian church after His ascension is an example of putting this principle into action. He recognized the God-like hidden gifts and talents in this diverse group of men and women and cultivated the development of those attributes. At times he was stern in his holding followers accountable for their progress in developing their servant leadership skills and dispositions, but that is a reflection of the importance of these individuals and not an application of Theory X principles.

Karen's mindset about the nature of human beings finds ultimate expression in her approach to management. The same is true of any Christian manager. What they have already determined about their employees is expressed in their leadership styles. For example, not fostering employee input, not recognizing employee accomplishment, and being unwilling to listen to employee concerns, may say more about what Karen believes about the value and potential that human beings possess (as a result of being made in the image of God) than what Joe, Kenny, or Gary believe about leadership.

That does not mean that Christian managers must always operate according to Theory Y principles. In fact, some Theory X assumptions are supported by Scripture. A study of Moses' leadership style in leading the Israelite nation out of Egypt and the forty year journey in the desert; or of Nehemiah's style in the rebuilding of Jerusalem reveals the use of some Theory X concepts. Some circumstances are best handled by a strong central command structure. For example, in confronting a raging fire a fire chief will not poll the workers and allow for employee feedback on the correct course of action. The fire chief is less worried about being considered a tyrant than in making an expeditious command decision to save lives. To do otherwise would be unethical. That leadership styles should match individual circumstances is the mandate of Christian ethics.

The Servant Leader

For this reason, many Christian managers have adopted the leadership style Jesus suggested as a model for greatness. He said, "Whoever wants to be great among you must be your servant" (Matthew 20:26). Servant leadership allows the manager to be flexible in style, adapting to the needs of the situation, as in the example of the fire chief. However, it is crucial to note that this flexibility is in *style* of leadership only. Ethical principles must be upheld even in an emergency. This flexibility should never be confused with situational ethics, in which hypocrisy, dishonesty, immorality, and other actions done for personal or corporate gain are made to seem ethical.

Servant leadership generally rejects the "top-down" mentality of a Theory X manager. It assumes that the role of a leader is to facilitate the work of followers. However, a servant leader also may respond authoritatively when the situation calls for decisive action for the good of employees or the organization.

> *servant leadership:* Assumes that the role of a leader is to facilitate the work of followers who are generally self motivated. The servant leader generally engages in participatory management.

Servant Leadership in the Workplace

A servant leader managed the care of several patients in a nursing home facility. The majority of the time she behaved in a very gentle and caring manner with those under her care. When Mr. Jones refused to take his medication, she exercised her authority firmly and strictly. "Because I care for my people," she explained, "I have no choice but to insist that he take his medication."

Similarly, a factory supervisor modeled servant leadership and became known for his participatory style among the workers. Because he cared for people and wanted the best for them, he listened attentively to his employees' personal and job-related problems. When it was necessary to correct them, he did so gently and compassionately. However, when tornado alarms sounded at the plant one afternoon, his concern for the well-being of others caused him to bark orders, ignore questions, and demand immediate action.

An office manager usually exercised a participative style of leadership and accommodated the input of those under her supervision. Her supervisor informed her that the company risked losing an important customer if the employees could not complete a difficult and time-consuming task ahead of schedule. Because her servant leadership style had gained the respect of employees, she was able to organize the work, announce the plans, and complete the task in record time without employee objection.

Charting a Course

The key to ethical leadership thus involves flexibility of approach for the ultimate good of others. The servant leader constantly searches for ways to assist employees in the effective performance of their tasks. Some servant leaders prefer to invert the traditional organizational chart in order to remind themselves of their ultimate responsibility (see Figure 11.2). In the inverted chart, the leader's role as servant to managers and employees is emphasized by placing the servant leader below those being lead. The leader has the responsibility to listen to the input of subordinates and to facilitate their success in their part of the company's enterprise.

Figure 11.2

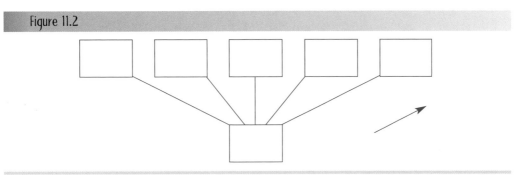

The arrow on the right side of the chart reminds servant leaders to consider rotating the chart from time to time. This prompts servant leaders to remember their roots as ethical Christian managers by adapting their leadership style to best suit the circumstances.

The servant leader generally assumes a participatory leadership role (see Figure 11.3). The leader becomes the quarterback on the team, not the team's coach or general manager. The leader motivates the team, gets dirty in the processes of give-and-take with the team, and does whatever task is necessary for the team to win. The leader understands the role of each team member and that all roles contribute to the success of the team. At times the servant leader may go alongside various team members and assist them in becoming successful team members. In short, the leader gets dirty hands in the real work world of subordinates.

Occasionally, the servant leader may face a crisis calling for immediate and decisive action (see Figure 11.4). The rotation of the chart demonstrates the servant leader's response. The leader has assumed a directive leadership posture, making decisions based on data from subordinates but with less direct participation by those subordinates. The leader becomes the coach on the stand high above the practice field that sees the big picture, makes decisions, and calls out orders to the assistant coaches for implementation by the team's offensive or defensive players.

Figure 11.3

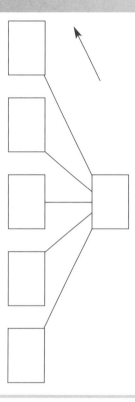

Once the servant leader has built quality employee relationships for the long term, employees willingly respond to directives in the midst of crisis. These employees realize that the servant leader will return to the more characteristic style of management as soon as possible. Ethical behavior demands it.

Figure 11.4

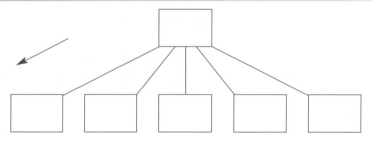

Toward an Ethical Christian Worldview

Mark 10:35-44

> Then James and John, the sons of Zebedee, came to him. "Teacher," they said, "we want you to do for us whatever we ask."
> "What do you want me to do for you?" he asked.
> They replied, "Let one of us sit at your right and the other at your left in your glory" (Mark 10:35-37).

Examining Jesus' teaching on the nature of greatness in biblical context yields an even clearer insight into the nature of servant leadership and the ethical responsibility of Christian managers to practice the servant style. This conversation arises when two of the disciples, James and John, ask Jesus for a blank check with regard to their role in His future kingdom. "We want you to do for us whatever we ask" (v. 35).

Immediately it is clear that James and John see themselves and their needs as the primary issue. Jesus points out that the real issue is service to others. "Whoever wants to become great among you must be your servant" (v. 44).

The teaching of Jesus in this situation is reminiscent of Paul's instruction in Romans 12:3: "For by the grace given me I say to every one of you: Do not think of yourself more highly than you ought . . ."

Clearly, James and John's lofty self-image establishes an unethical view of their role as kingdom leaders. Jesus encourages James and John to adopt an attitude of servant leadership. What if they were to refuse? Ironically, if they were to continue to interpret leadership as a vehicle for elevating their own status, they ultimately would find themselves even lower than before. Wise King Solomon observed centuries earlier, "A man's pride brings him low" (Proverbs 29:23).

Ethical Dilemma

How important is it for a manager to be a servant-leader?

Therefore, Karen's leadership style is ethically important to her employees and to the organizational structure of West Park Apartments. It is also important to Karen and her managerial future.

Ask the Pro

Mark Yoder is shift manager at an urban McDonald's restaurant. He has worked at this McDonald's location for three years, the last two as a manager. In addition to his job, he is a student at a local community college, studying toward a degree in Computer-Aided Drafting. He is active in his local church.

When he was promoted to manager at seventeen years of age, he was the youngest person ever to hold this position among the state's nine northern McDonald's stores. The authors believe that experience makes Yoder uniquely qualified to discuss the West Park Apartments' case. The results of our conversation appear below:

Q: Karen's age seems to be undermining her ability to lead at West Park Apartments. Do you have any thoughts on that problem?

Yoder: When I first started as manager, I was only seventeen. I was with older employees who had been working here longer. Some of them didn't like the idea of me telling them what to do.

Q: Would that be worse for Karen as a female?

Yoder: I suppose that would have an effect. At least in my situation, some of the guys kind of looked up to me.

Q: Is Karen handling the leadership role correctly?

Yoder: When you have people who don't really respect you, you have to find ways to gain their respect. She doesn't have to beat on folks all the time. Eventually, they will come around if she just keeps doing what it takes to get the job done.

Q: Is there a particular place Karen should adjust?

Yoder: I think she was hard on Gary. She should have listened to him. When people have been here longer than I have, I try to give them the benefit of the doubt because of their experience. I would try to listen to him.

Q: Is it hard being a Christian in a management role?

Yoder: Sometimes. For example, the other day I had to send a woman home. She takes care of two children. But, I get paid to follow the rules. It's sometimes hard to decide what is the right thing to do.

You Be the Consultant

Answer the following questions in light of Karen's difficulties:

1. What ethical concerns do you have about Karen's leadership style? How might they be addressed? What course of action could Karen take to salvage her relationship with the maintenance crew in general?

2. Karen believes that adopting a servant style of leadership would be viewed as weakness by her staff. She fears that they will run roughshod over her. How do you respond?

3. What are the problems with servant leadership? Will it work in every situation? Is it possible to be an ethical Christian leader without being a servant leader? Support your answers.

4. In light of your ethical statement, how would you recommend that Karen deal with Gary in the upcoming meeting? What would an ethical egoist suggest? What would a Kantian suggest?

5. Which of the four ethical positions discussed in chapter 3 most closely parallels Karen's attitudes? Defend your response.

Endnotes

1. Douglas McGregor, *The Human Side of Enterprise* (New York: McGraw-Hill, 1960).

12

The Christian Manager
as Ethical Record Keeper

"The Lord detests lying lips, but he delights in
men who are truthful."

(Proverbs 12:22)

Chapter Challenges

A careful examination of Chapter 12 should enable the reader to:

- Recognize the importance of ethical record keeping.
- Define the managerial function of control.
- List the five characteristics of ethical record keeping.

Case Study

Ace Production Company

Jon gazed in amazement at the tub of parts. He estimated the tub to be eighty percent full. He had found the finished cams in a construction zone just east of the cam finishing area where one would not expect to find production parts. The tub had been covered carefully with cardboard to shield it from the view of passersby. "Buzz is hiding cams from day shift," he whistled to himself. "So that's how he does it."

Jon Warren supervised the twenty-three hourly employees on the second shift in the cam finishing area of Ace Production Company. Buzz Johnson held the same position on the first shift.

Cam finishing involved finish-grinding and heat-treating the cams in preparation for shipment to the assembly division. At the completion of the process, workers placed each cam in a shipping tub. Tubs uniformly held 250 cams. The labor-intensive nature of the work meant that the cam finishing area produced only three tubs or 750 cams when it ran at 100 percent efficiency for an entire eight-hour shift.

Production control calculated efficiencies based on ready-to-ship completed tubs rather than individual parts. As a result, Jon's area might produce 700 parts on a given evening, but since those completely filled only two tubs, reports revealed a dismal 67 percent operating efficiency. Just fifty more parts would have completely filled another tub and yielded 100 percent efficiency.

The Efficiency Battle

For several months Jon had been under pressure from his general supervisor, Karen O'Neal. Karen had reminded him that over the last year his shift's efficiency had averaged only 82 percent

"Look, Jon, I know it can be done. Buzz has a 97 percent efficiency for the same period," Karen challenged. "Your efficiency is declining, while his is increasing. You have simply *got* to get out more tubs of finished cams."

"Karen, those reports are misleading," Jon argued. "Night after night I leave a tub half or two-thirds full for Buzz to begin with in the morning. Yet consistently he has just finished a tub near the end of his shift. He leaves only a few dozen parts in the bottom of the next container for my people."

"It may seem like that," Karen said, her voice reflecting compassion. "But we have been through this before. The number of parts remaining at the end of each shift will average out. Over time, you gain as many as you lose."

Jon tried to convince the production control staff to devise a single part count measure of efficiency. However, the engineers saw no need to tamper with the current accounting procedure. "If it ain't broke, we ain't got time to fix it," one production controller had declared with finality.

So, the situation remained the same, with Buzz consistently winning the efficiency battle between the two shifts. "I just know something is wrong," Jon told his lead man and truck driver, Joe. "But, I haven't been able to figure out what is going on. I think that Buzz has found some way to fudge the numbers."

Now, with the discovery of a nearly complete and apparently hidden tub of cams, Jon believed he had discovered how Buzz developed such a strong efficiency report.

"I finally figured out what the first shift crew is up to," Jon told Joe later that same evening. He described finding the nearly completed tub hidden in the construction zone. "In the morning, he will simply bring his work back in and finish the tub. Then he will run what he needs to complete the tub we have left him. By mid-morning the first shift will have two tubs complete with six hours production time remaining."

"That sly old fox!" Joe said with a degree of admiration. "You've got to hand it to him for figuring a way to beat the system. But what are we going to do now that you've caught him, Jon?"

"I'm not sure," Jon admitted. "We could just go pick up that partial tub and get a great efficiency today."

"But tomorrow, he will find another hiding place for his partial," Joe finished the thought. "And unless we find them every day, the problem isn't solved."

"That's right," Jon said. "I suppose we could just find a hiding place of our own. Two can play this game—except it's not a bright move if the big bosses find out."

"We only have three hours of production time left," Joe mentioned. "What do you want me to do?"

On Background

Keeping Accurate Records

The managerial function called *control* embraces many aspects of the company's operations such as performance appraisals, productions statistics and standards, and the budgetary systems. In all of the control functions, the collection, storage, and usage of clear, accurate and appropriate information is vital. Arguably, no single function consumes more of a manager's day-to-day activity than record keeping. Certainly no other task poses such ethical challenges. Sometimes the records involve accumulated production, as in the dilemma facing Jon Warren. On other occasions, the manager may be called upon to record costs incurred for an expense report. At still other times, personnel records and matters of training or discipline become the issue. This emphasizes the need for accurate records and their collection and storage based in the company's values and their appropriate use in triggering the company's motivation system with its inherent rewards and punishments. Failure to plan and provide for these aspects of record keeping creates "gray areas" of decision making that may lead to unethical decisions.

> *control:* Managerial function that includes performance appraisal, production statistics, and budgetary systems.

One manager reportedly interviewed a representative from several accounting firms before selecting one to perform bookkeeping functions for his fledgling business. A colleague inquired, "What was it in the interview process that convinced you to select this particular accountant?"

"Well," responded the manager, "I ask each accountant the same question. What does one plus one equal? All but one interviewee gave the answer as two. The accountant I hired was the only exception."

"What was that accountant's answer?" quizzed the surprised colleague.

"He responded with a question of his own. He asked, 'What do you need it to equal?'"

Similarly, another accountant who served as treasurer of a nonprofit corporation once boasted to the executive officer, "I can make the monthly report reflect whatever you want me to. Just let me know."

Perhaps there is some truth to this adage, "Figures never lie. But, liars do sometimes figure."

The Five Characteristics of Ethical Record Keeping

The same ethical standards apply to every record-keeping situation. We have summarized these as the five characteristics of ethical record keeping.

Ethical Records Must Be Understandable

The first characteristic of ethical record keeping is to make records comprehensible. When an ethical record keeper is responsible for an organization's records, those records can be properly interpreted without undue difficulty. In contrast, records that require explanation on the part of the record keeper do not reflect ethical activity.

One company's personnel files included an intricate coding system. This allowed officers to quickly compile the racial statistics for the quarterly affirmative action report required at division headquarters. Despite the fact that the data served a positive purpose, the procedure raises ethical questions. The data included in those personnel files was not readily understandable to observers.

Ethical Records Must Be Verifiable

The second characteristic of ethical record keeping is their verifiability. In today's office, backup files are essential in the event of a computer malfunction. Backups also serve the secondary purpose of verifying the accuracy of records in the event the ethics of record keepers are called into question.

While receipts for certain purchases may not be required with an employee expense report, they do provide necessary verification in the event of an inquiry.

Ethical managers will attach such documentation to file copies in order to demonstrate accuracy in record keeping.

Ethical Records Must Be Timely

In addition to being understandable and verifiable, ethical records must be timely. While a manager may occasionally fall behind in record-keeping tasks, records generally must be produced in an expeditious fashion.

For example, consider the manager who is required to keep a mileage log. The Internal Revenue Service (IRS) and others consider these logs most accurate when they are kept in the vehicle and created on a trip-by-trip basis. Of lesser ethical value are those logs generated in the office at the end of the month.

One sales manager was required to file an annual report of business activity. However, he failed to keep the records necessary to accurately complete the report. In response to each question, he would do the best he could to recall twelve months of activity and fill in the report while thinking aloud. "I reckon about seven calls made" or "I reckon about three hundred parts ordered," he would say. He jokingly referred to the report as his "reckon about" report.

The ethical record keeper avoids "reckon about" reporting by making timely data entries. Serendipitous to timely reporting is that it requires much less of the manager's time than attempting to re-create the facts later and from memory.

Ethical Records Must Be Complete

Fourth, ethical records must be thorough and complete. Record keepers create a paper trail of data and activity. Incomplete records leave holes in that trail and open the door to moral compromise.

The production control authorities at Ace Production have established a flawed system that invites fraudulent and incomplete record keeping. Since Jon and Buzz can only count full tubs of completed parts, the actual production count is misleading. On any given shift, from one to 249 parts may be unaccounted for. Such holes in the records have set the stage for Buzz's unethical behavior and Jon's current dilemma.

Ethical Records Must Reflect Accountability

Ethical record keeping occurs when the record keeper is accountable. The basic management principle that every worker must be accountable to one—but only one—superior applies especially to record keepers.

One nonprofit corporation hired a local firm to perform basic accounting duties, including ledger activity and check writing. As a safeguard, an employee of the nonprofit performed banking operations and delivered deposit slips to the accountant. On a day-to-day basis, the procedures worked efficiently, effectively, and ethically. However, at the end of the fiscal year, the same accounting firm performed the nonprofit's annual audit. The public record of the nonprofit's good performance essentially was the result of the accounting firm's self-audit. While this procedure is legal in the strictest sense, the practice lacks the ethical characteristic of accountability.

Ethical records are always understandable, verifiable, timely, and complete. They reflect the record keeper's accountability. The ethical record keeper will always record that 1+1 = 2, not "whatever you want it to equal."

Ethical Records Are Always

- Understandable
- Verifiable
- Timely
- Complete
- Reflective of Accountability

Toward an Ethical Christian Worldview

Acts 5:1-10

Many Christians surmise that the death of Ananias as recorded in Acts 5 teaches the importance of proper stewardship. A closer look reveals an even deeper ethical issue at work.

> *Now a man named Ananias, together with his wife Sapphira, also sold a piece of property. With his wife's full knowledge he kept back part of the money for himself, but brought the rest and put it at the apostles' feet.*
>
> *Then Peter said, "Ananias, how is it that Satan has so filled your heart that you have lied to the Holy Spirit and have kept for yourself some of the money you received for the land? Didn't it belong to you before it was sold? And after it was sold, wasn't the money at your disposal? What made you think of doing such a thing? You have not lied to men, but to God."*
>
> *When Ananias heard this, he fell down and died* (Acts 5:1-5).

Ananias' judgment does not stem from his refusal to give, but from his unethical report of the income he received from the sale of property, as well as the lie this inferred. The phrase "kept back part of the price" in verse 2 is actually a single Greek verb sometimes translated "embezzled." It usually implies a secret theft from a much larger total. This word also appears in Titus 2:10 where slaves are told not to "steal" from their masters. Interestingly, in this context the opposite of stealing is demonstrated with the phrase "showing that they can be fully trusted."

Clearly Ananias sinned because he gave an inaccurate report on the sale of the property not because of his inadequate stewardship. He lied. In this case the lie is magnified because it is directed towards representatives of the body of Christ, the church, as well as the Holy Spirit.

The improper reporting stemmed from a conspiracy between Ananias and his wife Sapphira. She is judged to be as guilty as her husband and meets an identical fate.

About three hours later his wife came in, not knowing what had happened. Peter asked her, "Tell me, is this the price you and Ananias got for the land?"

"Yes," she said, "that is the price."

Peter said to her, "How could you agree to test the Spirit of the Lord? Look! The feet of the men who buried your husband are at the door, and they will carry you out also."

At that moment she fell down at his feet and died (Acts 5:7-10).

Whether these deaths resulted from divine judgment or natural causes has prompted a great deal of speculation through the centuries. Some believe that Sapphira died of shock from the combined loss of her husband and the revelation of her own evil intent. Others argue that her death was the result of the immediate and decisive wrath of God. Either way, the accounts reveal the clear position of the early church on the issue of ethical reporting.

While the deaths of Ananias and Sapphira are among the first references in the early Christian church to the vital importance of ethical reporting, the Old Testament had long suggested a similar message to the Israelite community. For example,

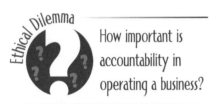

How important is accountability in operating a business?

Proverbs 20:23 declares, "The Lord detests differing weights, and dishonest scales do not please him." Clearly, God's preference is that His people use ethical and honest accounting in all of their dealings. How Jon decides to respond to his real-life industrial dilemma will reveal the importance he places on God's standard.

Ask the Pro

James Wilson is plant manager of the largest of the Midwest popcorn processors. He is a graduate of the Purdue University School of Agriculture with a degree in food business management. James has seventeen years of experience in the food manufacturing industry.

The company where James is employed is a world leader in popcorn production and has been a privately held, family-owned business for seventy-five years. In addition to the Midwest plant, the company has a plant in Rojas, Argentina.

Along with his wife, James attends church regularly, where he teaches children occasionally and volunteers frequently. The couple has three elementary-age daughters.

The authors asked James to discuss the Ace Production case and business ethics in general from the perspective of a Christian in industrial management. The results of our conversation are below:

Q: Jon at Ace Production has a problem with a coworker. How should he handle that problem?

Wilson: He needs to engage Buzz face to face. I think I would find him now, even at home and asleep. I'd get in my vehicle and drive to his house if necessary. "We have to talk."

Q: That sounds confrontational.

Wilson: It doesn't need to be. In fact, if handled properly, Buzz could become an ally to get the system changed appropriately. I would encourage him to work with me to get management to find a better way to track efficiency.

Q: What better ways would you recommend?

Wilson: We use five Key Performance Indicators that ensure accountability and become a template for success. Every person, every work group, every shift, every department is measured by the same quantifiable standards. They are quality, safety, machine efficiency, labor efficiency, and scrap.

Q: So this scenario could not happen in your organization?

Wilson: It better not!

Q: Do you believe the production control engineers are ultimately responsible for this situation?

Wilson: Only partially. Jon did not engage his superior properly to present his ideas. A good manager must impact the business in a positive fashion by making sure his thoughts are heard. He should have made sure his ideas on calculating efficiency were considered. A dynamic leader gets heard.

Q: Does being a Christian in the industrial world impact any of that?

Wilson: I am proud of who I am. A big part of that comes through my walk with Christ. I express that at work in a variety of ways. The key components include engaging people. That's what Jesus did. He went to the lost wherever they were. Also, one must be consistent. I am so grateful to work for a company that allows me to be consistently Christian.

You Be the Consultant

As you consider Jon's dilemma, answer the following questions:

1. How would you advise Jon to respond to Joe's question? What longer-term plan would you advise Jon to implement following his discovery of the hidden cams?

2. Should Jon inform production control or Karen, the general supervisor, of his find?

3. Should he mention it to Buzz? Why or why not?

4. Answer questions 1 and 2 again. This time assume these positions:
    a. utilitarianism

    b. Kant's categorical imperative

    c. ethical egoism

Special Assignment

Personal Ethics Statement Update

Considering the cases explored in chapters 9 through 12, reexamine and rewrite your personal ethics statement in the space below. Be certain that your statement adequately addresses issues that may arise in staffing, appraising employee performance, leading, and record keeping.

Statement of Personal Ethics	
Name _____	Date _____

13

The Christian Manager as Ethical Disciplinarian

"He who ignores discipline comes to poverty and shame,
but whoever heeds correction is honored."

(Proverbs 13:18)

Chapter Challenges

A careful examination of Chapter 13 should enable the reader to:

- Understand the purpose and principles of employee disciplinary action.
- Develop an ethical approach to employee discipline.

Case Study

Sagamore County Mental Health Association

"What is this trash?" Sue Yaton angrily demanded as she stormed into the office of her supervisor, Paul Novak.

"Now, Sue, calm down, and we will discuss the matter rationally," Paul responded.

"You calm down if you want to," Sue continued. "But I'm furious, and someone is going to hear about this." She slammed a memo from Paul down on the desk. "This is garbage, and you know it!"

Paul's memo to Sue indicated that he had placed a written warning in her file for insubordination. While the memo and the written warning did not indicate the circumstances, Sue knew the matter stemmed from an incident with Ivan Westmore, one of Sue's clients.

A Legal and Ethical Obligation

As case manager for Sagamore County Mental Health Association, Sue managed a caseload of twenty-two mentally handicapped adults. Her responsibilities involved making sure clients received the benefits available to them from state, county, and local agencies. She worked with these agencies to assure that none of her people were granted less than full citizenship rights because of their disabilities. Her task also included making sure the clients functioned as nearly as possible at their full capacity.

Some of her clients were severely disabled and required close supervision on an ongoing basis. Others, like twenty-six-year-old Ivan Westmore, were only mildly challenged. Ivan held a regular full-time job and lived in his own apartment. However, he did struggle with money management. Thus, he qualified for five hours of assistance each week to make sure he was not cheated during such activities as banking and shopping.

Ivan had developed an infatuation with a sixteen-year-old girl who lived in his neighborhood. Although he referred to the girl as "his woman," most observers doubted the seriousness of the relationship. The girl's father had become sufficiently alarmed to ask a judge to issue a restraining order against Ivan. The court had granted the father's request, and it had fallen to Sue to explain to Ivan that he must stay away from the girl or face contempt-of-court charges. She was confident that Ivan understood the court order and its implications.

A few weeks later during a routine interview, Ivan revealed to Sue that he and the girl had recently gone together to a movie. He discussed their date with enough clarity that Sue became convinced that he had violated the court order, and the two had become involved in a consensual sexual relationship.

As soon as she had reason to believe that Ivan had violated the restraining order, Sue believed she had a legal and ethical responsibility to notify the authorities. "Ivan," she said, looking steadily into his eyes, "do you understand that what you are doing is wrong and that I have to notify the sheriff?"

"Go ahead, Miss Sue," Ivan responded. "I'm willing to get in trouble, and my woman will wait for me until I get out."

A Heated Disagreement

While Sue's legal obligation seemed clear enough to her, Paul argued that Sue should look the other way on the matter. "Look, Sue," he instructed, "we have a mental health levy before the voters in less than thirty days. Something like this in the papers could get blown all out of proportion and threaten all of our jobs. Quit asking the kid about his sex life and forget what you already know."

"You're suggesting I violate the law," Sue argued. "I have no choice but to report what I know. If the voters can't sort out right from wrong, we'll just have to find alternative funding."

"No!" Paul demanded angrily. "I'm not *suggesting* anything. I'm giving you a direct order. Forget Ivan's sex life."

Later that same afternoon, Sue filed a report with the Sagamore County Sheriff's Office. As required by office procedures, she put a copy of the report in Paul's mailbox. Now she stood red-faced with anger in Paul's office.

"A written warning for following the law and doing my job correctly is a cheap shot!" she shouted.

"If you continue to raise your voice to me, I'll increase your discipline to a day off without pay," Paul responded.

The battle over disciplinary action at Sagamore County Mental Health Association was heating up.

On Background

Progressive and Positive Discipline

Both Sue and Paul have made and/or are about to make ethics-related decisions. Paul believes he has used *disciplinary action* appropriately in order to deal with an insubordinate employee. Sue finds Paul's instructions inappropriate. She feels justified in her behavior and would argue that Paul's disciplinary action falls outside the bounds of propriety. The two disagree on several ethical fronts. A better understanding of the process of employee discipline may provide a starting point toward finding common ground.

Reasons for Employee Discipline

In establishing ethical discipline procedures, experts generally group employees into four categories: employees who are ineffective, employees with personal problems, employees involved in on-the-job criminal activity, and employees who violate company policy.

Ineffectiveness

Sometimes supervisors must deal with employees whose skills are inadequate for the job to which they are assigned. Sometimes employees may have the necessary skills, but utilize them in an ineffective manner. The ethical manager carefully analyzes each situation to make sure that discipline does not become a substitute for coaching and adequate training.

Personal Problems

A second category requiring disciplinary action involves employees with off-the-job personal problems that directly or indirectly impact job performance. Alcohol abuse may create an attendance problem; drug abuse may lead to unsafe work habits; marital difficulties may cause on-the-job lapses of concentration or overall ineffectiveness. For the Christian manager, this area touches the key concept that all individuals, regardless of their personal actions, have true value because they are God's creation and are made in His image. To discard employees with personal problems as if you were throwing away yesterday's newspaper is denying human value. Real ethical questions for the manager are: How do I provide Christian discipline? (this includes corrective measures as well as punitive ones—while protecting the interest of fellow employees and fulfilling my fiduciary responsibilities to the company's owners and suppliers)

In dealing with these kinds of employees, the ethical manager must make certain that discipline does not become a substitute for appropriate counseling. One manager made no distinction between an employee who failed to report for work because he was in the county drunk tank, and another employee who failed to report in order to attend a parent's funeral nearly 200 miles away. "If they're not here; they're not here," he growled. "I got no use for them." Most of us would agree that disciplining without regard to an employee's circumstances or record is unethical. This statement emphasizes the interdependence of record keeping and disciplining aspects of a managerial control function and how failure to recognize that interrelatedness can set the stage for inappropriate and often unethical decisions.

On-the-Job Crime

A third category requiring employee discipline involves the growing problem of on-the-job crime. Stealing from employers, embezzling funds, disclosing trade secrets, and misusing expense accounts or company credit cards all fall within this category. Often law enforcement authorities intervene, relieving the employer of disciplinary action. Ethical managers recognize the employer's responsibility to minimize opportunities for illegal behavior. Increasingly, companies utilize industrial security techniques, including security education, fraud control, and appropriate checks and balances.

Company Policy Violations

A fourth reason for employee discipline often is the most difficult to administer. It includes employees who violate company policy or supervisor instruction. Paul believes Sue fits into this category. In order to determine appropriate discipline for such violations, the ethical manager must be certain that company policies and instructions have been clearly communicated to the employee. For example, when orienting new employees, many managers take a pro-active approach. This goes beyond the typical walking tour of the facility, introduction to key personnel, filling out tax and insurance forms, and the giving of a policy manual. The pro-active manager invests company time in an in-depth orientation to policies and procedures at the hiring phase and a periodic review of policies throughout the employee's time with the company. Special attention is given to orienting the employees to new policies and procedures as they develop.

When this pro-active policy approach is utilized, it reduces the opportunity for unethical managerial practices when policies and procedures are not followed, it helps the honest employee not to make mistakes through ignorance, and it gives management firmer ground to stand on in case of employee or union appeal, or court action challenging management's disciplinary actions. This practice or similar ones intentionally address the question, "Is it ethical to discipline employees for violating policies or procedures that have not been taught to them?" These approaches also comply with the philosophy that quality management equips its employees with the knowledge, skills, and resources to successfully do their required task. Is it ethical to do otherwise?

Progressive Discipline

When employee discipline becomes necessary, the ethical manager generally uses a four-stage progressive discipline approach.

1. First violations often result in a verbal warning or disciplinary discussion. This is the most common of all disciplinary actions, and often brings about the necessary correction.

2. When verbal warnings fail to create the necessary changes in behavior, the ethical manager next may issue a written warning. A copy of the warning is placed in the employee's personnel file and presented to the employee. This form of discipline is most effective when the written warning is presented as soon as possible after the infraction.

3. If these two steps fail to produce the intended change, some firms utilize a third step, the disciplinary layoff. Ranging from a few hours to a week or more, a disciplinary layoff means the employee is ordered to take time off without pay. Sometimes this step is divided, allowing for progressively longer periods of layoff reflecting the severity of the infraction or of repeated offenses.

4. The final step in the progressive discipline process is termination— after other efforts to produce changed behavior have failed. Work guidelines and rules, including those instituted by the government and collective bargaining agreements, make disciplinary discharge extremely difficult to implement. However, where these safeguards do not exist, unethical managers may see termination as the solution to every employee problem, whether it is for one or multiple infractions, or some other non-discipline-related issue.

Positive Discipline

A relatively new approach to employee discipline focuses on future behavior rather than past infractions. Called *positive discipline*, it recognizes that people do make mistakes, yet it de-emphasizes the use of punitive action in favor of written reminders, pro-active interaction with the employee, and positive reinforcements for appropriate employee behavior. The ultimate discipline, discharge, may still be employed when circumstances warrant.

Positive discipline suggests that employees wish to be positive, contributing members to the society within their company. This results in more frequent and voluntary compliance with company policies and procedures, leading to worker satisfaction and positive worker contributions toward meeting the company's goals and vision. A key belief is that this intrinsic desire can be activated, leading to more appropriate employee behavior and productivity.

This approach has roots in elements of the work of Abraham Maslow, Fredrick Herzberg, and B.F. Skinner. Maslow's contribution was to identify the basic needs of individuals from the very basics necessary to sustain life to the higher human elements that add personal meaning and value to life. Herzberg studied employees and their companies, identifying workplace policies and characteristics that cause worker frustration and discontent, and examining human motivators related to employees' desires emanating from the workplace. Working in behavioral psychology, B. F. Skinner identified the relationship between positive and negative actions that eliminate current undesired human behavior or initiate new desired behaviors.

In this approach, management might establish a rewards system to reinforce appropriate employee response to company policies and practices. For example, cash bonuses or a company banquet may reward employees who have perfect attendance for the year, have committed no violations of company policy during the year, and have exceeded minimum annual productivity expectations. These activities are designed to prevent undesirable employee behavior from occurring.

Herzberg's work suggests other positive, preemptive measures that short-circuit the need for employee discipline by altering of the work. Two examples are reducing monotony by rotating workers from one repetitive work task to another or providing workers with an understanding of how their work contributes to the success of the company and the good of society. In short, emphasize the concept that work should build human dignity.

When an employee is guilty of behavior that violates company policy or procedures, the company looks at the causes of the behavior as well as the cost and affects of the behavior. For example, if an employee has a chronic absenteeism problem, counseling and possible treatment for an identified root cause such as drug addiction may be the appropriate company response instead of firing the employee. This is a human approach to discipline that is in part based in economic reality. If the company has a capable employee and has made a major investment in the training of that employee, positive discipline with related expenditures may be the cost-effective way to meet company needs.

This approach to discipline also respects the employee as a person of dignity and personal and professional potential. It is interesting that of the eleven definitions of "discipline" in the American College Dictionary, only two directly relate to the use of punishment or a negative approach to discipline while the other nine relate to the teaching and training aspects of discipline.[1] Positive discipline does not wink at inappropriate behavior. It identifies inappropriate behavior, confronts it, records it, and even uses data collection for employee termination. However, it also looks for positive remedies and emphasizes the belief that human beings will respond in appropriate ways when they are treated as persons of dignity with personal and professional potential. There is an underlying belief that when employees are managed and disciplined in a positive, pro-active way, both the employee and the company benefit.

Systems in the company can set the stage for more opportunities of either ethical or unethical decision making, as evidenced in the area of employee discipline. Kant's concept of treating people with dignity while upholding several universal rights and various contractual rights such as due process and fair and accurate data gathering, requires management to develop well-defined and functional systems. Managed by administrators who view man as made in God's image and who practice a redemptive philosophy of discipline designed to respect the dignity of employees, these systems can help employees overcome personal problems, attitudes, and ineffective work habits.

Toward an Ethical Christian Worldview

Hebrews 12:5-11

In Scripture, God's discipline always involves helping one of His children to do better. This is most clearly stated in the following verses from the book of Hebrews.

My son, do not make light of the Lord's discipline,
and do not lose heart when he rebukes you,
    because the Lord disciplines those he loves,
and he punishes everyone he accepts as a son.*

Endure hardship as discipline; God is treating you as sons. For what son is not disciplined by his father? If you are not disciplined (and everyone undergoes discipline), then you are illegitimate children and not true sons. Moreover, we have all had human fathers who disciplined us and we respected them for it. How much more should we submit to the Father of our spirits and live! Our fathers disciplined us for a little while as they thought best; but God disciplines us for our good, that we may share in his holiness. No discipline seems pleasant at the time, but painful. Later on, however, it produces a harvest of righteousness and peace for those who have been trained by it (Hebrews 12:5-11; *Proverbs 3:11, 12).

The Greek word *paideia*, translated "discipline" in this passage, has the same root as the English word pediatrics. This word implies the training or instruction a caring parent might give to a child. Interestingly, the passage suggests that discipline from God should be considered as evidence of His love. Just as a loving parent disciplines a child, so God disciplines in order to help His children improve.

Similarly, discipline meted out by a caring employer who desires to train, instruct, and improve the performance of an employee meets the scriptural parameters of ethical discipline. By contrast, revenge or reprisal, while often confused with discipline, are in reality much different and are by definition unethical.

One manager sought some way to get rid of a person he perceived as a problem employee. He went through the progressive discipline steps, but his mind had been made up before he even began the process. "This troublemaker has to go," he declared. His preconceptions meant that the discipline he administered was only intended to fulfill the demands of a rulebook, not to improve the employee's performance. Such discipline does not meet the scriptural guidelines of proper ethics.

A Teachable Spirit

In addition to the difference in the way ethical discipline is administered, there should also be a difference in the way ethical discipline is received.

Proverbs 13 suggests that even ethical discipline may not have the desired effect. Much depends on the attitude with which that discipline is received. "He who ignores discipline comes to poverty and shame, but whoever heeds correction is honored" (Proverbs 13:18).

One manager concluded that this verse points to the importance of a teachable spirit. Ethical discipline designed to gain an improvement in performance has neutral or even negative results in the life of an employee who lacks a teachable spirit. Looking again at Sagamore Valley Mental Health, we must first determine whether or not Paul intended to bring Sue to a place of improved performance. Was his motivation caring? Did he want to make Sue a better employee, or did he have a different agenda?

How can an employer's disciplinary action be above reproach?

Then we must ask whether Sue demonstrated a teachable spirit? Whether or not Paul's discipline met the ethical requirements of propriety, Sue had a responsibility to receive the discipline in an ethical manner.

Ask the Pro

Nancy Quan is a Family Case Manager in the Child Protection Division of Family and Children. In that capacity, she is called upon to investigate allegations of abuse or neglect. Prior to being at the Child Protection Division, she worked for six years in providing private foster care. For more than four of those years, she was a supervisor.

Nancy graduated from Taylor University with a bachelor's degree in psychology. She has attended church her entire life. At her church, she has served as secretary, board member, Sunday school teacher, and worship leader.

Nancy agreed to review the situation at Sagamore County Mental Health from her perspective as a social work practitioner and also from her experience as a supervisor. The authors sat down with Nancy at her office for the following exchange.

Q: Paul thinks Sue made a poor decision. Do you agree?
Quan: I had a bit of a struggle deciding what she should have done. In my state, sixteen is the age of consent. There actually would be no crime in

this situation. If I were Sue (knowing there had been no crime, but aware of the restraining order), I think I would have called the girl's father and let him know that his daughter had made a bad decision, and that the restraining order may have been violated. On the other hand, if the child were fifteen instead of sixteen, Sue would have had an obligation to report what she knew—because in that case a crime had been committed.

Q: Where do the supervisor's instructions come in?

Quan: The law is a higher standard than what the supervisor says. I would try to talk it out with Paul. I might even go to his manager so that I wouldn't surprise anyone when I did what would have to be done.

Q: Let's look at the case from the supervisor's position. Did Paul act appropriately?

Quan: I can't imagine a supervisor telling an employee not to report something like this. That is wrong. But, Sue certainly over-reacted. She didn't demonstrate the right attitude in the way she told her supervisor that she didn't agree with his decision.

Q: But he is concerned about the levy. Does he really have any choices?

Quan: Since the levy is an issue, what still raises an ethical dilemma— but is much more likely to occur—is an attempt to get Ivan off the caseload, so that the office is no longer associated with the entire mess. That is still unethical if he needs the services. Personally, my value system would just cause me to say, "Tough. Forget the voters. Turn him in."

Q: You mentioned your value system. Tell me about values. What role do they play in your work?

Quan: For me, it is very hard to separate values from what I do at work. I have had coworkers who believe church life is church life, and work life is work life. They never combine the two. That is impossible in my life. All my decisions include my values. I can't imagine making a decision separate from values.

Q: Are there ever times when you are tempted to compromise those values?

Quan: I didn't realize when I started in this work how many times I would be put in a situation where I *could* compromise. You have to know clearly and in advance what you believe, and then stand up for what's right, regardless of the cost. You might get a reprimand. You might even lose a job. You need a support group of people who share your values and help hold you accountable.

You Be the Consultant

Examine the ramifications of this ethical dilemma in light of these questions:

1. From the position you adopted in your statement of ethics, do you believe Paul handled employee discipline in an ethical manner? Explain.

2. Do you find Sue's report to the sheriff on Ivan's sexual behavior ethical? Explain.

3. Paul's concerns about a funding levy are not at all uncommon in government-funded agencies. What role should ethical concerns play in gaining public support? What are the limits?

4. Assume the role of a mediator. How should Paul and Sue handle their current differences? Would your mediator role be different if you were a Kantian? Explain your answer.

5. Compare and contrast employee discipline from the points of view of ethical egoism and utilitarianism.

6. How do you view the positive discipline approach used by some firms? Is it more or less inherently ethical than traditional approaches to discipline? How would one who uses Kant's categorical imperatives respond? How would one who is committed to cultural relativism respond?

Endnotes

1. The American College Dictionary, (New York: Random House, 1963), p. 344.

14

The Christian Manager as Ethical Communicator

"Out of the same mouth come praise and cursing.
My brothers, this should not be."

(James 3:10)

Chapter Challenges

A careful examination of Chapter 14 should enable the reader to:

- Define communication.
- Explain six principles of communication.
- Identify four rules for ethical communication.

Case Study

Samoya Enterprises

Herb Walker left Mr. Samoya's office and walked toward the production floor with a smile on his face. At last the years of long hours and loyal service were about to pay off. Herb had worked for Samoya Enterprises for ten years, having hired in as a night watchman while still a student at the local community college. Once he had earned his degree, he joined the twenty-five employees who made up the Samoya hourly production staff. Two years ago, Mr. Samoya had promoted him to production manager. In that capacity Herb's responsibilities included supervising his previous colleagues on the assembly floor. However, what Herb had just learned in a private meeting with Mr. Samoya promised to be the biggest career break of his life.

"Herb," Mr. Samoya said, "what I'm about to tell you must stay in this room. If our employees get wind of it—well, frankly, it could unravel the whole deal. I've decided to sell the business to Widget Industries, our biggest competitor. They have made a very attractive offer that will allow me to retire comfortably."

Herb spoke frankly. "Of course, I'm happy for you, Mr. Samoya, but what about the rest of us?" he asked.

"That's why I wanted to see you, Herb. Widget intends to transfer you to Capital City as plant manager of their operation up there. Congratulations! It's a great move for you, and you deserve the opportunity."

Herb stammered a bit, but finally found the words to respond, "Me? Plant Manager? Thank you, sir! I appreciate the opportunity. I am sure that your recommendation carried a lot of weight. I won't disappoint you, Mr. Samoya."

"I know you won't, Herb," Mr. Samoya said. "Now, don't forget, not a word of this to anyone."

"Of course, sir. Mum's the word. By the way, what does this mean for the rest of the people here at Samoya?"

Mr. Samoya shifted uncomfortably. "A few will have jobs if they are willing to transfer to other Widget Industry plants. Most will be dismissed, I'm afraid. But Widget has plans to grant a severance package of a full month's pay."

"One month?" Herb answered. "But, Mr. Samoya, some of these people have been with the company more than twenty years, and—"

"I realize this won't be easy," Mr. Samoya interrupted. "But, that's business, isn't it, Mr. Plant Manager?" he said with a wink. "Now, remember, no one is to know about any of this until the papers are signed."

Between a Rock and a Hard Place

Once on the production floor, Herb could scarcely contain himself. His thoughts tumbled boisterously in his head. "Imagine me, Herb Walker, Plant Manager!" The excitement must have shown on his face, because several people commented on how happy he seemed.

"You look like the cat that swallowed the canary," Joyce Wilson, Herb's office clerk, commented.

"Just having a great day," Herb responded cheerfully. Joyce had become a close personal friend of Herb and his wife Mindy over the past year. When Joyce and her husband had gone through a rather nasty divorce, Herb and Mindy had befriended Joyce. They had helped her make the transition to single parenting. She had even stayed at their house for a few weeks until she could find an affordable apartment. Herb and Mindy were responsible for her becoming involved in their church and were beginning to see some remarkable changes in Joyce's life. Both Herb and Mindy agreed that Joyce had become like a sister to them.

"I'm pretty excited today, too," Joyce continued. "I'm taking a very big step this week."

"What step is that?" Herb asked, his mind still on the plant manager position.

"I've decided that you and Mindy are right. It is time for me to take addtional steps in emotional adjustments. I'm going to take your advice and take action on some new goals for my life."

"That's great," Herb responded sincerely.

Joyce continued. "So, tonight I'm meeting with a real estate agent after work to take a second look at a little house just a couple of blocks from the plant. I've carefully calculated a budget, and my paychecks here at Samoya Industries total just enough to meet the monthly payments. I'm going to buy a house!"

"You're what?" Herb exclaimed in a voice that was louder than he intended.

"I'm going to buy a house!" Joyce repeated, grinning. "Isn't it marvelous?"

Facing her, Herb bent slightly and braced his hands on Joyce's desk. "Joyce, you can't," he said in a solemn, strained tone.

"Why not?" Joyce asked with a puzzled look.

On Background

The Principles of Interpersonal Communication

On the spur of the moment, Herb might dismiss Joyce's question. He could say, "Just surprised, that's all," and move the conversation to another topic for the time being.

Very soon, however, Herb must make a serious ethical decision. Should he keep Mr. Samoya's confidence, ensuring that he is given the plant manager position? Or should he tell Joyce what he knows and prevent a friend from making a potentially devastating personal financial mistake?

As Herb contemplates his options, he will want to consider some important facts related to organizational ethics and to organizational communication. Simply defined, *communication* is the interaction between two or more individuals. When two individuals are involved in the communication process, such as the meeting between Herb and Mr. Samoya behind closed doors, *interpersonal communication* takes place.

Patterns of Interaction

Most often, groups of people gather together and develop patterns of interaction. We refer to these patterns and the social collectives in which they occur as *organizational communication*. Sometimes the formal or informal rules for interpersonal interaction within an organization shape the way communication takes place.

> *interpersonal communication:* Interaction between just two individuals.
>
> *organizational communication:* Formal and informal rules within an organization that shapes the way interaction occurs.

Regardless of the organizational rules for communication in place at Samoya Enterprises, Herb would benefit from understanding six basic principles of interpersonal communication.[1]

Principle #1: Communication Occurs over Time

Reading about Herb Walker's dilemma, we examine the events as if they occurred in a vacuum—as if this particular interaction is the only one that has ever occurred between Herb and Mr. Samoya. In reality, an ongoing process of interaction has led up to this verbal transaction. Herb likely will evaluate the current situation by looking back over the process that preceded it, perhaps asking himself these questions:

- "Has Mr. Samoya ever asked me to keep secrets before?"
- "How did he react when I challenged him in the past?"
- "Is he likely to be open to input from a subordinate?"

Similarly, Herb may need to evaluate the process of communication he has established over time with Joyce. His questions might include these:

- "How much does Joyce trust me to give her good advice?"
- "How well can she keep a secret?"
- "How flexible is she in her decision making style?"

Communication is a process, not a single isolated conversation. Realizing that can help Herb make a better decision on an ethical course of action.

Principle #2: Personal Motives Are Significant

Herb undoubtedly will have to do some self-analysis. He will want to explore how he feels about the pending promotion, and how much he is willing to sacrifice in order to gain it.

- Would he willingly sacrifice his friendship with and ministry to Joyce?
- Would he sacrifice his personal integrity?
- Would he sacrifice his reputation with the other employees at the plant?

In the final analysis, only Herb can answer these questions. On a personal level, every manager ultimately has to answer these and similar questions.

Principle #3: Effective Communication Reduces Uncertainty[2]

Joyce undoubtedly has come away from her conversation with Herb Walker more confused than ever. Based on earlier conversations, she thought that Herb and Mindy felt she was ready to take the next steps in adjusting to a new lifestyle. Now, based on Herb's facial expressions and his exclamation at her announcement, she wonders if he really believes she should buy a house. Maybe she misunderstood. Maybe Herb and Mindy don't think she's ready to handle that kind of responsibility.

In part, Joyce's confusion stems from the fact that Herb has not communicated very effectively. Effective communication decreases rather than increases the level of uncertainty. Consider two people who meet for conversation on a particular subject. In Figure 14.1, the people are each represented by a circle. The figure demonstrates in the overlap of the circles a "meeting of the minds" prior to their conversation.

Figure 14.1, Meeting of the Minds

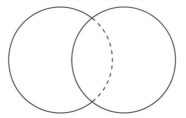

Figure 14.2 shows that the area of mutual understanding has grown as a result of effective conversation. Notice that when communication is effective, the area of overlap increases. The commonality has grown. There is a greater "meeting of the minds" than prior to conversation.

Figure 14.2, Effective Communication

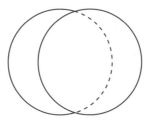

Figure 14.3 demonstrates what may have taken place between Joyce and Herb as a result of their conversation. Joyce's common area of understanding has decreased because ineffective communication has left her uncertain about their standing with one another.

Figure 14.3, Ineffective Communication

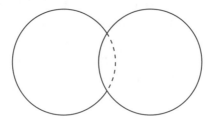

Principle #4: Communication is Non-returnable

Two children playing war in the backyard may trade insults. One child yells, "You take that back!"

The other finally admits, "Okay, I take it back."

The problem is solved. In the minds of children, it is as if the insults were never uttered.

By contrast, most adults recognize that it is impossible to "take back" that which has been uttered. Words, like thick smoke in a strong breeze, quickly cover a large area in a community or organization. Herb will need to proceed very carefully as he addresses either Joyce or Mr. Samoya. Little room exists for error in this communication; while communication can be amended or explained, it cannot be returned.

Principle #5: Communication Includes Both Content and Relationship

Herb will do well to realize that every communication event includes aspects of *content* and *relationship*. For example, suppose a student walks into a business ethics class and announces, "Take out a sheet of paper. We're going to have a quiz." Members of the class likely will jeer or simply ignore the student. They figure the student either misunderstands his role or is attempting to entertain them.

Imagine the totally different response of the class when the professor enters and makes the same announcement. There may be groans and mild objections like "You never told us" or "It's not in the syllabus." But even as the groans are uttered, the sheets of paper are taken out.

How could two people get such strikingly dissimilar reactions to exactly the same words? The answer involves the relationship aspect of communication. While the content of the communication is identical in both cases, the relationship of the speaker to the hearer differs. The response depends upon both the content and relational aspects of the communiqué.

Herb will need to analyze two relationships as he decides what course of action to follow. His relationship with Mr. Samoya is that of a subordinate to a superior. However, additional aspects are a factor. How have the two interacted in the past? Have they ever socialized? If so, do they share a friendship as well as a professional relationship? Does Mr. Samoya share Herb's faith?

Similarly, Herb's relationship with Joyce will make a great deal of difference in how she responds to him. Does she see him as a co-equal friend, or a powerful superior? Has he given her good or bad advice in the past? Has the year of peer counseling she has received from Herb and Mindy helped her to become independent, or does she find herself dependent on them?

Principle #6: Ethical Communication Is Never Risk Free

Regardless of how he decides to solve this dilemma, Herb is about to take some risks. Because it is impossible to determine how all parties involved will receive or interpret what is being communicated, it is impossible to determine all of the short- and long-term consequences of a communication. On one hand, he may risk his job and a promotion. On the other hand, he may risk his friendship with Joyce and the relationship that he and Mindy have developed with her. Despite the risks, Herb has an obligation to discover an ethical approach for solving this situation. Joyce has the universal right to be told the truth and to be treated with dignity. The Christian ethic calls for fair and honest actions between the Christian and others. The mandate to "do unto others as you would have them do unto you" requires that a solution must be found that treats all parties in an ethical way.

Ethical Communication: Four Rules

As Herb seeks an ethical solution to his dilemma, he may benefit from considering four general rules for ethical communication.

1. ***Ethical communicators never intentionally deceive.***[3]

    Every member of an organization always has an ethical responsibility to tell the truth. Certainly, Herb is not honor-bound to tell all that he knows. He has a responsibility to protect the confidentiality of information shared by others. A common managerial dilemma revolves around protecting the confidentiality of one party while properly informing other interested parties. In the case of personal information, this is given legal force by privacy laws. However, if he is ethical he cannot tell falsehoods either to Joyce or to Mr. Samoya.

2. ***Ethical communicators do not purposely harm others.***[4]

    Herb has an ethical obligation to those with whom he communicates to ensure that he does not intentionally harm them. Added to this is the principle of malfeasance, or the carrying out of a task that you have no right to do. These conflicting important principles established the dilemma in the Herb Walker case. If he reveals what he knows about the pending sale, Mr. Samoya's sale could be jeopardized. If he remains silent, Joyce could find herself facing serious financial harm.

3. ***Ethical communicators practice "Golden Rule" communication.***

Herb must sort out what he would want to have happen if he were Mr. Samoya. Similarly, he will need to put himself in Joyce's situation. How would he want her to communicate if the circumstances were reversed? Finding a solution that satisfies the "Golden Rule" of communication in both relationships will be difficult.

4. ***Ethical communicators consider the organizational culture.***

All organizations have a unique organizational culture, including Samoya Enterprises. In some organizations, an employee is rewarded for standing on principle and insisting on doing what is right. For example, a Christian company may support an employee who discovers that a potential customer intends to sell the company's products in a way that is in opposition to the Christian company's biblically-based mission statement. Even at the risk of losing the potential customer's business, the Christian company recognizes the long-term benefits of remaining true to its mission statement.

In another organizational culture, this same employee might be expected to take whatever action is necessary to ensure profitability instead. He could not expect to be rewarded for placing principles above profits. Since Herb has worked at Samoya Enterprises long enough to know the company's expectations, he will have to include that knowledge in his analysis of what course of action to take.

Ethical Communicators

- Never intentionally deceive
- Do not purposely harm others
- Practice "golden rule" communication
- Consider the organizational culture

Toward an Ethical Christian Worldview

James 3:3-10

When we put bits into the mouths of horses to make them obey us, we can turn the whole animal. Or take ships as an example. Although they are so large and are driven by strong winds, they are steered by a very small rudder wherever the pilot wants to go. Likewise the tongue is a small part of the body, but it makes great boasts. Consider what a great forest is set on fire by a small spark. The tongue also is a fire, a world of evil among the parts of the body. It corrupts the whole person, sets the whole course of his life on fire, and is itself set on fire by hell.

All kinds of animals, birds, reptiles and creatures of the sea are being tamed and have been tamed by man, but no man can tame the tongue. It is a restless evil, full of deadly poison.

With the tongue we praise our Lord and Father, and with it we curse men, who have been made in God's likeness. Out of the same mouth come praise and cursing. My brothers, this should not be (James 3:3-10).

What Makes a Man Perfect?

In this passage James implies that our words are the key to Christian perfection. A person who learns to control what he says has learned to please God. He is considered to be a perfect man.

The structure of this passage is similar to the structure Jesus uses in Matthew 5. The command to use direct speaking is followed a few verses later by His encouragement to please God by means of perfection:

Simply let your "Yes" be "Yes," and your "No," "No"; anything beyond this comes from the evil one (Matthew 5:37).

Be perfect, therefore, as your heavenly Father is perfect (Matthew 5:48).

To make his point, the James passage includes three illustrations. The first relates the use of a bit in a horse's mouth. A bit is a small thing compared to the overall size of the horse, yet that much smaller device controls the entire animal. The next illustration is an example from the maritime world. A rudder is a small part of a sailing vessel, yet that small part determines the course of the entire ship. In yet another illustration, readers are asked to consider a tiny spark that has the ability to set an entire forest ablaze. The tongue—like a bit, a rudder, or a spark—is small but can cause big things to happen, either good or bad. While it is a small part of the body, it controls the entire human being.

Having established the importance of direct conversation to the believer, James then declares that "no man can tame the tongue" (v. 8). Were this the last word on the matter, the reader would be discouraged indeed. However, the writer continues with a solution to the communication problem.

Who is wise and understanding among you? Let him show it by his good life, by deeds done in the humility that comes from wisdom. . . . the wisdom that comes from heaven . . . (James 3:13, 17a).

While it is implied that human beings cannot tame the tongue, God working in and through human beings can facilitate a change in the use of their tongues. Additional illustrations demonstrate the absurdity of trying to tame the tongue through self-will. Fresh water and salt water do not come from the same source. Olives cannot grow on fig trees, nor figs on grapevines (vv. 11-12). Similarly, righteousness does not emanate from an unrighteous being. Only those totally controlled by God have the ability to speak in ways that please Him (vv. 15-18).

Ethical Dilemma

What happens when interpersonal communication runs the risk of harming others?

As Herb searches for the best course of action in communicating with Mr. Samoya and Joyce Wilson, he will want to consider the importance of godly communication.

Ask the Pro

Before retiring in 1996, Clarence Southcutt served as a high school principal for twenty-four years. Prior to that, he was an assistant principal for four years. Currently, he chairs the board of directors of a local bank.

Clarence and his wife have been active in the local church they attended since 1959. He has served the church on a variety of committees and in other leadership roles. The authors asked Clarence for his insights on the Herb Walker case. Our conversation follows:

Q: Before we talk about the solution to this dilemma, let's discuss the case itself. How "real life" is this scenario in your estimation?

Southcutt: There are tremendous parallels to real life. I have certainly been asked to keep secrets. And, sometimes, you can do that. But, when it affects people's lives, income, or retirement, that's a totally different story. For example, the severance package in this case is totally inadequate. Employees need time to prepare for elimination of their jobs.

Q: Are you suggesting that if Herb doesn't talk, he is a part of that inadequacy?

Southcutt: Yes.

Q: How would you analyze Herb Walker's dilemma?

Southcutt: Remember, Herb came up through the ranks of this business. He has worked with people at all levels. He probably was raised in the local community. He has an obligation to the people with whom he has worked.

Q: You mean as a Christian?

Southcutt: No, I think he has that obligation whether he is a Christian or not.

Q: So, what should Herb do?

Southcutt: Herb needs to go to Mr. Samoya and say, "I can't keep this confidence under these conditions. I have too much at stake to remain silent. It's not just about my promotion to plant manager, but about all these people who are involved."

Q: Won't that cost him the promotion?

Southcutt: If it does, so be it. That's the downside. I think he is likely to lose the position. On the other hand, no one can take away his education and experience. They can only take his integrity, if he allows it. I think it is possible that Mr. Samoya might have an even greater respect for Herb. He may call the new owners and say, "Wow, you have really got something in that Herb Walker. Let me tell you about his integrity."

Q: Is there no middle ground? Could he sit down with Mr. Samoya and say, "I need your permission to tell just one woman"?

Southcutt: Well, I suppose he could, but I don't think that is enough. All the people he has worked with trust him. I think he has an ethical responsibility to tell the people what he knows that is about to impact their lives.

Q: Did Herb overstep his boundaries and get too close to Joyce as an employee? Did he violate a good ethic with regard to fraternization?

Southcutt: No, I don't think so. As a Christian, he was reaching out to someone in need. That's what we are called to do.

Q: How about Mr. Samoya? Did he behave unethically when he said, "I'm going to tell you something, but you can't tell?"

Southcutt: That's harder to say. I'd like to know more about him and his motivations. I do think that when Herb heard those words, they should have acted as a "red flag." As soon as he heard those words, he should have been on guard. Sometimes, you can agree to abide by that, but sometimes you have to say, "Sorry, I can't agree to keep quiet." That's where Herb is now. He must find a way to tell what he knows.

You Be the Consultant

Help Herb decide on the best course of action by studying and answering these questions:

1. Is Herb's relationship with Joyce appropriate? What are the ethical limits of employee fraternization?

2. What are the ethical limits in receiving or keeping secrets? Should Herb have stopped Mr. Samoya before he ever received the information about the sale of the business?

3. What do you think is Herb's best course of action at this point?

4. How might a follower of utilitarianism advise Herb to handle this situation? Compare and contrast that advice to what might be expected from the position of cultural relativism.

5. Is your personal statement of ethics adequate to deal with this situation? Defend your answer.

Endnotes

1. Emory A. Griffin, *Making Friends (& Making Them Count)* (Downers Grove, IL: InterVarsity, 1987), 18-24.
2. Charles R. Berger and Richard J. Calabrese, "Some Explorations in Initial Interaction and Beyond: Toward a Developmental Theory of Interpersonal Communication," *Human Communication Research* 1 (1975): 99-112.
3. Gary L. Kreps, *Organizational Communication*, 2nd ed. (New York: Longman, 1990), 250.
4. Ibid.

Notes

15

The Christian Manager as Ethical Team Builder

"Two are better than one,
because they have a good return for their work . . ."
(Ecclesiastes 4:9)

Chapter Challenges

A careful examination of Chapter 15 should enable the reader to:

- Understand the concept of a work team.
- Identify several characteristics of a work team.
- Recognize four important rules of ethics for work team leaders.

Case Study

Pit Stop Northeast

"We think it would be fairer to Randy and we're all willing, so we propose to start tomorrow and rotate on a daily basis." Al Jenson spoke for the group, addressing regional manager Fred Bayon during the weekly staff meeting at Pit Stop's northeast branch.

Pit Stop operated five establishments at various locations throughout the city. Each location offered ten-minute oil changes and a variety of services and automotive accessories to busy auto owners. As regional manager, Fred provided general supervision to all five locations. He visited each of the five as necessary to order inventory and deal with any personnel issues or customer complaints.

Pit Stop Northeast operated without a site manager. A team made up of four employees handled day-to-day operations. Fred suggested the team approach when the site manager quit nearly a year ago. Although the other four Pit Stops continued to have a single site manager in charge of the daily operation, Northeast did well so far using Fred's model. In fact, the success of the team approach at Northeast had captured the attention of corporate management. The team idea was now being tried in other cities. Fred believed he was in line for a promotion as soon as there was an opening at the corporate headquarters.

Fred encouraged the team concept at Northeast. For example, he paid a monthly bonus to the store manager of the store that reported the most sales volume. At Northeast, he reminded the four employees to think like a team and split the bonus among each of the four members.

A Perplexing Proposal

Listening to Al and seeing the looks on the faces of the other Northeast team members, Fred found himself thinking, "For the first time, my teamwork idea is about to present some difficulties."

At Northeast, each employee had specific job responsibilities. The same was true at all Pit Stop locations. Fred believed this concept worked especially well at Northeast. Since there was no site manager, each employee was personally responsible for one of four specific areas.

Operator one was the pit operator, whose job included all of the under-car duties. He pulled the oil plug and performed the grease gun work. Of the four jobs, the pit operator's job was the dirtiest and most unpleasant. On a busy day, operator one often did not have time to come up to ground level for several hours. Randy Temple worked the pit at the Northeast location.

Bruce King was the second operator at Northeast. He swept the inside of the vehicle and cleaned the windows inside and out. It was also operator two's job to check the tire pressure on each vehicle.

The third operator performed the under-hood functions, which included checking fluid levels and belts. In addition, operator three put oil back in the vehicle. Al Jensen worked this job at Northeast.

The key to sales at all Pit Stop locations was the fourth member of the team. Operator four interacted with the customers. In addition, operator four completed all the necessary paperwork and sold the customer additional services. The real profit at any Pit Stop location came through the sale of such accessories as wiper blades, bulbs, belts, hoses, and filters. Operator four noted the need for these items and gained the customer's approval for replacement.

A few months earlier, Fred had hired Stacy Jaggers to work as operator four at Northeast. Since Stacy had joined the team, sales had jumped significantly. She worked well with customers, knew automobiles, and projected a positive and confident image. While he was careful not to say so publicly, Fred believed he had demonstrated a "stroke of genius" when he hired a female to sell to the predominantly male customers at Pit Stop Northeast. In fact, Fred had been working on plans to replace the sales team members at his other stores with the most knowledgeable and attractive female employees he could find.

For the moment those plans took a back seat in Fred's thinking. The Northeast team had just made a proposal at the weekly staff meeting to begin a daily rotation of the four operators. That meant that three out of four days, Stacy would not be with the customers. Fred imagined that sales would plummet.

"Randy has such a dirty and nasty spot," Al said. "You have always emphasized that we are a team and should think creatively, with everyone being responsible for the whole operation. Well, we just think daily rotation would work well for us."

"Another benefit," Bruce added, "is that everyone will know every position. Remember last month, when Randy called in sick? It took us a couple of vehicles to become efficient because we weren't used to his job. This way, everyone will know every job."

Put on the Spot

"I don't know," Fred hesitated. "It seems to me that by rotating, no one will be responsible for anything.

"Just the opposite," Randy corrected. "Since we're a team, everyone will still bear responsibility for the entire operation. Besides, we will feel more like we really *are* a team—not just hear that word from you all the time." The group smiled knowingly.

"You *are* a team," Fred bristled. "I don't want to tinker with the most productive Pit Stop staff in the city. Also, you have earned the monthly productivity bonus the last three months. I wouldn't want you to risk losing that extra income."

After allowing the potential loss of revenue to sink in for a few moments, Fred continued. "Stacy, you're the best at what you do in the entire Pit Stop organization. Do you really want to rotate to the pit?"

"I'm willing," Stacy responded. "Not that it is my life's goal to work down there, but you *have* stressed teamwork. I'm willing to do my part for the team."

"What do you say?" Al challenged. "Can we rotate starting tomorrow?"

On Background

Work Teams

Fred's reluctance to wholeheartedly endorse the Pit Stop Northeast employees' idea for rotation may indicate a potential ethical problem. His reluctance also may demonstrate a misunderstanding of the *work team* concept.

> *work team:* basic production unit that builds tasks and organizations around processes instead of functions.

In *Human Resource Development*, Jeff Horsby says, "The basis of work teams is that jobs and organizations should be designed around processes instead of functions, and that the basic production unit should be the team, not the department."[1] Work teams build tasks and organizations around processes, leading to the achievement of organizational goals instead of functions within a department. At Pit Stop, the individual functions of four operators have remained the primary focus in spite of "team talk." Al, Bruce, Randy, and Stacy now propose shifting to a process orientation. They want to begin to view processing vehicles as paramount to each individual doing a particular task. They further believe that the adjustment will increase their satisfaction level in the workplace.

How Work Teams Work

Fred must recognize several key characteristics of work teams as he makes what could become a very crucial decision with ethical dimensions.

Work Teams Build Synergy

Synergy is a term that was developed in chemistry. It is the phenomenon that occurs when the effect of a combination of chemicals is larger than the sum of the individual effects of the chemicals. This is why your doctor may tell you not to take certain combinations of medicines or not to drink certain beverages and take certain prescription drugs at the same time.

This idea is applied to business when some type of team or cooperative approach is used. The synergetic result is that the people working together and building on each other's ideas and strengths will produce greater positive results than if these people had worked independently, assuming that the people are working toward a common, mutually advantageous goal. The strength of the combination is always greater than the sum of the strength of the independent parts. This concept is graphically demonstrated in a numerical formula. In highly effective work teams:

$$1 + 1 > 2$$

Work Teams Develop over Time

Fred also should consider that work teams take time to develop. No team becomes highly effective just because a manager orders it into being. Instead, work teams develop over time through several distinct and predictable stages. Most teams demonstrate at least four stages:[2]

Stage 1: Formation – groups develop the rules for interaction and become accustomed to working with each other.

Stage 2: Conflict – groups often grow tired of one another and threaten to separate due to conflict.

Stage 3: Integration – groups go back and forth between conflict and performance. Together, they develop the standards for effective operation.

Stage 4: Performance – groups set their own work goals and maximize their potential for productivity.

Characteristics of Ethical Team Leaders

- Clearly define the parameters of the team in advance.
- Exercise patience.
- Provide empowerment commensurate with responsibility
- Recognize individual personal responsibility for the team

Every highly effective group must pass through each of these stages on its way to maximum productivity. Managers must allow the process to continue through completion. For example, it may be tempting to abandon the work team concept during the conflict stage. This stage takes a great deal of time. Further, conflict resolution can seem to sidetrack the team from its main purpose. However, highly effective work teams have learned to work through the conflict stage, and subsequently, they are better prepared to anticipate and avoid conflict in the future.

Perhaps Northeast is closer to the performance stage than Fred realizes. He also should consider that the recent increases in productivity might be more directly attributable to group performance than to the gender or skills of one individual team member.

Work Teams Meet with Resistance

Finally, Fred needs to be aware that the most common barrier to work team performance is a lack of management commitment. Most managers verbally endorse the team approach, but demonstrate a high resistance to change when organizational work groups are actually implemented.

In some cases, circumstances justify such resistance. Highly specialized functions, for example, do not lend themselves to cross-functional work teams that utilize cross-training among the various team tasks. For example, if one member of the Pit Stop team was required to read high-tech instruments or perform some other task requiring a high degree of training, the cross-functional team concept might prove less useful if all team members did not have the same level of training.

Work Team Ethics

In addition to understanding these basic background facts on work teams, Fred needs to consider four important ethical aspects of work teams.

1. *Ethical team leaders clearly define in advance the parameters of team activity.* From the beginning, they ask and answer these kinds of questions:

    - Is the team ongoing or temporary in its breadth of operation?
    - Is the team empowered to make changes or only to make recommendations?
    - Does the team have product development authority?
    - Can the team adjust current marketing strategies?
    - Does the team have authority to alter work rules?
    - Is the team permitted to discipline one of its own members?

All such questions should have clearly communicated answers early in a work team's development.

2. *Ethical team leaders exercise patience.* Since teams do not instantly attain high performance, management must allow for the development of work team effectiveness. Ultimately, synergy kicks in, but the development curve may be longer than the team leader intended.

3. *Ethical team leaders provide empowerment commensurate with responsibility.* Teams often are held responsible for certain job-related decisions or processes, but are not provided adequate resources of time, money, or personnel to accomplish the task with maximum effectiveness. The ethical team leader acknowledges the need for an appropriate level of resources.

4. *Ethical team leaders recognize their personal responsibility for the productivity and decisions of the team.* Team building can become a hiding place for ineffective managers who declare, "I'm not responsible for that. I gave it to a team." With teams, as with individuals, managers may delegate authority, but not ultimate responsibility.

Toward an Ethical Christian Worldview

Ecclesiastes 4:9-12

Two are better than one,
*   because they have a good return for their work:*
If one falls down,
*   his friend can help him up.*
But pity the man who falls
*   and has no one to help him up!*
Also, if two lie down together, they will keep warm.
*   But how can one keep warm alone?*
Though one may be overpowered,
*   two can defend themselves.*
A cord of three strands is not easily broken (Ecclesiastes 4:9-12).

The theme of the entire book of Ecclesiastes involves the futility of selfishness. Solomon found everything in life to be meaningless, or, as he put it, "Vanity of vanities" (1:2 KJV), until he discovered as the "conclusion of the matter: Fear God and keep his commandments" (12:13). In God, we discover purpose and meaning in life.

Ironically, as the writer struggled with his own selfish nature and the emptiness it brought to his life, he discovered something that brought temporary relief as he moved toward a more permanent solution in God. That temporary improvement involved teamwork.

The Threefold Cord of Teamwork

This biblical passage shows how teamwork yields several important positive results. These include accomplishment (verse 9), support (verse 10), warmth in the presence of cold (verse 11), and defense (verse 12). Each of these benefits comes in spite of the overall meaninglessness of life. In short, teamwork works.

Verse 12 states that a "threefold cord" is not easily broken. If it is true that two heads are better than one, then aren't three heads an even more beneficial arrangement? Solomon seems to think so.

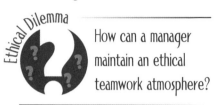

How can a manager maintain an ethical teamwork atmosphere?

Clearly, this wisdom passage suggests the value of teamwork. However, the limits of teamwork are not addressed. At what point do the advantages of specialization and hierarchy of leadership outweigh the advantages of teamwork? That is the question that Fred Bayon must answer at Pit Stop. Apparently, his answer must be decided very quickly.

Ask the Pro

Carmen Medina is in her eleventh year as the head volleyball coach at a university. Her lifetime record is 415 wins and only 110 losses. Coach Medina has led teams to the National Tournament four times, achieving an Elite Eight distinction ten years ago. She holds a doctor of education degree from Northwestern University.

Carmen grew up in a small-town church, where she continues to play an active role. She has served in recent years on a variety of committees and has assumed a host of leadership responsibilities.

The authors sat down in the University Grill with Medina to discuss the team development concepts of the Pit Stop case. The results of that conversation follow:

Q: What are the issues of this case as you see them?

Medina: There is a conflict between allowing people autonomy to carry on, and having someone who is responsible for keeping the main goal or mission statement before them. It appears to me that rotating, as they perceive it, might put people in jobs for which they are not qualified. You might say this is an idea that threatens the quality control of the business.

Q: Does the team-building concept have natural limitations?

Medina: Of course. Ultimately, there has to be someone in charge. Decentralization is great, but all the goals have to stay in harmony or it won't work.

Q: Since the goal on the volleyball court obviously is to win, is such a scenario unlikely?

Medina: Not at all. At Pit Stop the goal is financial gain. The problem is that employees, like players, have different perceptions of how they can best achieve that goal.

For example, a freshman in our system usually takes very little leadership on the court. A few years ago a freshman was a defensive starter and a very verbal leader. The captains took charge in an early match and simply told her to keep quiet. As leaders they were attempting to instill proper respect for program process and to form a functioning unit. However, the results during a match were devastating. The freshman became timid and non-communicative. We unraveled. I had to step in and say, "As a team we have some misunderstandings about leadership. Let's talk about how we lead and the best way to communicate with one another."

Q: So, like Fred Bayon, you had asked for a team attitude, then stepped in and said, "Wait a minute, that's not exactly what I had in mind."

Medina: Exactly! Now, the key for Fred is communication. *How* he says "Good idea, but we're not doing it" is very important.

Q: How would you suggest he approach that?

Medina: I would bring them all into the process, since they are all stakeholders in the decision. I would focus on the part of their recommendation that is good. Fred needs to explain that he must retain enough decision making power to accomplish business goals. I might suggest a compromise where they perform dual roles rather than a full rotation. That uses the best of their idea within limits, and keeps the rotation from allowing people to be in areas where they are not qualified.

Q: Do you see a gender ethics issue in this case?

Medina: I looked at that very carefully, because it seems to be on the borderline. However, as it stands I don't see one. I wonder if some of Stacy's coworkers aren't suggesting that she ought to do some of the dirty work, too. But, if Fred isn't asking her to dress a certain way in order to get the attention of the male customers, or something like that which is not discussed here, then I think he's okay. It could be that she is a good "people person" regardless of gender.

You Be the Consultant

As you consider Fred's concerns, examine them in light of these questions:

1. What are the ethical considerations Fred needs to make as he contemplates the proposal of the Northeast team? When might an ethical manager refuse to adopt a team proposal?

2. How would you characterize Fred's attitude toward Stacy and her performance? Is his attitude ethical? Why or why not? Would a Kantian agree? How about an ethical egoist?

3. What stakeholders need to be considered as Fred makes the decision about rotation? What are the implications to each stakeholder?

4. What will Fred do if his ethical position resembles utilitarianism? Kantian ethics? Ethical egoism? Cultural relativism?

5. Based upon your statement of ethical position, what advice would you give Fred Bayon? Is your statement adequate for this dilemma? Explain your answer.

Endnotes

1. Jeff Hornsby, *Human Resource Development* (Muncie, IN: T.I.S., 2001), 98.
2. P. Buhler, "Group Membership" *Supervision* (May 1994): 8-10.

16

The Christian Manager as Ethical Motivator

"So we rebuilt the wall till all of it reached half its height,
for the people worked with all their heart."

(Nehemiah 4:6)

Chapter Challenges

A careful examination of Chapter 16 should enable the reader to:

- Recognize the difference between motivation and manipulation.
- Understand the characteristics of ethical motivation.

Case Study

Worker's Benefit Insurance Company

Jim Johnson glanced at his watch as he pulled into the driveway at 1104 South Street. He didn't want to be late for his very first appointment. Last Friday afternoon, he finished the two-week orientation course with Worker's Benefit Insurance Company. This beautiful Monday morning marked his first day as a full-fledged claims adjuster. Worker's Benefit had assigned Jim to a five-state area to handle all of its disability claims.

Worker's Benefit specialized in low-cost disability insurance for blue-collar workers. Usually the policies were sold door-to-door in lower middle-class neighborhoods like the one in which Jim now found himself. Often the agents made weekly premium collection visits at the homes of the insured.

The policies were a specialized disability insurance that promised to pay only in the event of a work-related injury. The schedule of benefits varied depending upon the extent of the disabling injury. For example, the company promised to pay $100 per month for life for the loss of a finger. The benefits increased to a maximum of $2,000 per month for life in the event of a total and permanent disability.

Jim's task as claims adjuster included verifying the disability by means of personal interview and medical record research. In addition, he represented Worker's Benefit in an attempt to "buy out" legitimate claims by offering up-front cash settlements. Of course, the buyouts cost the company less in the long run than the promised monthly benefits.

In his very first full-time job since graduating from college, Jim anticipated handling several large buyouts very soon. The old-timers said that claims adjusters made a name for themselves in the company and increased their opportunity for advancement by arranging buyouts that saved Worker's Benefit huge sums of money. These buyouts also were advantageous to Jim. Besides his small cash salary, Worker's Benefit would pay him a percentage of the savings in the form of a bonus for each buyout. If he could favorably handle a few major claims, Jim hoped to repay the bulk of his education loans in just a few months.

An Up-Front Settlement

Jim knocked on the door of the little bungalow belonging to Moses Engels. Since the verification of total and permanent disability was not in question, during today's visit Jim hoped to convince the fifty-seven-year-old Engels to take significantly less than the $2,000 per month which the policy provided for him. The actuarial outlook revealed that Worker's Benefit stood to pay Moses nearly $400,000 in lifetime benefits.

Moses Engels' daughter, Sherry, greeted Jim at the door. "Thank you for visiting us, Mr. Johnson," she said as she showed Jim to a chair in the cramped and cluttered living room. "May I bring you some coffee?"

"No thanks," Jim responded. "If you don't mind, I'd like to get down to business with your father."

"Dad will be right in," Sherry acknowledged. "Actually, my father has only a sixth-grade education and is not very adept at business matters. I work with him on all but the most routine decisions. While I don't have his power of attorney, my father and I get along very well in this relationship. Here he is now," she noted as Moses Engels entered the room.

Jim rose and greeted Engels. After some casual small talk, he got to his purpose in coming to the Engels home. "Worker's Benefit has authorized me to offer you a very handsome sum of money right now as settlement for your injuries. We regret seeing you waiting on all of those small monthly checks."

"There are a lot of medical bills right now," Moses responded. "One doctor charged me almost $300 for one office visit. Can you imagine a man making $300 an hour?"

"Ridiculous, isn't it, sir?" Jim readily agreed.

"Daddy," Sherry said "We've already talked about all those bills. I understand that they are a worry to you, but if I take care of those and pay off the house, then you will have all you need from your monthly check."

"Girl, that's nearly fifteen thousand dollars," Moses interrupted. "It ain't right for a grown man to take charity, especially from his own young-uns."

"Daddy, we'll talk later," Sherry said, speaking with finality. Turning to Jim, she continued, "Mr. Johnson, we are really not interested in any up-front settlements, regardless of how generous they may appear. My father needs the monthly cash flow to manage, now more than ever since the accident. Thank you, though, for coming."

She stood and extended a hand. It was clear the meeting had ended. Jim made his way to the door. It was not exactly the outcome he had hoped to report to Worker's Benefit in his first day's report.

Since Jim was not one to accept temporary setbacks as permanent defeat, within a few hours he hit upon an idea. Jim stopped at a local department store and purchased a large two-suit suitcase. After a couple of calls to the home office, he received a wire from Worker's Benefit for $15,000, which he exchanged for small bills. Carefully, he placed the money in the suitcase. After calling ahead to confirm that Sherry had left her father's house, he returned to 1104 South Street.

"Mr. Engels," he greeted Moses, "I've been thinking about our earlier conversation, and your very honorable desire to not take charity from your children. Worker's Benefit would like to help. I think I have found a way that you can pay those bills yourself. In fact, one quick signature and you could be debt free. May I come in?"

On Background

Motivation vs. Manipulation

The Worker's Benefit case describes the interaction between Jim Johnson and Moses Engels, two men who have very different goals and objectives with regard to a personal injury claim. At issue is ethical behavior in the area of *motivation*. Motivation comes into play when a claims adjuster meets a claimant. Of course, motivation is relevant in many other kinds of relationships; for example, between employer and employee, salesperson and customer, or parent and child. In fact, in any situation in which two people hope to convince one another of something, persuasion takes place. Therefore, motivation comes into play and ethics becomes an issue.

The Motivation Continuum

Before attempting to define ethical motivation, we should review the concept of motivation in general. The word motivation comes from the root word "motive," something that moves or compels us to action. Motivation occurs along a continuum between the behavioral extremes of inner drive and manipulation. Figure 16.1 demonstrates this continuum.

Figure 16.1. Continuum of Motivation Possibilities

Continuum of Motivation Possibilities

Inner Drive				Manipulation
-10	-5	0	5	10

We often associate motivation with varying degrees of natural inner drive. We sometimes say, "She is highly motivated" or "The position requires a motivated self-starter." Such statements recognize an innate characteristic related to degrees of ambition. For example, Jim Johnson seems to be motivated by a drive to become a successful claims adjuster, one who intends to pay off certain education loans in the process. Moses Engels, on the other hand, appears to be motivated by the desire for independence. Presumably no one dangled these goals before either man. Instead, these goals are internalized as part of the individual's makeup.

Manipulation

At the opposite end of the motivation continuum is *manipulation*. In its most benign sense, to manipulate means to manage or utilize skillfully. However, today the word manipulation often carries negative overtones. We call someone who attempts to control a situation to his or her own advantage a "manipulative" person. At its most extreme, it becomes coercion. For example, contracts executed at the point of a gun have long been held to be invalid due to duress. One party *manipulated* rather than *motivated* the other to sign the contract.

> *motivation:* Drive that compels a person to action.
>
> *manipulation:* Extreme form of motivation that is sometimes seen as coercion.

Ethical Motivation

It seems clear that manipulation is not ethical. What requires more careful analysis is determining which behaviors along the continuum of motivational possibilities are ethical, and which fall outside the bounds of acceptable ethics. In *Communication Ethics: Methods of Analysis*, authors James A. Jaksa and Michael S. Pritchard say, "We want persuaders to be honest, disclosing important and relevant information for the case at hand."[1]

In looking at what constitutes ethical motivation, we offer the following standards for analysis.

Ethical Motivators Communicate Their Own Goals

In and of itself, the desire to be successful and to make money is not unethical. In fact, Nobel laureate and economist Milton Friedman argues that making money may be the ethical thing to do in some circumstances.[2] Dr.

Friedman has often stated that a primary fiduciary responsibility of managers is to make as much money as possible for the company's owners without breaking the law or violating moral standards. Making consistent profits is good for the economy and protects the jobs of the employees. However, attempting to hide profit-oriented motives behind more altruistic intentions is unethical.

For example, a used car salesman may say to a prospective buyer, "I really could care less about the commission I make; I just want you to have the best car possible." That salesperson may be viewed with greater suspicion than a competitor who declares, "Of course I want to sell you a car! That's how I make my living. But, I also hope to help you find the best car possible."

Ethical Motivators Consider Others' Goals

One manager's ethical statement declared that the key to leadership lies in finding out what people want and then helping them obtain those things. He took the position that the nature of the things desired made no difference whatsoever. As long as he helped others achieve these desires, he felt that he was behaving ethically.

Obviously, that manager holds a rather extreme understanding of ethical behavior. Some people want things that are illegal. Others may want what is not in their best interests. This is an inadequate view in that it has no boundaries and it does not require the manager to confront the issues at hand. However, the ethical motivator considers the "ethicalness" of the other person's goals as they relate to the greater good before developing a motivational strategy.

Experts in motivation generally categorize people's desires according to levels of need. Maslow's Hierarchy of Needs, explained in his landmark 1954 work, *Motivation and Personality*, is an example of this concept. It suggests that there is a hierarchy or ranking of importance of human needs. Maslow listed them, in order of importance, as these: physiological, safety, love, esteem, and self-actualization.[3] Until one level of need has been satisfied, the next level does not serve to motivate.

Our most basic needs are *physiological*: food, water, and avoidance of pain, which serve to keep our bodies healthy and alive. If these needs are not met, a person will typically be consumed with a desire to meet them and will be able to care about little, if anything, else. Those who have experienced the temporary trauma of "having the wind knocked out" of them know that in that moment of airlessness nothing matters but the desire to breathe. Homeless people will search restaurant dumpsters for leftovers, their need for food overwhelming any embarrassment they might feel.

According to Maslow, the next need is for *safety*, to have security and stability in what can be a chaotic world. Abused children often have developmental problems. They "freeze" at the point at which the abuse began, unable to seek satisfaction of their higher needs. Students living in high crime areas often are more concerned with their day-to-day safety than with their teachers' urgings to "live up to their potential." What good is it to study for a test if I won't be alive tomorrow to take it?

Love and belonging needs follow safety. Humans crave interaction, acceptance, and membership in groups. Once the basic physiological and safety needs are met, humans reach out to other humans for validation and support. To what lengths did you go as a teen to be accepted by your peers? Think of the social groups to which you belong, and how you would feel if you were rejected by one of them.

Next is the *esteem need*. Humans desire recognition for their abilities and achievements, both from within themselves and from others. Reaching a certain goal or mastering a particular skill makes us feel good about ourselves. We also want others to acknowledge our successes. A man who has received a promotion and a hefty salary increase may purchase an expensive car. The unspoken message to all who see the car is, "I make a lot of money and I am successful. I have power."

The final need Maslow discussed is *self-actualization*. This need drives people to seek their true purpose in life, to "be all they can be," to rise above the mass of humanity and be different, and better.

If one wishes to motivate employees, it is a good idea to identify their level of need and address it. This practice will help avoid the managerial error of trying to motivate employees with false motivators, rewards that management believes to be of interest to employees but are really not. The higher needs of love, belonging, self-worth, and prestige are often ignored by managerial approaches to motivation that rely solely on financial rewards such as pay increases, increased medical or retirement benefits, or child care. Maslow's thesis would say that these types of motivators lose their potency as employees' personal and family situations improve to the point that survival issues are not as pressing. When these basic needs are met, the managers must recognize it and develop motivation strategies that address the self-fulfillment issues in the employees' professional lives.

The needs of an individual must be met at one level before that person is motivated to move to the next level. Recognizing the level of need in others helps the motivator to be successful. Such awareness also increases the necessity for ethical motivational behavior. An ethical manager will regard employees as God-created individuals, and will exercise care in the use of that knowledge in open, non-manipulative ways. This knowledge of employees can be used in negative ways since many company systems divide motivation into reward and punishment systems. To a person that the manager knows is having trouble providing the basic needs for her family, the threat of time off without pay may be a very effective motivational tool. But is use of that knowledge ethical?

Ethical Motivators Are Skilled Listeners

Ethical motivators recognize that others' thoughts and words provide clues to their goals. In addition, the careful listener has a built-in barometer for determining whether or not communication is being properly understood.

Most people agree on the importance of listening. Surprisingly, many managers fail to listen effectively. One can learn to become a better listener. Learning to listen more effectively sets the stage for more ethical motivation. Three keys aid the manager to improve listening:

1. Listen with all of the senses. Listen to the verbal communication and read both body language and facial expressions as well. Someone may respond to you, "Oh, I'm fine," while at the same time wringing her hands and blinking nervously. These physical signs tell you that the person is *not* fine.

2. Control *thinking speed*. We think three times faster than we speak. The good listener fills the available time with feedback that enhances communication. This may be through analysis of the speaker's content, reflecting on the emotions that the speaker's content or delivery style is evoking, and other thought processes that focus on the speaker and the information being communicated. Sadly, many people merely let their minds wander to other topics when someone else is speaking.

3. Delay evaluation. Skilled listeners avoid jumping to conclusions about what the other person is saying. They postpone evaluation until they have totally digested the message.

Ethical Motivators Balance Rewards and Punishments

Experts agree that both rewards and punishments can serve to motivate effectively. For example, the reward of more money can motivate an employee to work longer hours. The fear of being fired can motivate an employee to avoid making personal phone calls during work hours.

Ethical motivators utilize a combination of rewards and punishments to motivate. Using only punishment may serve to cheapen human life. Punishments also may lose their effectiveness over time. Using only rewards may ignore the original nature of every human being. The Bible is replete with examples of people such as Adam, David, and Solomon who illustrate this point. They received the positive rewards of God, but despite these rewards, they deviated from desired behavior.

Even when using these four guidelines to ethical motivation, managers often face difficult decisions in the area of motivation. Motivating people means exercising power over others. Walking the continuum between inner drive and manipulation can present great challenges to the Christian manager who seeks to apply an integrated ethic to the area of motivation.

Ethical Motivators

- Communicate personal goals
- Consider the goals of others
- Listen
- Balance rewards and punishments

Toward an Ethical Christian Worldview

Nehemiah 4:6

So we rebuilt the wall until all of it reached half its height, for the people worked with all their heart (Nehemiah 4:6).

Perhaps nowhere in Scripture is there such a powerful account of motivation than in the book of Nehemiah. According to the book that bears his name, Nehemiah, who was a Jew, initially served in the palace as cupbearer to the Persian king, Artaxerxes. The Jews had been taken into exile by the Babylonians in the sixth century B.C. Later, Babylon was defeated by Persia and exiles were then allowed to return to Jerusalem.

The first wave of Jews returning under the leadership of Zerubbabel began to rebuild the Temple. The work started and stopped, finally resuming in 520 B.C. Ezra led a second group of exiles to Jerusalem in 458 B.C. and focused on re-establishing the Law in Jewish society. But the walls of Jerusalem were still in ruins and the safety of those "back home" weighed heavily on Nehemiah. Once convinced of his God-appointed role to rebuild, Nehemiah gained the permission of the king to lead a work team to Jerusalem in 432 B.C. The walls had been in ruins since the fall of Jerusalem in 586 B.C. With Nehemiah's capable leadership, the monumental task of completing the wall was accomplished in just fifty-two days!

A Mind to Work

Nehemiah acknowledged that the accomplishment was because the "people worked with all their heart" (4:6). The King James Version of the Bible translates the same phrase, "the people had a mind to work."

After a century-and-a-half of inactivity, why did the people all of the sudden have a mind to work? The answer lies clearly in the superior motivational skills of Nehemiah. He caused the people to see the divine appointment under which they labored. He gave appropriate recognition and credit to those who achieved goals.

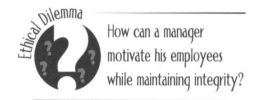

Ethical Dilemma

How can a manager motivate his employees while maintaining integrity?

He effectively divided the labor to facilitate incremental accomplishment. He skillfully overcame obstacles—whether physical, mental, or emotional. In short, he proved to be a superior motivator.

As Jim Johnson seeks to motivate Moses Engels and others in order to accomplish his life goals, he might well take a lesson from Nehemiah. One has to wonder how the godly Nehemiah would view Johnson's approach thus far.

Ask the Pro

Randell Sweetser sold his first policy as an independent insurance agent twenty-two years ago. Today, his office services over 5,000 policies for automobile, home, health, life, and business insurance and has grown to the second largest agency of its kind in his state.

Randell holds a bachelor's degree in business management from a Christian liberal arts university. He and his wife have four children. He attends a large church and serves on the board of directors of its private school.

The authors asked Randell for his perspective on the situation at Worker's Benefit Insurance Company. The results of that conversation appear below:

Q: How realistic is the Workmen's Benefit scenario? Surely, what Jim Johnson is trying to do in this scenario would not be attempted in real life.

Sweetser: You'd be surprised. I'm not directly involved in the claims process, but there are certainly individuals and companies out there who search for ways to avoid paying a claim. One of the reasons I chose the company I am with is that it is a fair company. This scenario would not develop.

Q: Is Johnson's behavior against the law?

Sweetser: No, but he has crossed a line of ethical propriety. The daughter made it very clear that Moses needs the monthly cash flow. For Johnson to go back later when the daughter is not there and blatantly appeal to Moses' emotions is wrong.

Q: Nevertheless, if it's not illegal, won't he get away with it?

Sweetser: If Johnson lived in my state and were turned into the Department of Insurance by the daughter, in my opinion he would very likely be suspended or, at a minimum, put on probation.

Q: So, is this such an ethical breach that even a secular worldview would identify it as wrong?
Sweetser: Yes.

Q: Are there issues in your business in which being a Christian does lead to a different conclusion?

Sweetser: Being a Christian is not something you wear around on your sleeve like a WWJD bracelet. Asking "what would Jesus do" is all right, but the truth is you can bend the answers to benefit yourself. Being a Christian means treating people right—all the time. I think living the Golden Rule is very important in business.

Q: Isn't that just good business?

Sweetser: Of course, but it is also a way of life. I deal with real human beings. Some folks in my business deal with computer screens or statistical tables. With people you have to add the element of compassion. Relationships become much more important for a Christian in business.

You Be the Consultant

As you consider Jim Johnson's actions, answer these questions:

1. How would the limits of ethical motivation differ between those whose ethics are derived from utilitarianism and those whose ethics come from cultural relativism?

2. Compare and contrast Kantian ethical motivation with what ethical egoism would say about ethical motivation.

3. Has Jim Johnson behaved ethically in his offer to Moses Engels? Why or why not? Would his offer be more ethical if he had made it in the presence of Moses' daughter? Would the offer be more ethical if it were for more money? If so, at what dollar amount does propriety begin?

4. Is Workers Benefit's "buyout" approach ethical? Why or why not? Provide biblical as well as philosophical evidence to support your answer.

Endnotes

1. James A. Jaksa and Michael S. Pritchard, *Communication Ethics: Methods of Analysis* (Belmont, CA: Wadsworth, 1985), 35.
2. Michael E. Hattersley and Linda McJannet, *Management Communication: Principles and Practice* (Boston: McGraw Hill, 1997), 211.
3. Maslow, Abraham. "A Theory of Human Motivation". Psychological Review 50(1970):370-396.

Special Assignment

Personal Ethics Statement Update

Re-examine your personal statement of ethics and determine what changes are necessary in light of the case studies you have examined in chapters 13–16. Rewrite your statement, incorporating any changes and assuring that your statement will encompass issues that may arise in the areas of employee discipline, communication, team building, and motivation.

Statement of Personal Ethics

Name _____   Date_____

17

The Christian Manager as Ethical Marketer

"May the words of my mouth and the meditation of
my heart be pleasing in your sight."

Psalm 19:14

Chapter Challenges

A careful examination of Chapter 17 should enable the reader to:

- Understand and be able to implement five questions of ehtical adverstising.

Case Study

Dupont Men's Wear

All Men's Suits **10% Off!**	**Back to School Special!** • • • • • • • • • • • • • **Boys' Jeans $19.95**
Get Ready for Fall! *Check Out Our Complete* *Line of Flannel Shirts*	**Baseball Caps** *Reduced Now* *Starting at only $7.95*
DUPONT MEN'S WEAR *On the Courthouse Square • Downtown Doville*	

Ryan put the finishing touches on the ad for the Sunday paper as Karen, Ryan's wife and business partner, entered the office. "Working on the ad?" she asked, looking over his shoulder.

"Just finished," he responded. "What do you think?"

Karen studied the ad carefully. "Looks okay," she responded somewhat tentatively.

Ryan and Karen had recently taken over Dupont Men's Wear, and were learning the retail business together. Karen's father, Ralph Dupont, had founded the clothing store and operated it for forty-five years. Three months ago, he had suddenly decided that it was time for him to retire.

Both Ryan and Karen had worked part-time as sales associates at the store, but had little experience in the details of operating a small business. Nor was Ralph any help. He verbalized only one stipulation when he handed them the keys and signed over the inventory. "Don't call me. I've done my time. Good luck!" He had not come into the store since.

In fact, not too many others had come into the store either. Dupont's was situated on the courthouse square of the small town of Doville. Doville was the county seat where forty years ago the area was a hub of activity. Today, much of the traffic could be found at the outskirts of town where several national chain stores were located. Ryan and Karen were learning the hard way that doing retail business in Doville's downtown area was a very difficult challenge.

An Advertising Question

"I certainly hope this ad generates some activity," Ryan mused. "Cash flow has become a major issue in the last few weeks."

"I realize things are tight," Karen said. "That's why I'm wondering about a 10 percent discount on men's suits. I'm not sure we can afford that much of a discount. After all, selling suits to Dad's repeat customers has kept us going so far."

"You're right," Ryan responded. "So we need to go with our strength. My plan is to price every suit at least 10 percent higher before we run this ad. That way, the advertisement will generate sales, but after we discount at the register, we will be right back to our regular price."

"I don't know," Karen said. "That plan sounds questionable to me. How does this idea fit into our ethics statement and our agreement to operate the business with genuine Christian values?"

Both Ryan and Karen had been Christians since their dating days. They were active in their local church and took living their faith very seriously. When they took over the store, they had agreed to honor the Lord in everything they did. They had carefully crafted a statement of ethical behavior that served as their guide to decision making.

"I don't see any problem," Ryan replied. "As long as we get the suits marked up before we run the ad, it's just a routine price increase. Besides, we aren't twisting anyone's arm to buy at the new price. We just offer the suits and the customer makes the decision to buy. What is non-Christian or unethical about that?"

"You make it sound so proper," Karen said. "So, why do I feel like a kid sneaking a cookie from the cookie jar?"

Ryan shrugged. "Probably because it is business, and as we have agreed a hundred times before, you are just too sweet for the tough decisions of business." He gave her a quick kiss on the cheek. "Now, what do you say? Shall we get busy and mark those suits up?"

On Background

Ethical Advertising

In these early days of operating Dupont Men's Wear, Ryan and Karen have come face-to-face with one of the most controversial ethical dilemmas managers face. Some automatically consider advertising to be unethical. Others see it as just a necessary part of doing business. Some argue that advertising is neither ethical nor unethical.

Advertising attempts to create a need. An ad works when it generates a consumer's a desire for something, or a desire for more of something. Some Christians contrast the nature of advertising with this verse: "I have learned, in whatever state I am, to be content" (Philippians 4:11 RSV). Again, "Godliness with contentment is great gain" (1 Timothy 6:6 NIV). Some believe that any advertising contradicts the highest values of the Christian faith.

Others would argue that advertising simply serves to inform potential customers. The advertising itself does not alter a customer's freedom to choose. Some even hold that anything goes in advertising so long as it is legal. "Advertising is simply the exercise of free speech," some suggest. "An ad is no more or less ethical than any other information exchange, regardless of what that ad communicates."

Five Questions to Ask

Most managers with a desire to employ honest and ethical advertising practices fall between these two extremes. They will benefit, as will Ryan and Karen, from asking themselves five questions regarding advertising.

Is It Accurate?

Both ethical managers and the Federal Trade Commission agree that an ad must not be false or misleading. According to case law and federal regulations, total impression of the ad provides the key. To be considered ethical and legal, the total impression must not be false or misleading. For example, advertising a particular headache remedy as a cure for a headache may be improper advertisement if the product only temporarily masks the symptoms of a headache.

Is It True?

Marketers interested in an ethical approach will also consider whether an ad tells the truth. Here subtle distinctions become important. Generally, the buying public anticipates and even expects a certain amount of "puffery" or "puffing up" to accompany a product's advertisement. A certain amount of exaggeration is considered acceptable and within the boundaries of ethical propriety. Misrepresentation, on the other hand, is both illegal and unethical.

Consider, for example, an advertisement that declares a particular briefcase to be "one of the finest leather cases made." If the case is made of imitation leather, the ad is untrue and unethical. However, if it is made of genuine leather, the "one of the finest" descriptive aspect will probably be viewed as puffery, but still ethical.

Is It Clear?

A general guideline in ethical advertisement is that the ad must be clear, even to those of a lower intellectual capacity. To intentionally confuse in order to deceive is not ethical. A travel agency advertisement offered a free Florida vacation with every purchase of a teddy bear. When potential buyers investigated they discovered that the teddy bear cost $2,500. In reality, the agency was offering a Florida vacation with a free teddy bear. While technically not illegal, most people would consider this ad to be unethical.

An advertising approach may be ethical if it is deemed to be so outrageous that no serious buyer would be confused. Those who drink a certain sports drink, for example, don't expect their perspiration to be the same color as the beverage—despite what the TV commercials depict. In cases like these, the advertisers are more interested in capturing the consumer's attention, creating humor, or exercising creative license than in attempting to confuse the consumer.

Is It Offensive?

Perhaps the most difficult item on the advertising ethics checklist involves the issue of offense. Since nearly everything is offensive to someone, the concept of community standards has been established to determine an ad's potential to offend. Community standards have certainly changed over time. What the majority of Americans found offensive thirty years ago often is considered harmless today.

Further, the concept of community standards requires geographic definition. For example, does a state university student body constitute an independent community? If so, does the school's newspaper determine the appropriateness of a particular advertisement on the basis of that community alone, or does it consider the impact on the larger community outside the campus? Concerning issues that cross the line of propriety, the larger community often has a lower tolerance than a campus community.

Perhaps the Christian manager would benefit from considering a biblical standard over a community standard. While community standards change over time and geographic area, Scripture remains unchanging.

Is It Harmful?

Ethical advertisers acknowledge their responsibility to protect consumers. Of special interest in this category is the issue of potential harm to little children. For example, some years ago the courts determined that advertisements for alcoholic beverages potentially harm children. As a result, such ads have been banned from those publications catering to persons under eighteen years of age. More recently, "watchdog" groups have raised questions as to whether or not tobacco products carry the same risk of harm to minors.

Some would argue that certain snack foods threaten the health of children. Should companies that manufacture these commodities be forbidden to advertise on the basis of potential harm? When does interpretation infringe on the constitutional right of free speech? Free speech applies to advertisers, as well as to Americans in general. This right must be safeguarded.

While there may be other considerations that bear on the issue of ethical advertising, Ryan and Karen would certainly do well to begin with this checklist in determining the ethics of their Sunday paper advertisement. While applying these and other principles, they may also wish to consider this comment from LaRue T. Hosmer in *The Ethics of Management*: "If it does not break the law it is only the beginning point in making ethical decisions and not the ultimate standard."[1]

Ethical Advertisers Ask:

- Is it accurate?
- Is it true?
- Is it clear?
- Is it offensive?
- Is it harmful?

Toward an Ethical Christian Worldview

Matthew 21:12-13

Jesus entered the temple area and drove out all who were buying and selling there. He overturned the tables of the money changers and the benches of those selling doves. "It is written," he said to them, "'My house will be called a house of prayer,' but you are making it a 'den of robbers'" (Matthew 21:12-13).

The vivid details with which all four gospel writers describe Jesus' cleansing of the Temple makes it one of the most dramatic accounts in all of

New Testament literature. However, some misunderstanding of his motivation continues to create confusion in the modern church. Many conclude that Jesus' purpose involved the elimination of buying and selling in the Temple area. Thus, they strictly enforce a no-sales-in-the-church-building policy in support of Jesus' attitude.

In quoting Jeremiah 7:11, ["You are making it a den of robbers"], Jesus seems to indicate a different purpose. His behavior is designed not so much for the elimination of commerce in the Temple, as the elimination of dishonest commerce in any location.

A Matter of Principle

In Jesus' day, the court area surrounding the Temple proper included a market where goats and sheep were sold for sacrifice. The law required that only sacrifices declared by the high priest to be "without blemish" were appropriate for sacrifice. Everything purchased in the Temple court, often at grossly inflated prices, was guaranteed for approval. By contrast, even the finest animals carried onto the premises from outside were certain to be rejected. Such abuse of power to achieve personal economic advantage stirred Jesus' displeasure.

Similarly, every adult male had to pay an annual Temple tax of half a shekel. The tax had to be paid with a Phoenician coin. Since daily commerce operated in Greek or Roman coinage, most people had to get their money changed. Priests who operated the exchange tables were permitted to charge as much as a 15 percent fee for the exchange. Jesus objected to the impact of such unscrupulous behaviors on the common people.

Ethical Dilemma

How can a manager meet the marketing demands of his business ethically?

Since the cleansing of the Temple clearly was about honesty in dealings at the table of commerce, Ryan and Karen at Dupont Men's Wear should examine their advertising practices in light of Jesus' decisive action. The question they should ask themselves is, "Does our intended advertising match the behavior of the Temple priests in this passage, or does our behavior rise above such unscrupulous dealings?"

Ask the Pro

Bill Miller is the owner/manager of Miller's Do-It-Best Hardware. His grandfather began the business over 80 years ago. Bill started working in the store after graduating from college. At that time, his father and mother owned the business. After working with them for about ten years, Bill purchased this two-employee operation about 20 years ago.

Bill and his wife attend a community church located in their small town where they team-teach a fourth-grade Sunday school class. The couple has four teenage children. The authors sat down with Bill at the store to discuss business ethics in general and the Dupont Men's Wear case in particular. Here are the results of that conversation:

Q: Ryan and Karen seem to be under enormous pressure because of their location. You operate in a very small town at a time when much larger high-volume stores seem to be the norm. Can you sympathize at all with them?

Miller: Oh, of course. We don't even have a grocery store here, so people shop in the larger county seat. It would be nice to have the traffic that is generated by a large department store next door. On the other hand, repeat customers happen because of what you do, not because of where you are. We simply highlight the differences between our store and the chain competitors.

Q: What differences?

Miller: Service. Honesty. Integrity. Principles like treating customers fairly and having what they want. But I think it would be easy to sit and criticize Ryan for his mistake. After being in the business for thirty years, I have made some similar mistakes. You think, "It won't hurt to do this. It's no big deal." Sometimes, you learn the hard way.

Q: So you do think Ryan's approach is a mistake?

Miller: I don't think it will work, for one thing. Whether it's right or wrong is another issue. But, simply from a business standpoint, I don't think it will work. Most of his customers are going to be smart enough to figure this one out and it also creates a bad precedent.

Q: What do you mean by a bad precedent?

Miller: Well, this appears to be a rather insignificant thing that doesn't really matter. In reality it is a "red flag." Scripture is quite clear that small things do matter. All one has to do is give the devil a toehold, and he will make himself at home in your life or your business. It's like the story about the camel sticking his nose under your tent. What differences does a little nose make? But, in the long run, it can make a lot of difference. What starts out as a little insignificant thing can become much more than that. You have to be very careful, because in business you face little things every day.

Q: Does a Christian in business face those little things differently than a non-Christian might?

Miller: I think it is just good business to follow Christian principles. The biblical worldview works. It is practical.

Q: That almost sounds like it is necessary to be a Christian to succeed in business.

Miller: I suppose you can be a perfectly good businessman and not be a believer, but you can also be a good Christian and operate your business effectively.

You Be the Consultant

Examine Ryan and Karen's approach to advertising in light of these questions:

1. According to your statement of ethics, is Ryan's plan for generating sales ethical? Why/why not? How would someone who has adopted utilitarianism respond? How would someone who operates from ethical egoism respond?

2. How would you evaluate Karen's statement, "I feel like a kid in the cookie jar?" Are feelings an adequate measure of ethical standard?

3. Suppose Ryan visits with others in the retail sales business and discovers that his plan is rather common. Would that change your answer to question one? Why or why not? In which ethical positions would such information have an impact?

4. Which system of ethics would most likely consider community standards when determining ethical propriety? Defend your response.

Endnotes

1.   LaRue Tone Hosmer, *The Ethics of Management*, 3rd ed. (Chicago: Irwin, 1996), 75.

18

The Christian Manager as Ethical Negotiator

"Live in peace with each other."

(1 Thessalonians 5:13)

Chapter Challenges

A careful examination of Chapter 18 should enable the reader to:

- Recognize the circumstances that necessitate negotiation.
- Be able to compare and contrast win/win and win/lose negotiation strategies.

Case Study

Decker and Associates Real Estate

"You're staying late again," Tonya said, turning off her office light and heading for the front door.

"Just hoping the phone will ring after hours," Jay responded. "Everyone advises it's the best way to make sales happen in the first few months."

The two visited near the reception desk and switchboard of Decker and Associates Real Estate. As licensed real estate agents, both Tonya and Jay comprised part of the "and associates" who worked in the large real estate office of principal broker, Tom Decker.

Tonya had been involved in real estate sales for more than ten years. During the first six years, she continued teaching fifth grade at a local elementary school. She worked part time at real estate and built a large client base. As her experience and the number of referral clients grew, she eventually took the plunge and quit her teaching job, devoting herself full-time to a career in real estate sales. She was the top producing agent at Decker and Associates and one of the leading salespeople in the area. Tonya had a reputation for tough, no-nonsense business. As a dedicated professional, she worked hard on behalf of her clients and as a result earned a six-figure income. Earning that much in commissions was no small feat, considering that she listed properties at only 6 percent of sales in a market where the average home sold for only $73,000.

Jay had worked in real estate sales only three months. Though he had grown up in the local community, he had been away for five years earning a degree in business at the state university. Since returning, he had married his high school sweetheart and now rented a desk at Decker and Associates. Like all new agents, Jay enjoyed very little repeat or referral business. As a result, he spent a lot of hours knocking on doors in high-turnover neighborhoods, or like this evening, sitting at the front desk after hours waiting for the phone to ring.

"You're doing all the right things," Tonya encouraged. "But it takes a few months to get rolling. Don't get discouraged."

"Thanks," Jay said. "Coming from you, that means a lot. I'm really not discouraged. I had my first closing earlier this week, and had a big break on a cold call today."

"Great!" Tonya responded sincerely. "What happened?"

"I was knocking on doors over on McGregor Avenue. You know the routine, 'I'm looking for a property in this neighborhood for a client. Do you know anyone in the area who might be willing to sell?'"

"Don't tell me that line actually worked?" Tonya said, chuckling.

"It may have," Jay answered. "I found a couple who said they were anxious to sell if I could find them their dream home on the south side."

"Marvelous," Tonya said, "What do they consider a dream home?"

"They need a four-bedroom, two-bath house. It looks as if they may be looking in the $150,000 range," Jay reported.

"Did you say McGregor Avenue?" Tonya asked. "I'm working with a couple on McGregor too."

"Really," Jay responded with genuine interest. "What are your folks looking for in a move up?"

"They also want a four-bedroom, two-bath home," Tonya answered. "In addition, she is really big on an eat-in kitchen, and prefers country style. He insists on a family room large enough for a pool table."

Jay could not disguise the shocked look on his face. "It can't be," he said, his voice expressing his confusion. "Are we both working for the same couple?"

"I wouldn't think so," Tonya said. "I've been helping the McCartys for nearly six months."

"But it *is* the McCartys I ran into today," Jay said with dismay. "Tonya, I had no idea. They never mentioned another real estate agent. I'm showing them a house later this evening."

On Background

Few Clear Industry Boundaries

Both Jay and Tonya make their living on commission sales. Gaining the McCartys' business is very important to them. While real estate agents can be very aggressive, there is a tacit, ethical understanding that under no circumstances should an agent solicit another agent's client.

Some in the real estate business would argue that Jay has done nothing unethical. "If Tonya had taken care of her buyers," they might say, "they would not even have responded to Jay's cold call sales pitch."

Others suggest that Jay had an ethical responsibility to first ask the McCartys if they were involved with any other agents. They maintain that the highest ethical standards demand that Jay ascertain for certain that no competitor, certainly not one in the same office, be undercut by his sales techniques.

These differences in point of view have become severe enough that many states have adopted new licensing regulations allowing for a buyer's broker. Under these legal requirements, unless Tonya has a signed contract with the

McCartys, she has only a prospect, not a full-fledged client. Most real estate professionals would continue to honor her link to the McCarty family as a matter of professional ethics and courtesy.

An Awkward Situation

Regardless of the legal requirements for maintaining a client/agent relationship in their state, Jay and Tonya now find themselves in an awkward but not uncommon situation with regard to their future course of action. Of course, at issue are any commissions resulting from the sale of a new home to the McCartys. In addition, listing and selling the McCartys' current residence could add thousands of dollars to the potential dispute. Jay and Tonya are about to enter into a period of negotiation necessitated by the presence of three circumstances:[1]

1. *Conflict of interest*. When no conflict exists, there is no need for negotiation. In the Decker and Associates case, both Jay and Tonya have a keen interest in finding the McCartys a dream home, thus earning a handsome commission.

2. *No automatic solution*. If Decker had a policy book covering such circumstances, then the outcome of this dilemma would be less ambiguous. In the absence of policies or an established set of rules, negotiation remains a necessary next step.

3. *Opportunities for compromise*. There are several possible solutions. These range from deciding that the first to work a deal owns it, to the proverbial "finders, keepers" answer. Most of the potential solutions will result in some degree of dissatisfaction for Tonya, Jay, or both. To avoid conflict, a compromise seems necessary.

Negotiation Strategies

In the presence of any of the three circumstances above, parties who face potential conflict are in a position to negotiate. If Jay and Tonya have been trained in negotiation competence, they may recognize and implement an ethical course of action.[2] If not, they each automatically will adopt a negotiation strategy in the next few moments.

> Their course of action likely will follow one of two paths:
>
> *win/lose strategy:* Conflict negotiation strategy based upon the assumption that when one person gains a benefit the other must lose in corresponding fashion.
>
> *win/win strategy:* Conflict negotiation strategy based on the assumption that it is possible to maximize benefits for both parties simultaneously.

Win/Win Strategy

They might adopt a *win/win strategy*. Using this negotiation approach, the two believe that a solution exists, one that will maximize mutual benefits. Jay and Tonya will search for a solution that is good for both of them. In order to use a win/win approach, emotion will need to take a back seat to reason. Both Jay and Tonya will have to be open to persuasion—both in being persuaded as well as in trying to persuade the other.

Win/Lose Strategy

More than likely, at least one of the Decker associates will adopt a *win/lose strategy*. Sometimes called zero-sum negotiation, the win/lose strategy is based upon the belief that only one McCarty commission exists. Who gets it or how to divide it up is the real issue. What one gains under this approach, the other automatically loses.

A summary of the comparisons between win/win and win/lose strategies appears in Table 18.1.[3]

Figure 18.1. Comparisons of Win/Win and Win/Lose

Comparisons of Win/Win and Win/Lose
Negotiating Strategies

Win/Win	Win/Lose
Emotions Interfere	Emotions Benefit
Common Interests Pursued	Individual Interests Pursued
Cooperativeness Encouraged	Competitiveness Encouraged
Trust and Mutuality Enhanced	Power and Control Desired
Consulting Developed	Demanding Emphasized
Relationships Strengthened	Relationships Diminished

Some may argue for one approach over another. They may see one or the other approach as more ethical or more effective, regardless of the circumstances. Experts in negotiation believe that the most appropriate strategy will vary from one circumstance to another. Negotiators also note that selecting an appropriate strategy depends to a great extent on the counterpart's choice of strategy. One can see the differences between diplomacy and war in the geopolitical world. This can also apply to the business world in the contrast between friendly mergers and hostile takeovers. In a hostile takeover situation the aggressor may say that the forced acquisition is in the best interest of both companies, but the characteristics of the takeover are found in the Win-Lose column of the above table. The bullying tactics and the loss of independence of the acquired company are clear evidence of the lack of a win-win philosophy. The extreme example is when the newly acquired company is dissolved and its capital and other resources sold at a loss to provide tax benefits for the aggressor company.

Strategies and Outcomes

Figure 18.2. Likely Outcomes for Strategy Selections

		Jay's Choices	
		Win/win	Win/lose
Tonya's Choices	Win/win	positive for both	best for Jay worst for Tonya
	Win/lose	worst for Jay best for Tonya	neutral for both

Table 18.2 demonstrates the possible strategy choices for both Jay and Tonya, along with the likely outcome for each combination. This case is based on an actual situation that existed between two agents. If the senior agent, Tonya, claims her rights based on rank in the company and first contact with the customer, she risks animosity between herself and Jay as well as possibly the homeowner. She could get all the commission or cause the homeowner to lose confidence in the agency and seek help from a competitor agency. If Jay sticks to his guns and bases his right to the listing on currency and the apparent fact

that the homeowner has lost faith in Tonya's ability to sell the house, he will probably gain the commission and a powerful adversary within his own company. In the win-win scenario, the two agents would talk things through and develop an agreement that would not jeopardize the sale and would benefit them both financially as well as build cooperation between them instead of animosity. This win-win situation was adopted in the real-life situation, and the results were beneficial to all three parties.

Toward an Ethical Christian Worldview

Luke 12:57-59

> *Why don't you judge for yourselves what is right? As you are going with your adversary to the magistrate, try hard to be reconciled to him on the way, or he may drag you off to the judge, and the judge turn you over to the officer, and the officer throw you into prison. I tell you, you will not get out until you have paid the last penny* (Luke 12:57-59).

Jesus' words in Luke 12 certainly are designed to call attention to the spiritual rift that exists between God and man. He advises, "It is to your advantage to settle with God without going to the judgment hall." In an adversarial situation this passage suggests that reconciliation is good common sense. To throw oneself at the mercy of the court or some other kind of arbiter carries certain risks. Negotiating early guarantees more control over the situation for both adversaries, especially for the one with the least chance to win in court. This approach is generally beneficial within company structures and relationships. It is better for shop managers and individual workers to resolve work performance and human resource issues in a cooperative, mutually benefiting manner rather than bring in the union steward and setting up an "us versus them" relationship that requires a winner and a loser. What is the managerial goal? Is it to find the most effective way to meet both short and long term goals of the organization, or to prove who is in charge? Is it to find ways to respect all company employees because of their dignity based on their being made in God's image?

How does a manager maintain professional ethics and courtesy?

In the Decker and Associates scenario, Jay and Tonya also would be well advised to find a mutually beneficial solution without taking the matter before their managing broker or an even higher authority. Determining that solution may prove difficult when a commission is at stake.

Ask the Pro

Melvin Hornsby is the owner and operator of H&H Pro Audio, a company that sells and installs sound equipment for churches, schools, and businesses in a multi-state area. Melvin has owned this business for ten years.

Melvin and his wife attend a local church, where he serves as Sunday school superintendent and song leader. The couple also has formed a singing quartet called "The Master's Own." This group ministers regularly in area churches.

In addition to H&H, Melvin has been involved in commission sales for ten years in a variety of settings. Today, he manages the commission sales staff of H&H. It was his experience in commission work that first attracted the authors to him for advice on the Decker and Associates case. The result of the conversation appears below:

Q: From your experience in commission sales, how realistic is the Decker and Associates scenario?

Hornsby: This case is not uncommon at all.

Q: Do such matters usually work out well?

Hornsby: They can be uncomfortable. However, it is possible to sit down and discuss matters such as how much time we each have spent with these clients, and work out a compromise.

Q: How might those negotiations work?

Hornsby: Jay made a cold call and has spent a little bit of time with these people already. In addition, he has a showing scheduled. Tonya, on the other hand, has six months invested. Maybe a 60/40 or even a 70/30 split would be in order.

Q: Is that what the broker will impose if they can't work it out?

Hornsby: I think the broker will lean more toward giving Tonya the commission. She spent the bulk of the time and has been with him the longest. She would probably take the total commission if it comes to that.

Q: If she sees that developing, why would she bother to negotiate with Jay?

Hornsby: To keep peace, to keep a coworker as a friend, and to show respect for another. Everyone needs to do all they can to maintain positive attitudes between salespeople.

Q: Does a commission arrangement automatically set up competition?

Hornsby: Yes, but that doesn't necessarily mean it's bad. Commissions allow you to see in your paycheck how you are doing. Commissions serve as a motivator.

Q: In your experience, what are the chances that Jay and Tonya will voluntarily negotiate this matter in a mutually beneficial way?

Hornsby: It is possible to work it out, but usually one needs a manager to intervene.

Q: In a more general way, what is the biggest challenge to you as a Christian in business?

Hornsby: As a Christian, I have certain standards. For example, I prefer not to solicit bars. It's a choice not to pursue that type of a business for a sound system installation. Of course, there is some lost income, because bars usually need elaborate sound and lighting systems. Some employees have quit working for me when they realized the company was not going to seek that type of business because they wanted to capitalize on the revenue that can come from a bar. As a business owner and salesman, I think that standard still leaves 98 percent of the country as potential customers. I believe in having some standards and sticking to them. That's important!

You Be the Consultant

Examine Jay and Tonya's situation in light of these questions:

1. What course of action would you advise Jay to take in his negotiations with Tonya? How would you advise Tonya?

2. Is it possible for Jay and Tonya to find a win/win outcome in this situation? Defend your answer.

3. Let's say that Jay and Tonya cannot find an agreeable solution. The matter goes before the principal broker in the firm, Mr. Decker. He asks for your advice in dealing with the dilemma. How will you advise Decker? Explain why.

4. Is either the win/win or the win/lose strategy inherently more ethical than the other? Explain. How would your answer differ from a utilitarian perspective? How would your answer differ from the perspective of ethical egoism?

5. Imagine that at Decker and Associates you are the broker charged with developing a policy manual to prevent conflicts such as Jay and Tonya now face. Using your ethical statement as a basis, decide what policies the manual should include.

Endnotes

1. Jensen Zhao, *Managerial Communication* (Muncie, IN: T.I.S., 2001), 30. .
2. Roger Fisher and Scott Brown, *Getting Together: Building a Relationship That Gets to Yes* (Boston: Houghton-Mifflin, 1988).
3. Zhao, 31.

19

The Christian Manager as Ethical Global Citizen

"The earth is the Lord's, and everything in it,
the world, and all who live in it."

(Psalm 24:1)

Chapter Challenges

A careful examination of Chapter 19 should enable the reader to:

- Recognize the ethical environmental issues facing managers.
- Understand three global ethical responsibilities facing today's managers.

Case Study

The Ken Eastland Farm

Ken Eastland looked carefully down the half-mile lane leading to his barnyard. Although few strangers came around this part of the farm, Ken had heard rumors in town that Environmental Protection Agency (EPA) representatives were working in the area again. There was a need to be especially careful in the mixing of herbicides.

The EPA had spent a great deal of time in Ken's county since the Rock Creek fish kill a few years ago. Unidentified chemicals in the creek had killed fish for nearly twenty-five miles downstream. That summer Ken and every other farmer in the area had been suspect in the investigation. Just to be safe, everyone seemed to be overreacting—diluting herbicides and right-of-way sprays to well below the label's recommended proportions. As a result, weeds threatened to take over the county! Now, with the heat off for the most part, Ken had quietly returned to his more normal practice of increasing the recommended strength.

Of course, Ken cared about the environment. In fact, he had several large fields near the river. For years, he had always sprayed according to label instructions. No regulator had to tell Ken the impact of runoff in those locations. The effects were obvious. However, Ken found certain other regulations for the use of chemicals ridiculous. "It's hard enough to make a living on a small farm," Ken complained to a friend recently, "without Uncle Sam protecting the weeds on the farms of good citizens."

"Good morning!"

Ken turned with a start to face a tall, well-dressed stranger. "What are you doing sneaking around?" Ken gruffly demanded.

"Sorry to startle you," the stranger apologized. "I am Jerry Kirkwood from Worldwide Employment Services."

"Sounds like some government agency," Ken responded suspiciously.

"Hardly," Jerry smiled. "We are a private employment agency that matches farmers such as you with the plentiful supply of inexpensive farm labor around the world."

An Interesting Proposition

Ken's anxiety turned to curiosity. He moved Jerry away from his mixing operation by offering his hand as he stepped outside the barn. "What's on your mind?" he asked Jerry.

"I thought you might be needing some help," Jerry answered.

"You're looking for a job?" Ken asked with surprise. "We don't get too many applicants here, and I don't recall ever seeing a farmhand applicant in a shirt and tie."

"No! It's not me," Jerry said, smiling warmly. "My firm represents men from Honduras who are new in this country and looking for a better life."

"Sorry," Ken said. "I've got enough on my mind without having to watch for border agents because I've hired illegal immigrants."

"I assure you, all of our people have appropriate entrance papers and work permits," Jerry continued. "In fact, many will be studying toward United States citizenship very soon."

"I don't get it," Ken confessed. "What's the catch?"

"No catch," Jerry responded. "Honduras is one of the poorest countries in this hemisphere. Many of its people do whatever is necessary to come to our land of opportunity. My company loans them transportation money and locates farm jobs where they can earn $6 per hour. An hour here is two days' pay in Honduras for most workers. And, they're familiar with working from sunup until sundown."

"The hours sound right for this farm," Ken quipped.

"This and every family farm in America," Jerry continued. "The Honduran work ethic matches the need of America's family farms. That is the basis of our work at Worldwide Employment Services."

"A couple of questions come to my mind," Ken said.

"Good," Jerry responded. "Worldwide Employment Services has absolutely nothing to hide. We're happy to answer your questions."

"Well, first off, what's in it for you? Is this Worldwide-whatever a charity? How do you make a living?"

"Our income is derived from two sources," Jerry explained. "Like any other employment agency, we collect a small finder's fee from the employing farmer. In most cases the fee is only $300, and we don't expect that for six weeks. That gives you plenty of time to make sure your help works out before you pay us. Then, we also ask you to withhold 10 percent from the employee's weekly check. That's how the farmhand repays our travel and opportunity loans."

"Ten percent off the $6 leaves a fella only $5.40 per hour to live on," Ken calculated. "There's no way he could make it."

"Of course he can," Jerry argued. "You or I couldn't, but that's more money than these folks have ever seen. They usually live ten or twelve to a house and eat beans and rice. It's just like home for them, except here they have money for the beans."

"Sounds almost like slave labor," Ken observed.

"Not at all," Jerry said. "No one has to sign up, and no one has to stay. Any time they want to repay their loans and move on, they are free to do as they please. They just recognize a great opportunity. I hope you will too."

"Check with me in a few days," Ken said. "With 1,200 acres of corn and beans and a few head of cattle, God knows I could use the help. But right now, I have chemicals to mix."

On Background

Issues of Environment and People from Other Countries

The twenty-first century has seen rapid increases in transportation and communication technology. Business once focused on the repeat customers of a single small town. Today, the marketplace has expanded to planetary dimensions. Increasing ethical tensions arise along with marvelous new opportunities. For example, as a relatively small-scale farmer and businessman, Ken currently faces two ethical questions with worldwide dimensions.

The first tension involves environmental issues. On one hand, increasingly tight governmental regulations designed to preserve the environment have threatened business and industry. National attention was drawn to the Northwest a few years ago. Preserving the habitat of an endangered species, the spotted owl, threatened logging concerns and the families that depended on logging for their livelihood.

On the other hand, when business has been allowed to police itself, all too often the environment has suffered. Oil spills, hazardous material dumping, and unscrubbed air emissions are examples of environmental abuse.

The Christian and the Environment

A Christian in business recognizes that human beings are the pinnacle of God's creation. In Genesis 2:28, God gave humans, represented by Adam and Eve, rule and dominion over all creation. Recognizing God's call to rule as good stewards, Christians especially should recognize an ethical responsibility to conserve God's creation. This requires Christian businesses to adopt in-house procedures and purchasing practices that reduce the strain on nature's resources. Not only is this being a good steward of God's resources, but in many cases such practices will increase the company's bottom line by reducing waste.

Christians also acknowledge that dominion implies rule and lordship. This means that human beings do not have to be subject to the rest of the creation. Many would say that the spotted owl controversy in the forests of the Northwest is an example of this concept being out of balance. Environmentalists were able to shut down much of the timber industry, causing economic hardship to the region and especially to the thousands of persons who lost their jobs and homes. The well being of a bird was given precedence over that of humans. However, this concept does not relieve man of the responsibility to examine both short- and long-term effects of his interaction with nature and natural resources—and to make decisions that reflect responsible use of God-given power.

The Christian and People from Other Countries

The second global ethical issue facing Ken concerns the responsibility of American business managers to people from other countries. Such issues usually fall into one of three categories:

1. Ethical dealings with foreigners as customers
2. Ethical dealings with foreigners as employees
3. Ethical dealings with foreigners as suppliers of non-human resources

As with environmental concerns, ethical managers can arrive at vastly different conclusions about these issues. An examination of the expiration dates on domestically processed foods such as peanut butter and canned fruits in supermarkets in many third world countries, will often reveal recent shipments of goods that are six months or more beyond expiration date. Wholesale dealers would probably argue that the USDA set unnecessarily stringent standards and that these food products are safe for human consumption for many months or even years to come. They would say that there is no health risk and therefore their practices do not violate ethical principles. Others may argue that because of the United States companies' superior economic strength, they are using less powerful nations' homes as a dumping ground for foods that the United States government declares not safe for its own peoples' consumption. They may say, "You are violating our dignity as God's creation for selfish economic gain."

The practices of using foreign employees here in the United States at a time when so many jobs ·are being outsourced to second and third world nations raises ethical questions in the minds of many Americans. Is it ethical to further strain the fragile economic status of our unskilled labor force by encouraging foreign unskilled labor to come to our country? Is the motive of finding a cheaper labor pool to expand the profit margins of already prosperous companies an ethical one? Is it ethical to continue the existence of poverty and slums by seeking out a workforce that is willing to live in misery with the hope of helping their loved ones back home by sending small amounts of money from their low paying jobs here in the United States? On the other hand, is it ethical to deprive our companies of a workforce that is willing to do jobs that many United States citizens are not willing to do? Is it ethical to deprive hard-working foreigners of the opportunity to better their standards of living or that of their families? Is it ethical and/or against the interests of the United States to deprive it of people who often serve as the source of new creative energies that keep our country from becoming stagnant and thus adversely affecting all Americans in the long run? These are just a few of the thorny issues that surround the use of cheap foreign labor here in the United States and only tangentially touches the use of cheap labor forces in other nations.

One of the hottest issues in third world countries is what those countries often view as exploitation of their natural resources by more economically superior and, generally, more militarily powerful countries. These third world countries question the ethicalness of the lion's share of the benefits going to the foreign companies or citizens of the receiving countries instead of those of the country that owns the natural resources.

Adding fuel to the fire, the economically powerful country often decides to build factories in the third world country to process the raw materials before exporting them. This is often done to reduce the cost of shipping to the developed country. The ethical questions then revolve around the wages paid and the emissions standards put into practice. Many third world citizens believe that the United States companies are really not interested in helping the local economy or people, but that they wish to use the third world country as a dumping ground for pollutants that would not be permitted in the United States. They question whether these companies are being godly stewards of nature and whether they are respecting the dignity of their fellow human beings. Again we can see that providing the proper balance between fiduciary responsibilities—to stockholders, local employees, and consumers and responsibility to God's creation including citizens of other countries—is a difficult process that does not happen without earnest effort. In seeking ethical responses, Christian managers should consider Cain's question to God, recorded in Genesis 4:9, "Am I my brother's keeper?" The answer throughout Scripture is a resounding, "Yes."

Finding A Way Through the Maze

Christian managers honestly strive to find their way through the maze of conflicting expectations, barriers, and economic performance pressures that are part of the modern business environment. The authors recommend the general principles enumerated in the list below as beginning guidelines for making ethical decisions regarding people from other countries. It is also recommended that ethical concepts from classical philosophy (see chapter two) as well as the manager's own personal statement of ethics (see chapter four) be employed in this decision making.

1. At minimum, decisions should follow the laws of the host country. This does not exclude taking the higher road of biblical principles if the local laws violate God's Word or are a lower standard.
2. Decisions should promote the general welfare of all people involved.
3. Decisions should be designed to treat each human being as the business person would want to be treated.

Toward an Ethical Christian Worldview

Psalm 24:1

The earth is the Lord's, and everything in it, the world, and all who live in it (Psalm 24:1).

The Bible declares in this verse and elsewhere that the planet and everything on it belong to God. Human beings have been given the unique role among created beings to oversee God's creation.

In the Genesis account, man is the capstone of the creation event. All other beings are created first, as if in preparation for God's ultimate creative stroke. Further, human beings are the only products of creation made in the image of God (1:27). God instills the importance of this fact in the following verses:

God blessed them and said to them, "Be fruitful and increase in number; fill the earth and subdue it. Rule over the fish of the sea and the birds of the air and over every living creature that moves on the ground." Then God said, "I give you every seed-bearing plant on the face of the whole

earth and every tree that has fruit with seed in it. They will be yours for
food. And to all the beasts of the earth and all the birds of the air and all
the creatures that move on the ground–everything that has the breath of
life in it–I give every green plant for food" (Genesis 1:28-30).

In verse 28, the words "subdue" and "rule" represent a delegated authority
by God for man to tend to the care of the planet. Apparently, this precludes the
abuse of God's creation because God described the process as "very good" later
in the narrative.

Ken Eastland does have an ethical responsibility and a moral right to
oversee his farmland. He must determine whether the application of chemicals
in violation of label directions constitutes an abuse of that authority.

Ethical Dilemma

How does a manager
exhibit global citizenship?

Similarly, in Genesis 4, God holds Cain
responsible for the well being of his
brother, Abel. The implied answer to Cain's
question, "Am I my brother's keeper?" is a
resounding "Yes." Ken Eastland also must
decide whether people in Honduras are best
served by participation in, or rejection of, the Worldwide Employment Services
program.

Ask the Pro

Shane Davis farms approximately 2,200 acres, which has been his
livelihood for forty-five years. His son now helps him run the farm. They grow
corn and soy beans, along with the occasional specialty crop.

Davis and his wife attend a small town church where he has held a variety
of positions over the last twenty-six years. He currently serves as chair of the
administrative council of the church.

The authors ask Davis to evaluate the Ken Eastland case in light of his
farming experience. Our conversation follows:

Q: How realistic is the dilemma in which Ken Eastland finds himself?

Davis: No farmers I know would adjust spray rates. Improperly used, chemicals can contaminate the soil. We have to live here a long time. We take better care of the land than that. Even if a farmer increased a rate, it would cost more money for little or no increase in effectiveness.

Q: So, there is a business reason as well as an ethical one not to increase chemical application rates?

Davis: Oh, yes!

Q: What about the question of hiring farm help?

Davis: I think something here isn't right. It isn't clear that it is illegal, but it doesn't sound right to me. A man working for a subsistence or lower rate of pay won't last long. I would stay away from that situation.

Q: Isn't Ken likely to need the help?

Davis: Yes, but if it were me, I would hire someone nearby who needs a job. I'd look for someone who knows the machinery and how to run it. Without speaking Spanish, I couldn't even instruct a Honduran employee properly.

Q: So the Ken Eastland situation seems an easy decision to you?

Davis: Good farmers simply don't "cut corners." It doesn't pay.

Q: What are some ethical problems with which farmers do struggle?

Davis: Spraying on a windy day is a big issue. Label directions warn that my soy bean spray could kill a neighbor's corn if it drifts. That becomes a real issue when a farmer has a large area to spray in a short time—especially if wind speed is borderline, say ten or twelve miles per hour. One must get the work done, but also be a good neighbor at the same time.

Q: So, how do you solve the problem?

Davis: Even the best solutions don't always work. A few years ago, I sprayed most of a field on a borderline day, but I left the rows nearest my neighbor for a calmer day. I still don't know how, but the spray ruined twelve to twenty-four rows of his corn on that calm day. Even when you try to do the right thing, there are things that arise which one must make right.

You Be the Consultant

Answer the following questions as you study Ken Eastland's situation:

1. Preservationists believe that the environment should be left as nearly as possible in an unaltered pre-human state. Conservationists believe that humans should manage the environment for the good of all species, using such tactics as controlled hunts and the burning of certain vegetation. Which position most closely matches your ethic? Which position parallels Genesis 2:28? Explain why.

2. What advice would you give Ken Eastland about the use of herbicides on his farm? Why? How might the advice of one who follows cultural relativism differ? Why?

3. What answer do you believe Ken should give Jerry Kirkwood about hiring a Honduran immigrant? What are the ethical issues to consider in this decision? How does your statement of ethics deal with those issues? How might one who holds to Kantian ethics respond? Why? If you held to utilitarian ethics, what might your response be? Why?

4. Describe an ethical process for filling the need in the United States for low-skilled labor. Defend your position with an eye to your personal statement of ethics. How would a Kantian ethicist view your response? Defend your answer. How would a utilitarian view your response? Why do you think so?

Notes

20

The Christian Manager as Ethical Human Resource Administrator

"Everyone must submit himself to the governing authorities,
for there is no authority except that which God has established."

(Romans 13:1a)

Chapter Challenges

A careful examination of Chapter 20 should enable the reader to:

- Identify key elements of the Americans with Disabilities Act.
- Identify key elements of the Family Medical Leave Act.
- Recognize three possible courses of action in response to laws regarding the ethical treatment of employees.

Franks and Barnes Engineering Consultants

"Thank God, it's Friday," Ron Franks said as he headed for the parking lot of Franks and Barnes Engineering Consultants.

"With one less draftsman, there would be a lot more rough weeks," responded his partner, Jeff Barnes.

"That is definitely true, but we might save our company by letting him go," Ron said.

"It appears we have no real choice," Jeff agreed. "It is sad it has to happen. Maybe another idea will develop over the weekend. See you Monday, partner."

"See you Monday," Ron responded. "Have a great weekend."

Ron Franks and Jeff Barnes began their engineering consulting business more than thirty years ago in the basement of Ron's first home. The two had met at one of the finest engineering schools in the Midwest, and had enjoyed college life together as fraternity brothers. The business had steadily grown over the years, gaining a reputation for reasonable fees and exceptional service. Franks and Barnes now employed two graduate engineers in addition to Ron and Jeff, three clerk-assistants, and eight draftsmen.

Several years ago, during a time of unprecedented growth, the business moved into a large Victorian-style house just a block from downtown. The historic three-story brick structure provided ample room for the business and left a very positive impression on visitors and passersby.

Neither Ron nor Jeff had any training or interest in issues related to human resource management. In fact, they viewed the business aspects of their operation, in general, as just a necessary evil—something they had to put up with if they wanted to practice engineering. They saw themselves as engineers, first and foremost. Management and business matters were relegated to a distant second place.

"We're just engineering geeks," Ron had joked to Rhonda Sutton when he contracted with her firm to manage such matters as payroll, employee benefits, and accounting.

"And we love handling business for you geeks," Rhonda assured him with a smile.

The Implications of Accommodation

There was no joking about the knot Ron felt in his stomach when he looked out the window of his office on Thursday afternoon. He had been keeping an eye out for Jannette Lynn, with whom he had scheduled an interview. Franks and Barnes had just signed a lucrative contract to design a shopping center in Ohio. The additional business made it possible to hire another draftsman. Jannette had responded to the Franks and Barnes' advertisement in a national trade journal. Her résumé demonstrated impeccable credentials. She had an impressive combination of experience and education, and offered several excellent references. Ron had enjoyed a pleasant conversation with the candidate on the phone, but she had not mentioned a wheelchair. But there she sat in a wheelchair on the sidewalk in front of the Franks and Barnes building, looking at the menacing fifteen steps leading to the front door.

Fortunately, Ron recovered quickly and bounded down the steps to greet Jannette. He suggested that they meet together over coffee at a restaurant less than a block away. He made it appear that he always conducted interviews in that handicap-accessible facility.

Throughout their conversation, Ron contemplated what Jannette's presence might mean to Franks and Barnes. In addition to the front steps to the main entrance, he visualized the computer-assisted drafting area located on the third floor. The cost of making the building accessible could reach nearly a quarter of a million dollars. In addition, the historic charm of the old structure could be lost in the process. "Somehow," he thought, "I have to find a way to get rid of this potential employee."

A quick call to Rhonda Sutton after the interview confirmed his suspicions. "Of course, you fall under the Americans with Disabilities Act (ADA)," she said. "The law clearly states that the act applies to employers with fifteen or more employees. Your firm currently is at fifteen, so you meet ADA requirements—which means you need to accommodate the needs of this woman if you hire her."

The next morning Ron and Jeff outlined a plan. It would mean working more hours personally than either of them desired. In addition, it could cost the company in overtime to draftsmen. While they had never been much for long-term business plans, the current situation made it clear that the company would seek no new business in the foreseeable future. Although this troubled them, they were more worried about the cost of the alternative.

"How do we explain this to Billy?" Jeff asked, referring to Billy Asbury, one of their draftsmen. Billy had been with Franks and Barnes for three years. He did fine work and had earned outstanding job reviews.

Ron responded, "I'll say something like this: 'Billy, I'm sorry, but you were the most recent draftsman hired and business is such that we have no choice but to let someone go.'"

On Background

Americans with Disabilities and Family Medical Leave Acts

Ron and Jeff are apparently moving toward a decision with serious ethical as well as business ramifications. Rhonda and any others who may advise them will need to have some background on the *Americans with Disabilities Act* (ADA).

> *Americans With Disabilities Act:* 1990 federal law applying to businesses with more than fifteen employees and requiring accommodation for employees with physical or mental impairments.

As Rhonda suggested, ADA applies to employers with fifteen or more employees. Passed in 1990, the act is administered and enforced by the Equal Employment Opportunities Commission. According to ADA, employment discrimination is prohibited against individuals with disabilities who are able to perform the duties that every other employee must do. That prohibition against discrimination holds even if the employer must change the work environment, redesign the job, or alter work schedules.[1]

The act covers "both physical and mental impairments affecting one or more life activities."[2] However, no accommodation is required for a person who does not meet minimal stated job qualifications. For example, had Jannette Lynn applied for an engineer's job, no accommodation would have been required of Franks and Barnes. Since she meets and exceeds stated qualifications for the draftsman position, however, accommodation would certainly be required.

A special provision does exist which allows an employer to plead undue hardship.[3] In reality, however, the Equal Employment Opportunities Commission (EEOC) has demonstrated reluctance to allow the successful use of that provision. Further, undue expense has specifically been eliminated as a reason for hardship.

Rather than search for exceptions, however, ethical managers recognize their responsibility to assist those with physical or mental hardships. Many find that the act does not severely limit their businesses. Even before the act was made law, they voluntarily behaved in accordance with its provisions, which merely describe what they had long held to be a part of their social and

Christian responsibilities. Their view of the merits of treating people as they wished to be treated and belief in biblical and social norms for treating humans with dignity had been guiding principles.

It is true that accommodation and compliance with ADA guildelines may cost an enormous amount of financial resources. Such costs can seriously erode the bottom line of any business. Some managers question this use of profits with potential for return to stockholders or other owners. They raise legitimate questions about whether it is ethical to hire a person who could cost the company a great deal in accommodation, rather than employ an equally qualified non-disabled alternate, thus freeing funds for updating equipment or research and development activities that would benefit all present and future employees.

Another federal mandate that divides employers who seek to perform ethically is the *Family and Medical Leave Act* (FMLA) of the early 1990s. That Act provides up to twelve weeks of leave to eligible employees for the birth or adoption of a child, the care of a sick family member including a spouse, child, or parent or the care required for one's own health concerns.

> *Family and Medical Leave Act:* Federal law applying to most businesses with fifty or more employees and requiring those businesses to allow up to twelve weeks of unpaid leave for family emergencies.

Many employees and some managers see the fact that the act provides only for unpaid leave as a serious limitation. They would prefer to see provisions for compensation during an employee's time off. Others applaud the fact that the act guarantees employees the same or an equivalent position and conditions upon their return. Some businesses are put under severe strain when a highly skilled worker takes twelve weeks off at a critical time in the company's operations or times of employee shortage to care for an eligible relative. The Family and Medical Leave Act applies to firms with fifty or more employees within seventy-five-miles. While legally exempt, smaller companies may see an ethical responsibility and a benefit in voluntary compliance. This may be especially true in regions with a shortage of qualified workers or in close-knit organizations where employees and management have both personal and professional ties.

When society enacts ethical treatment of employees through laws such as the Americans with Disabilities Act and the Family and Medical Leave Act, companies can choose one of three major courses of action:

1. ***Minimum compliance with the letter of the law.*** Often the rationale is stated that "My decision is ethical because it complies with the related law." If that is always true, then the "separate but equal" clause as expressed in the Supreme Court decision *Plessy v. Ferguson* (1896) that established segregated seating on public buses and trains as well as separate restrooms in department stores led to ethical treatment of African American citizens. La Rue Hosmer's assertion that "The law is a guide to managerial decisions and actions, but it is not enough" certainly nullifies the use of the law as the sole definer of ethical behavior. Ethical managers should also consider Dr. Hosmer's assertion that the absence of a law protecting the rights and dignity of employees is not an excuse for lack of ethical action on the part of management.[4]

2. ***Compliance beyond what the law requires.*** The ethical manager chooses this option and goes beyond a legal compliance approach and employs a values-based approach that reflects biblical and philosophical ethical principles.

3. ***Noncompliance with the law.*** It is sad to say, but some managers select the noncompliance course of action. Refusing to consider the ethical and legal implications of these acts, they choose instead to find ways to skirt the intent of the Americans with Disabilities Act and the Family and Medical Leave Act even though they carry harsh penalties for noncompliance.

Toward an Ethical Christian Worldview

Romans 13:1-3

Everyone must submit himself to the governing authorities, for there is no authority except that which God has established. The authorities that exist have been established by God. Consequently, he who rebels against the authority is rebelling against what God has instituted, and those who do so will bring judgment on themselves. For rulers hold no terror for those who do right, but for those who do wrong. Do you want to be free from fear of the one in authority? Then do what is right and he will commend you (Romans 13:1-3).

Believers have a responsibility to the government. Matthew 22:15-22 records an occasion when Jesus was asked by His enemies, "Is it right to pay tribute to Caesar, or not?" (v. 17b)

He responded by borrowing a coin to use as an object lesson and asking them whose image appeared on the coin. "Caesar's," came the reply.

"Then," Jesus continued, "give to Caesar what is Caesar's, and to God what is God's" (vv. 21-22).

In this exchange, Jesus left no room for doubt—His followers were to obey the government. Paul, however, goes beyond simple obedience in his exhortation to a young disciple named Timothy:

I urge, then, first of all, that requests, prayers, intercession and thanksgiving be made to everyone–for kings and all those in authority, that we may live peaceful and quiet lives in all godliness and holiness. This is good, and pleases God our Savior . . . (1 Timothy 2:1-3).

Of course, Ron Franks and Jeff Barnes maintain that they are following the strict interpretation of the law. They might further argue that excessive government interference threatens the success of their business. What you

Can a manager succeed as an ethical human resource manager?

must determine is whether Ron and Jeff have held to the spirit of Romans 13 or merely obeyed the letter of the law. Still further, you must ask, "Have they treated Jannette Lynn in an ethical manner, as well as a legal one?"

Ask the Pro

Karen Brown has spent the last five years as a loan officer in a credit union. Previously, she worked in consumer credit and finance positions for various financial institutions for twenty-six years.

Karen and her husband attend a local church, where she sings in the choir and teaches Sunday school to a preschool class.

She agreed to assist the authors with a discussion of business ethics in general, and the Franks and Barnes case in particular. The results of that conversation follow:

Q: Before we look at the Franks and Barnes case, tell us about your particular business. What are the ethical concerns associated with being a loan officer?

Brown: One of my biggest concerns involves people who are not ethical themselves, and then don't seem to understand when I can't help them. For example, I recently had a potential client who was self-employed and had not reported all of his income over the last several years. He became very angry when we were forced to make a loan decision on what he reported to the federal government, rather than what he tells us now is his true income picture. He had behaved unethically and couldn't understand that there were consequences.

Q: That situation involves someone else's unethical behavior. Are there ever pressures on you to do the wrong thing?

Brown: On the one hand, loaning people money is helping them achieve a dream or solve a problem. On the other hand, sometimes making a loan could get people into trouble. I don't want to loan to people when it is not in their best interest to borrow.

Q: How do you deal with that situation? Doesn't your employer insist that you make as many loans as possible?

Brown: Fortunately, my employer doesn't pressure me to lend. In fact, we have very conservative lending policies. In addition, I am often in a position to do financial counseling with a prospective borrower by encouraging people to develop a budget or wait a while for a new car or a bigger house.

Q: It sounds as if you have a very good relationship with your employer. Would you have the same attitude working at Franks and Barnes? How would you evaluate this case?

Brown: I think it is a sad situation when an employer is simply not willing to work with a disabled person and make that person an employee. What is even more sad is their decision to eliminate a very good draftsman from the staff just so they don't have to accommodate a potential employee who is disabled. There is a moral issue here but beyond that, they will lose business by being understaffed. Ironically, they are driven by money and are making decisions that in the long term will be very costly.

Q: Are you saying that ethical decisions are good business?

Brown: I'm saying that if you make solid ethical decisions, especially on behalf of your staff, they will in turn be profitable decisions for your company and for you as the employer.

Q: But, what alternatives do these managers have?

Brown: They could begin by viewing the expenditures necessary to accommodate this potential employee as investment rather than expense.

Q: Accomodation and compliance with ADA guidelines involves a lot of money. How far should they go? Do you see alternatives?

Brown: Of course, there are always alternatives. She might work from home. They might lease another office that is accessible for part of the staff. I just think they looked only at the expense and ignored both the potential income from this qualified draftsman's work and the company's future growth. The ethical action is find a way to accommodate her since she is qualified for the job.

You Be the Consultant

Answer the following questions as you analyze the situation at Franks and Barnes:

1. Is reducing their firm size to fourteen a good business decision for Franks and Barnes? Why or why not? Is it legal? Is it ethical according to your personal statement of ethics? How would one who has adopted Kantian ethics respond? Would a utilitarian react differently? How?

2. Propose an alternate plan that may work for Franks and Barnes. Defend it using your statement of ethics. Then respond to your plan on the basis of Kantian ethics, utilitarianism, and ethical egoism.

3. Suppose you were advising Jannette Lynn, Billy Asbury, and Rhonda Sutton in this matter. What might you suggest to each of them?

4. Admittedly, Franks and Barnes had "never been much for long-term business plans." In what way has that attitude led to the current crisis? Are there ethical implications of failing to plan? Defend your answer with principles from chapters 3 and 6.

5. Should a company like Franks and Barnes conform to the standards of the Family and Medical Leave Act, even if the company falls far short of the minimum fifty employees? Why or why not? Why do you believe such minimums are placed in the federal law? Are those reasons ethical? According to which ethical position?

6. How would a manager following Kant's Categorical Imperatives view the Franks and Barnes plan? How would the answer change for one who adopted ethical egoism or cultural relativism?

Endnotes

1. J. Freedley Hunsicker Jr., "Ready or Not: The ADA," *Personnel Journal*, August 1990, 80-86.
2. Jeff Hornsby, *Human Resource Development* (Muncie, IN: T.I.S., 2001), 109.
3. John M. Ivancevich, *Human Resource Management: Foundations of Personnel*, 5th ed. (Homewood, IL: Irwin, 1992), 101.
4. LaRue T. Hosmer, *The Ethics of Management,* 3rd ed. (Chicago: Irwin, 1996), 75.

Special Assignment

Personal Ethics Statement Update

Write a final draft of your personal ethics statement. Be certain that the statement covers all of the situations presented in the case studies of this book.

Statement of Personal Ethics

Name _____   Date _____

Conclusion

The journey toward becoming an increasingly ethical manager is intertwined with becoming an increasingly self-reflecting searcher for ethical and spiritual truth. To become an ethical manager, family member, or citizen, one must be a purpose-driven individual. There must be a desire to grow ethically, and that desire must have a proactive element that looks beyond the requirements of society. It is more than compliance to society's laws and to God's laws. Compliance is action that is often motivated by fear, or at best a justification for the manager's actions. Growth in ethics is not fear driven. It is the transforming of the reasons for the laws into the fabric of a belief system, a motivational system, and implemented actions. It is the inculcation of the underlying principles regarding the value of people, the upholding of the biblical absolutes, and the justice, love, righteousness, and other character traits of God into your being.

Knowledge of management theory and practice is not a guarantee of ethical management and decision making though it can be a contributor to the level of ethicalness found within a company. Insufficient knowledge and inadequate skill development in the managerial functions can set up situations where the various levels of management within a company may inadvertently make unethical decisions or set up systems, procedures which cause lower level managers and employees to think and/or they have no choice but to act against their ethical beliefs. A poor decision based on inadequate management knowledge can look harmless today but may force future managers in difficult situations where they are put under extreme pressure to ignore their ethical beliefs.

Ethical decision making requires a high level of personal discipline. The manager must be vigilant to exercise sound management principles and practices so as to minimize the opportunities for ethical dilemmas to occur. The manager must also be aware of how the company's actions and policies are affecting employees, vendors, customers, and other stakeholders. This requires always keeping one eye on the bottom line and the other on both the place involved in the business arena and the needs of society. These sound like simple things to do, but under the pressure of production schedules, investor expectations, and threats from global competitors, it requires purposeful discipline on the part of conscientious managers.

Having a statement of personal ethics to serve as a framework to guide ethical decision making is very important. A manager, father, wife, or whomever, should not have to stop and analyze his or her personal beliefs each time a decision needs to be made. However, since the ethical decision maker is a maturing individual, it is valuable to review personal beliefs periodically to see how they have matured and to adjust one's statement of personal ethics. Reflection is also very important to help see the degree of alignment between stated beliefs and actual practices in the crucibles of the business and personal worlds. Bible study, prayer, and reflection on beliefs and practices are key tools in maturing as an ethical decision maker.

There are two "Ps" that are very important in growth as an ethical manager. The first is practice. Knowledge of God's character and principles, skills in management and decision making, and ethical beliefs from the world of philosophy are of little value if they are not practiced. It is through practice that managers develop their proficiency in making ethical decisions and solving problems in ways that glorify God.

Reflective practice is the necessary ingredient for personal growth. Reflection allows for the testing of the manager's knowledge and skill levels and an analysis of ethical decision making and areas requiring improvement. This habit of reflecting on one's performance eliminates the repeated practice of ineffective, unethical, and inappropriate knowledge and skills in the workplace, home, and community.

The second "P" is process. It is very helpful to have an established decision making process that is followed faithfully in major decisions. By having such a process as a tool in managerial thinking, managers will find that it becomes a subconscious part of their decision making in the routine areas as well. The authors recommend the following guiding questions when facing a decision involving the company's economic vitality and the company's responsibility to the investors, employees, customers, vendors, community, and the environment.

1. Who are the people (stakeholders) that will be affected by the decision? They should be identified as those persons will benefit and those who will be hurt by the decision.

2. What are the company's and the affected stakeholders' economic needs or desires that are being affected by the decision? (Who stands to gain and who stands to lose economically by my decision?)

3. Is the situation causing the need for a decision violating a company policy or the law? Will my proposed decision violate company policy or the law?

4. Will my proposed decision violate my statement of personal beliefs—including biblical and philosophical principles?

5. When I consider stakeholders, economic issues, the law and my statement of personal beliefs, what appear to be the two or three best courses of action for me to take?

6. Of the courses of action listed above, which one will do the most good and the least harm to the company and the stakeholders while conforming to God's character and principles?

Continuous practice of this or a similar decision making process will provide more consistency in ethicalness for decision makers.

Notes

Glossary of Key Terms

Americans with Disabilities Act (ADA): 1990 federal law applying to businesses with more than fifteen employees and requiring accommodation for employees with physical or mental impairments.

business plan: Detailed written statement of a business that is comprised of a strategic plan and an operational plan.

categorical imperative: Two standards that must be satisfied according to Kantian ethics. The first is act only on a maxim that you would be willing to become universal law. The second is to treat others as an end not a means.

Christian worldview: Those principles, attitudes and values that impact every area of life and grow out of a conviction that Jesus Christ is Lord.

cognitive dissonance: Discordant act of mentally holding two opposing views simultaneously.

core values: Principles around which a business is established and maintained.

communication: Interaction between two or more individuals.

compensatory justice: Type of long term justice that emerges from compensation for injustices of the past.

conflict stage: Second stage of group or team development where team members often grow tired of one another.

content: Aspect of communication focusing strictly on the words that are spoken as opposed to the contextual relationship in which those words are spoken.

contractual justice: Justice that occurs when an exchange of promises creates a special relationship called a contract.

control: Managerial function that includes performance appraisal, production statistics, and budgetary systems.

cultural relativism: Ethical system maintaining that right and wrong differs according to events and circumstances.

disciplinary action: Process of dealing with employees who are ineffective, demonstrate personal problems, commit crimes or violate company policy.

distributive justice: Type of justice that emerges from questions regarding the distribution of wealth.

esteem needs: Fourth level of needs according to Maslow's hierarchy involving the need for recognition.

ethical egoism: Ethical system where the ethical decision is determined by the self-interest of the decision maker.

ethics: Science of moral values and responsibilities.

ethnocentrism: Belief that one's culture is superior to all others.

equality: Along with justice and integrity a characteristic of the holiness of God.

Family and Medical Leave Act (FMLA): Federal law applying to most businesses with fifty or more employees and requiring those businesses to allow up to twelve weeks of unpaid leave for family emergencies.

formation stage: First stage of group or team development where members develop rules for interaction and grow accustomed to one another.

fundamentalist view: View of scripture maintaining that biblical teaching is normative for today's culture except where the scripture specifically suggests otherwise.

hedonism: Worldview focusing on maximizing personal pleasure and minimizing personal pain.

holiness: Attribute of God that issues in equality, integrity and justice.

integration stage: Third stage of group or team development where members develop standards for effective operation.

integrity: Along with equality and justice a characteristic of the holiness of God.

interpersonal communication: Interaction between just two individuals.

interpretive view: View of scripture maintaining that the reader must determine the original intent of a passage and then apply that intent to today's moral choices.

issue of fact: Decisions that consider the truth or falsity of an assertion.

issue of policy: Decisions that consider what course of action should or should not be taken.

issue of value: Decisions that consider the relative worth or rightness of an issue.

justice: Along with equality and integrity a characteristic of the holiness of God.

Kantian ethics: Ethical system developed by Immanuel Kant and based upon categorical imperatives.

liberal view: View of scripture maintaining that a biblical teaching is applicable to today's moral choices when it is clearly the word of God and not the writer's viewpoint.

love needs: Third level needs according to Maslow's hierarchy including the need for interaction, acceptance and membership in groups.

manipulation: Extreme form of motivation that is sometimes seen as coercion.

mission statement: Succinct statement of the fundamental purpose of the company which becomes the guiding light for every organizational decision.

motivation: Drive that compels a person to action.

natural law: Truths that transcend culture and thus are the same for all human beings.

negative harm principle: Specialized application of utilitarianism where stakeholders health and safety is impacted.

operational goals: Specific goals which break an organization's plan into short term action statements. The operational goals combine to form an operational plan.

operational plan: Comprised of short term and specific goals of an organization designed to meet the strategic plan over time.

organizational chart: Visual representation of an organization's structure.

organizational communication: Formal and informal rules within an organization that shapes the way interaction occurs.

organizational level: Those needs of the organization that drive decision making.

performance appraisal: Systematic review of an employee's job-related strengths and weaknesses.

performance stage: Fourth and final stage of group or team development where team members establish their own work goals and maximize productivity.

personal level: Lowest variable that drives the need for ethical decisions.

physiological needs: Lowest level needs according to Maslow's hierarchy including the need for air and water.

positive discipline: Process of employee discipline focusing on future behavior rather than past performance by offering positive reinforcements for appropriate behaviors.

progressive discipline: Process of administering employee discipline that increases in severity with each subsequent infraction.

protected classes: Groups protected by the civil rights act of 1968 including race, color, national origin, religion, gender, familial status and handicap.

recruiting: Process that is the first step in staffing wherein people are encouraged to apply for an open or potentially open position.

relationship: Aspect of communication focusing on the nature of the interaction instead of the content of the words.

safety needs: Second level needs according to Maslow's hierarchy.

selection: The process of screening potential employees who have been recruited. The second step in staffing.

self actualization: Fifth and highest level of needs according to Maslow's hierarchy involving the need to maximize one's personal potential.

servant leadership: Assumes that the role of a leader is to facilitate the work of followers who are generally self motivated. The servant leader generally engages in participatory management.

situation ethics: Ethic developed by Joseph Fletcher stating that the ethical decision will vary from situation to situation.

societal level: Needs that drive decision making stemming from the society at large.

Socratic model: Process demonstrated by Socrates consisting of raising questions in such a manner as to elicit the most logical conclusion.

staffing: Basic managerial function usually broken down into recruiting, selecting and training of employees.

stakeholders: Individuals or groups who have a stake in a particular decision.

strategic plan: Process of identifying major goals, policies and strategies for an organization.

synergy: Effect is greater than the sum of the parts. 1+1>2

theory X: View of employees in the McGregor model of management. In theory X employees are viewed as lazy and incapable. They must be closely supervised.

theory Y: View of employees in the McGregor model of management. In theory Y employees are viewed as capable of self management and self motivation.

thinking speed: Rate at which a listener can process verbal words. Usually three times faster than the words are spoken.

three E equation: Efficiency + Effectiveness + Ethics = Profits + Long term stability

training: The process of orienting employees to their job and its expectations. The third step in staffing.

utilitarianism: Ethical system built upon the belief that the decision where the end positives outweigh the end negatives is always the most ethical.

vision statement: An expansion of the organization's mission which provides a statement of the perceived, achievable and measurable future.

win/lose strategy: Conflict negotiation strategy based upon the assumption that when one person gains a benefit the other must lose in corresponding fashion.

win/win strategy: Conflict negotiation strategy based on the assumption that it is possible to maximize benefits for both parties simultaneously.

work team: basic production unit that builds tasks and organizations around processes instead of functions.

Notes

Index

Acknowledgements

The authors gratefully acknowledge both their mothers, (Bertha Cummings Batson and Mary Brown Neff), who provided sound ethical teachings through biblical instruction and personal actions; and their wives, Anne Parks Batson and Nancy Meeks Neff, who encouraged the authors and proofread the early drafts. Additional gratitude goes to the successful business men and women who were interviewed in the "Ask the Pro" sections of the text.

About the Authors

Blake J. Neff

Blake J. Neff is an experienced university professor and academic program director who currently pastors the Van Buren United Methodist Church in Van Buren, Indiana and serves as an adjunct faculty member at Indiana Wesleyan University. He holds a business degree from Kettering University, a theological degree from Asbury Seminary, and a doctorate in communications from Bowling Green State University (Ohio). Neff's publications include *A Pastor's Guide to Interpersonal Communication* (Haworth Press) and *The complete Guide To Religious Education Volunteers* (Co-editor, Religious Education Press). He and Nancy, his wife of thirty-one years, have three adult children and four grandchildren.

Ted Batson

Ted Batson has extensive experience in international business in Central America where he served fourteen years in managerial roles in not-for-profit organizations. He has a sixteen year higher education academic administration career in a variety of public and private colleges and universities. Batson has designed and taught ethics courses at both the undergraduate and graduate degree levels for the past nine years at Indiana Wesleyan University. He holds a B.S. degree from The University of Southwest Alabama, a M.A. degree from the University of South Alabama, and a Ph.D. degree from the University of Southern Mississippi. Batson completed additional studies in theology at Asbury Seminary and serves as a lay pastor in the United Methodist Church. He and Anne, his wife of forty-three years, have four adult children and fourteen grandchildren.

Notes

Notes

Notes

Notes